Dickens the Craftsman

STRATEGIES OF PRESENTATION

Edited, with a Foreword by ROBERT B. PARTLOW, JR.

Southern Illinois University Press, *Carbondale and Edwardsville*
Feffer & Simons, Inc., *London and Amsterdam*

CONTENTS

The immediate response of English journalists and reviewers to the sudden, unexpected death of Charles Dickens in 1870 was shock and a sense of bereavement, perhaps best summed up, appropriately, in the *Times* for 10 June:

> One whom young and old, wherever the English language is spoken, have been accustomed to regard as a personal friend is suddenly taken away from us. CHARLES DICKENS is no more. The loss of such a man makes ordinary expressions of regret seem cold and conventional. It will be felt by millions as nothing less than a personal bereavement. Statesmen, men of science, philanthropists, the acknowledged benefactors of their race might pass away, and yet not leave the void which will be caused by the death of DICKENS. They may have earned the esteem of mankind; their days may have been passed in power, honour, and prosperity; they may have been surrounded by troops of friends, but however preeminent in station, ability, or public services, they will not have been, like our great and genial novelist, the intimate of every household.

Other newspapers and magazines wrote of the loss not only as of a personal friend, but as of the end of something deeply significant, even if not fully understood. The leader in the *Illustrated London News* for 18 June began:

> The death . . . of a great author whose books have given pleasure to more readers in his lifetime than those of any other English writer, is an event that stirs up mixed feelings in the mind. There is a sense of sudden loss. . . . There is an intimate and heartfelt consciousness of personal loss in the recollection

of our past frequent communion with a favourite
author, who has come to us a hundred times, bringing always new thoughts or new shapes of fancy, new
expressions of feeling. He will never again offer anything new for our entertainment, though we may turn
back to him as often as we please to let him repeat
what he has offered us before.

Among many other personal responses, Anthony Trollope's
is remarkable since he was not only a novelist himself but a
close friend of Dickens, only four years younger than the
Thackeray whose obituary he sorrowfully wrote in 1863
and three years younger than Dickens, whose obituary he
sadly offered up in *St. Paul's*. His last paragraph reads:

A great man has gone from us;—such a one that we
may surely say of him that we shall not look on his
like again. As years roll on, we shall learn to appreciate his loss. He now rests in the spot consecrated to
the memory of our greatest and noblest; and English
men would certainly not have been contented had he
been laid elsewhere.

Most of the editorials, obituaries, and articles written
within a few weeks of Dickens' death speak of him in much
the same way: a great man, a great writer, a friend to every
Englishman of every class, a man who contributed greatly
to his country, has died, and the nation is the less for that
death. Many of the published pieces memorialize him by
reviewing the more public characteristics of the man, by
perpetuating (sometimes by creating) a public biography.
Sir Arthur Helps' comments are typical of this approach;
his initial sentence is, "When a great man departs from us,
what we desire to know about him is not so much what he
did, as what he was." Like others, he mentions Dickens'
powers of observation, his imaginative powers, his punc-
tilious accuracy, his love of order and neatness, his toleration and kindness exhibited in real life as well as in his
writings, his lively interest in important public affairs, his

habit of telling the truth even to himself, his love of the poor and oppressed, and his talents as an actor and public speaker. Sir Arthur insists that

> I have done my best to describe Mr. Dickens as he appeared to me, and certainly I have not uttered one word of flattery. But who can describe a great man— or indeed any man? We map down his separate qualities; but the subtle combination of them made by Nature eludes our description; and, after all, we fail, as I have failed now, in bringing before the reader the full sweetness, lovingness, and tenderness, wit and worth and sagacity, of such man as Charles Dickens, whose death is not merely a private grief—unspeakable, irreparable—to his family and many friends, but a public sorrow which all nations unite in deploring.[1]

John Forster's massive biography of his longtime friend and colleague is, of course, the major product of this sort of response to Dickens, and, supplemented by the memorials, letters, reminiscences of other friends and colleagues: Frith, Grant, Jerdan, Kitton, Lady Ritchie, Fitzgerald, Sala, and others, has been periodically reconsidered by later biographers. In this respect all of them were carrying out the instructions left by Dickens in his will, quoted in part by Dean Stanley during his memorial sermon in Westminster Abbey:

> I direct that my name be inscribed in plain English letters on my tomb. . . . I enjoin my friends on no account to make me the subject of any monument, memorial, or testimonial whatever. I rest my claims to the remembrance of my country upon my published works, and the remembrance of my friends upon their experience of me in addition thereto.[2]

In all probability Dickens was alluding in his will to monuments like that of Sir Walter Scott, that pile of stone rivaled only by the Albert Memorial—and this wish was respected. But there are other forms of monumentalization almost inevitable after the death of a great man, especially if he was greatly loved or greatly admired. There seems to be some ingrained need to *fix* the man and his work, to abstract him as the sculptor does, to smooth out the rough spots, to establish a final pose and posture, to create a satisfying image of the man for his age and for the future. The real, mercurial, contradictory man was gone, interred and honored as a national figure; the memory of the man was lovingly recalled, explained, embellished, and gradually fixed; books, letters, manuscripts, remains, were deposited in the national archives as relics. There remained the task of estimating his lasting worth—and that began as soon as he was dead, indeed had begun among the journalists as early as the first reviews of *Pickwick Papers;* now the corpus of work was complete, and assessments could be made without fear of contradiction by the next series of numbers.

Noel Peyrouton's division of Dickens criticism into four types (biographical, historical, psychological, and analytical)[3] is useful here as it suggests, more sharply and briefly than George Ford's study,[4] the main areas with which critics and appreciators have concerned themselves. Broadly speaking, the early critics were not interested in the historical approach, primarily because they felt no need to recreate the times in which they, Dickens, and his readers were still living; books like those of G. M. Young, Humphry House, and G. M. Trevelyan[5] were supererogatory. Psychological analyses were not widely utilized until the development of Freudian and other systems made possible orderly investigation and evaluation of personality and behavior. The biographical approach was, as noted above, at once and easily available, and hence the first to be developed at length, though without the full information (such as the Ellen Ternan affair and the full significance of the blacking-warehouse experience) or the interpretive tools provided by modern methods.

What is most striking to the student who investigates

the early essays on Dickens' work is the prevalence of *literary* criticism (or, more strictly, critical response) which is remarkably similar to work being done in our time, though clearly less complete, less rigorous in method, and less penetrating. In a way it is possible to say that the work of Professors Butt, Tillotson, Monod, Fielding, Axton, and other scholars of the last twenty years is less than completely original; so too, one might add, the work of the editor and authors of this volume: Dickens has been considered a craftsman, an artist, even a poet, almost from the beginning of his career. As early as 1851 some reviewers and critics were discussing Dickens in terms of the art of the novel and not merely as a humorist, a reformer, or an entertainer; and by the 1860's and seventies many of the avenues now being assiduously explored were identified, though only sketchily mapped.

The reviewers who wrote the obituary notices in 1870 surely did not arrive at their conclusions about Dickens on the spur of the moment; what they said quite probably comprised the general conclusions of their group over the preceding twenty or thirty years. When they sat down to make their final pronouncements, they did not have to search for things to say about their long-familiar friend and mentor. As one editor said,

> His method of composing and publishing his tales in monthly parts, or sometimes in weekly parts, aided the experience of this immediate personal companionship between the writer and the reader. It was just as if we received a letter or a visit, at regular intervals, from a kindly, observant gossip . . . who would let us know from time to time what was going on. . . . This periodical and piecemeal form of publication, being attended by a fragmentary manner of composition, was not at all favourable to the artistic harmony of his work as a whole. But few persons ever read any of Dickens's stories as a whole for the first time; because everyone was eager to enjoy the parts as they

were printed, going on a twelve month or twenty months in due succession, and growing in popularity as the pile of them increased.[6]

Despite the demurrer about the organic unity of Dickens' novels, apparently a fairly common response during his lifetime and only recently disposed of, this reviewer insists that "he was not merely a writer of extraordinary talent and skill; but, he was also a man of genius—let us say a prose poet," an artist and painter with words, of the Dutch school of Ostade and Teniers and Jan Steen, "revealing not only the picturesque effects, but the interesting moral characteristics that lie in the commonest and even the basest forms of plebeian life."

To be accurate, the most common terms applied to Dickens and his work are "humorist" and "moralist," rather typically expressed in the *Spectator*:

> The greatest humourist whom England ever produced,—Shakespeare himself not excepted,—is gone. . . . Humour,—in his case certainly, and we believe it has almost always been so,—is a great solvent of all exclusiveness and intolerance, a great enemy to social, to moral, to religious bigotry. . . . He has taught us by his humour, as nothing else could have taught us, how full to overflowing what is called "vulgar" life is of all the human qualities, good and evil, which make up the interest of human existence.[7]

But a surprising amount of space in the journals is devoted to the literary aspects of Dickens' work, even to technical and stylistic elements. In fact, as I suggested earlier, many of the areas now being scrutinized were adumbrated at this time. The starting point seems to have been the realization that Dickens handled words in a fresh, exciting manner, like an artist, a prose poet, manipulating language to achieve the pictorial and emotional effects he desired. To be exact, most of the critics' emphasis was on the characters and the "political" content, that is, on the meanings expressed by those words, which is only to be expected in critical estimates of a novelist who is advocating "radical" solutions for current problems: the temptation to argue and scold is more than most of us can bear. This particular reaction can be observed in the Podsnappish article of Margaret Oliphant published in *Blackwood's* in 1855, ostensibly as a review of *Hard Times* but actually an analysis of Dickens' class bias by an upper-middle-class bluestocking who loves his "sweet" characters and genteel families but is awfully distressed by his hateful villains, his "disagreeable" people, his inability to draw members of the upper classes, and especially by his plebeian tone and standards.

David Masson and Walter Bagehot sit in the same superior seat as Mrs. Oliphant, wondering like Professor Cockshut "how a man with such a coarse mind became a master of his art,"[8] but with greater subtlety and attention to the art than to the coarseness. Masson uses the tactic of comparing Dickens and Thackeray (specifically *David Copperfield* and *Pendennis*) in one review,[9] a favorite tactic for many years afterwards, particularly among those critics more attracted to Thackeray than to Dickens. Thackeray is presented as a gentlemanly writer, with faults certainly, but with the faults of a gentleman.

> There is a Horatian strictness, a racy strength, in Mr. Thackeray's expressions, even in his more level and tame passages, which we miss in the corresponding passages in Mr. Dickens' writings, and in which we seem to recognize the effect of those classical studies through which an accurate and determinate, though somewhat bald, use of words becomes a fixed habit. In the ease, and, at the same time, thorough polish and propriety with which Mr. Thackeray can use slang words, we seem especially to detect the University man.

Masson has a kind of gentlemanly scorn for the economics of literature, for moneymaking (as the dominant motive of

the age) instead of the ardent search for artistic perfection:
"We do not often see now that effort at artistic perfection,
that calm resolution to infuse into a performance the concentrated thought and observation of the writer, and to give
it final roundness and finish, which did exist in olden
times. . . . The spirit of craft and money-making has
crept into our artistic literature." Such an observation would
seem to lead Masson to adverse criticism of Dickens as an
artist, but, to his credit, he analyzes passages from the two
novels being considered with scrupulous fairness; he comes
to the conclusion that somehow Dickens is the finer writer
qua writer, achieving effects that Thackeray never reaches,
especially in the presentation of settings and characters.
Near the end of his review he says,

> There is a large region of objects and appearances
> familiar to the artistic activity of Mr. Dickens where
> Mr. Thackeray would not find himself at home. And
> as Mr. Dickens' artistic range is thus wider than that
> of Mr. Thackeray, so also is his style of art more ele-
> vated. Thackeray is essentially an artist of the real
> school; he belongs to what, in painting, would be
> called the school of low art. . . . Dickens, on the
> other hand, works in the ideal.

Masson's importance here is that he insisted that Dickens
was, and should be seriously considered, an artist with
words. He even goes so far as to suggest that an examination of the manuscript of *Copperfield* might reveal much
about the character and artistic integrity of the author, "not
only haste or slovenliness, if there is any; but also tricks of
association, the intellectual connexions and minute flights
by which the author leaps from thought to thought and
from phrase to phrase."

Bagehot also implies strongly that Dickens was deficient in taste, probably as the result of not receiving a
regular education, that his inability to plan plots led to complete failure at times, and that his unfamiliarity with ladies

and gentlemen made him incapable of drawing an heroic person or delineating a love affair truly or speaking knowledgeably of professional life. Bagehot nevertheless insists that Dickens is a genius, albeit of an irregular sort, by which he apparently means nonclassical, non-Johnsonian. He sees Dickens as lacking the "definite proportion of faculties and qualities suited to the exact work . . . in hand," as a writer having an *odd* style:

> It is descriptive, racy and flowing; it is instinct with new imagery and singular illustration; but it does not indicate that due proportion of the faculties to one another which is a beauty in itself, and which cannot help diffusing beauty over every happy word and molded clause. . . . It is the overflow of a copious mind, though not the chastened expression of an harmonious one.

Dickens, Bagehot goes on to say, though not at home with ideas or theories, unable to grasp with "the delicate refinement and discriminating taste of the idling orders," and only too apt to become sentimentally confused, is one of the first order of writers for his powers of observation in detail and his vivification of characters.

> Mr. Dickens's genius is especially suited to the delineation of city life. London is like a newspaper. Every thing is there, and every thing is disconnected. There is every kind of person in some houses; but there is no more connection between the houses than between the neighbors in the lists of "births, marriages, and deaths." As we change from the broad leader to the squalid police-report, we pass a corner and we are in a changed world. . . . His memory is full of instances of old buildings and curious people, and he does not care to piece them together. On the contrary, each scene, to his mind, is a separate scene,—each street a separate street. He has, too, the peculiar alertness of observation that is observable in those who live by it. He describes London like a special correspondent for posterity.[10]

Bagehot, then, seems to view Dickens primarily as a journalist, the writer of the *Sketches by Boz* who turned to
novel-writing with little change in technique, but a journalist of genius, not a first-class novelist but a superb writer.

Many of the same positions and attitudes are reflected
in the reviews of the novels of the 1850's and sixties and in
the obituaries and retrospective reviews of the 1870's. Even
as early as this, then, there was general agreement that
Charles Dickens was more than an entertainer, that he was
indeed one of the great literary artists of England. The
Saturday Review critic, for example, remarks almost casu-
ally in his death notice that "Mr. Dickens . . . was to
himself always something more than an artist," and then
writes at some length about his moral stances, but he ends
his listing of the novelist's notable qualities by saying,
"Lastly, he was an artist who was not only fond of his art
and proud of his success in it, but who looked on art as
imposing duties and responsibilities on those who devote
themselves to it."[11]

The *Fraser's Magazine* reviewer likewise takes Dickens' greatness as a writer for an established fact, but a fact
that needs much discussion. The most interesting of his
observations are those concerned with Dickens' involvement in the theater, here seen as a powerful influence in
the conception and writing of his novels:

> His fondness for all matters theatrical was well
> known. He was himself the very prince of amateur
> actors, and in his readings his remarkable mimetic
> powers enchanted countless audiences on both sides
> of the Atlantic. In fact, a story of his is like a drama
> for the fireside, furnished not only with situations and
> dialogue, but with appropriate scenery, gestures,
> actions, byplay; the author, scene-painter, stage-
> manager, and moreover the whole company, tragic
> and comic, male and female, from "stars" to "supers,"
> being one and the same skillful individual. The figures
> impress one rather as impersonations than as persons.

> But how telling they are, and what a list of dramatis
> personae is that of the *Theatre National Charles
> Dickens!* . . . His way is to catch a type (and he has
> caught a wonderful number of distinct ones), grip it
> fast, put it into a number of appropriate situations,
> and illustrate by means of an endless play of fancies.
> . . . In fact, he was an artist. He decided on the
> *effect* to be produced, chose his point of view, and
> worked on steadily in his own way. Keen observation
> of facts, humorous seizures and often grotesque
> exaggeration of the salient points, brilliant *quasi-*
> theatric expressions of these; such was his method.[12]

As these observations prefigure the intensive analyses of
Professors Garis and Axton, so the following comments in
Macmillan's Magazine seem almost a summary of the work
of Professors Butt and Tillotson:

> He was one of the most precise and accurate men in
> the world; and he grudged no labour in his work.
> Those who have seen his MSS. will recollect what
> elaborate notes, and comments, and plans (some
> adopted, many rejected), went to form the basis of his
> works. To see those manuscripts would cure anybody
> of the idle and presumptuous notion that men of
> genius require no forethought or preparation for their
> greatest efforts, but that these are dashed off by the
> aid of a mysterious something which is comprehended
> in the word "genius." It was one of Mr. Dickens's
> theories, and I believe a true one, that men hardly
> differ in anything so much as in their power of atten-
> tion; and certainly, whatever he did, he attended to it
> with all his might.[13]

The work of Dickens scholars over the last twenty
years has been, in some large part, an extension and
elaboration of the insights of Victorian critics like those I
have cited. Of course our critical methods and standards
have been refined, we have developed a more accurate
terminology, our analytical techniques are more precise; of
course the results are more persuasive because more objec-

tive and more firmly based in accepted literary theory. I suggest, however, that it has long been acknowledged that Dickens is a major artist and stylist, and that the primary task of Professors Fielding, Miller, Tillotson, Ford, Monod, Nisbet, and many others, has been not to establish his artistry as a fact,[14] but to document it: to show in detail the operation of the creative imagination, to discover ever more subtle meanings imbedded in the complex language patterns, to weigh the pressures and influences operating on that mind, to discover the dimensions of his moral and artistic commitments—in effect, to move from intuitive generalizations to ever-finer discriminations of meanings and techniques for presenting meanings. As Edgar Johnson indicated,[15] there are four principal areas of investigation which today are most significant and which will probably prove most fruitful in the next few years: the mythic or fairy tale, the imagistic, the structural, and the thematic— all of which have as a basic assumption that Dickens' mind was richly poetic, that he was a careful craftsman, and that his novelistic structures are executed like paintings, with the careful attention to balancing of masses, colors, and figures, the same concern for total as well as local effect, which Frith and Egg strove for and achieved in their best canvases.

The authors of this volume and I have made the same assumption: the very title is intended to focus attention on this one aspect of Dickens and his work. We could have concentrated on a given technique in one novel or a group of novels, say image patterns in the later novels; or we could have chosen to work on several technical aspects of just one novel, say *Little Dorrit*. Instead, we finally decided to select only the area, Dickens' craftsmanship, and the authors undertook to investigate those aspects that they, not the editor, found most significant. The number and excellence of the papers submitted surprised me: the essays in this volume represent less than half of the papers that could have been printed. They are the best that my able and conscientious assistants, Professors Archibald Coolidge and William Axton, and I could choose for their intrinsic merit and for the way in which they complement each other. We think they make a real contribution to our understanding of Dickens' artistry, or craftsmanship if you will.

Harry Stone, for example, points out that repetitive patterns (recurrent images, situations, or attitudes) which crop up in novel after novel "are coterminous with the author's chief concerns and with his way of viewing the world; . . . such patterns can be used reflexively to provide fresh insights into his writings." This principle of analysis is not entirely new—others have investigated the recurrence of the prison pattern for example—but the analysis itself is a notably skillful utilization of biographical data, psychological knowledge, and literary analysis. Stone demonstrates that the love pattern in such fictions as *Dombey and Son, Great Expectations,* and *The Haunted Man* is only partly a matter of artistic necessity or planning for effect, and much more a reflection of Dickens' inner needs and fears and experiences. Dickens' extreme reaction to his private reading of Robert Browning's *A Blot in the 'Scutcheon,* Stone shows, must be studied in terms of the relationships between Dickens and his sister Fanny, between Dickens and Maria Beadnell, and between Dickens and Mary Hogarth—who, among them, established a pattern of abandonment and betrayal in love which is repeated time after time in his writings as Dickens "idealizes the lost paradise, broods over its loss, and yearns for its return."

Philip Collins' approach is from a different, opposed direction: Dickens' self-awareness as a writer, not by analysis of the novels themselves but by a careful study of his remarks in the various prefaces, in the letters, in his comments as an editor, and, most significantly and originally, by considering John Forster's reviews of his works in the

Examiner. Here Collins returns to the original sources I mentioned at the beginning of this Foreword, the articles and observations of those readers and critics who were reacting to the novels as they appeared. Collins' essay is a neat piece of scholarly detective work. There is, first of all, the necessity of proving that Forster actually wrote the unsigned articles being cited. Next, there is demanded some analysis of the relationship between Dickens and Forster, especially in the light of the former's known dislike of adverse criticism, a fact which made the task of a reviewer who was also a close friend very difficult. Finally, there is an extensive comparison of the *Examiner* reviews and the parallel passages in Forster's *Life*, in order to show what Forster felt free to say after his sensitive friend and subject was dead, that is, what revisions of his earlier remarks he felt himself permitted to make. The results do not, to be sure, demonstrate that Dickens was a remarkably lucid or penetrating literary critic or theorist; they do demonstrate that he was aware of many of the problems involved in his own peculiar relationship with the reading public, and they do reinforce the major contention of this volume, that Dickens' art is essentially poetic.

Robert Patten's essay is also a piece of detection, on a more limited scale and with an even more clouded problem: the genesis of *The Old Curiosity Shop*. The author uses every bit of evidence and considerable ingenuity sorting out the tangled threads of this piece of publishing history. Dickens the craftsman, in the sense here of the writer called on to solve technical and publishing difficulties, emerges clearly.

"Laughter and Pathos" is James Kincaid's quite different response to *The Old Curiosity Shop*: instead of investigating the genesis of the novel, he considers the structure of the completed work primarily in terms of the conflict of basic tendencies, conflict between those characters associated with peace and the static, and those associated with violence and the dynamic. Kincaid's contribution to the arguments of other scholars lies in his perception of the structural importance of Dick Swiveller; he is seen as far more than a figure of comic relief, indeed he is the sane alternative to, the acceptable middle position between the "Nell-force" and the "Quilp-force," neither of which is fully adult or fully liberated. This new sense of the basic structure gives, it seems to me, a new awareness of the basic meaning of the novel, a meaning not previously so clearly expressed.

Richard Dunn's paper, though rightly cautious in its assumptions, procedures, and conclusions, and deliberately kept on a small scale, is one of the first of what is sure to be a long line of investigations of Dickens as a *Victorian* writer and man, thoroughly a part of the practical, ongoing life of his time (as Fielding and Brice show in their study), thoroughly concerned in both theory and practice with the problems of an age in which almost everything was unprecedented. Dunn sketches out some of the parallels between Diogenes Teufelsdröckh and David Copperfield primarily in terms of the barriers to self-discovery, self-awareness, and self-fulfillment in the suddenly unstable nineteenth century; he concludes that Dickens' novelistic form permitted a somewhat fuller solution than did Carlyle's experimental techniques in *Sartor Resartus*.

"*Bleak House* and the Graveyard" is another step in the extensive investigation of K. J. Fielding and A. W. Brice into the factual backgrounds of Dickens' novels. We have long known that Dickens "borrowed" people, scenes, and events from other books, his own experiences, newspaper articles, and the like, but the task of securely and finally identifying them—and, more importantly, assessing their significance in the total achievement—is hardly begun. Nor is this a pedantic game that Fielding and Brice are playing: their avowed intention is to study the ways in which Dickens used topical issues "to lead himself and his readers into the heart of the imaginary world of his fiction," to consider the techniques by which local and topical details were universalized so that even those who miss the journalistic immediacy undoubtedly felt by the first readers of a novel, say *Bleak House,* still accept the graveyard as a deeply meaningful symbol, image, and plot-element. Like Collins and Patten, these authors present a carefully controlled mass of evidence to show Dickens' attention to the problems of health and burial grounds, and then proceed to demonstrate the ways in which the topical features are transmuted by the genius of the novelist into the larger forms of fictional truth. As George Ford has pointed out,[16] there is increasing need for scholars to explain allusions no longer understood by even the most widely read student. This is part of what Fielding and Brice do in this paper, but only part: they properly insist that allusions are not ends in themselves but parts of larger and continuously significant patterns of meaning—which is not a bad definition of the mode of operation of the artist.

The final two essays in this volume belong to a class or type of critical analysis which has already proved fruitful and which will doubtless be the major investigative method in the next few years: the technical, in the sense of study of the writer's techniques, such as structure, language in its myriad aspects, point of view. Richard Stang's essay considers *Little Dorrit* as the enormous elaboration of one central metaphor: "They seemed to have got on the wrong side of the pattern of the universe." This is not the same as saying, as others have, that Dickens is basically concerned with appearance and reality or saying that the novel is fundamentally ironic, but something more penetrating: a view of this novel (and, by extension, many of Dickens' novels) as an elaborate theme and variations, a view of the novel as a huge and intricated elaboration of a metaphor which is itself an apocalyptic vision. Stang's meticulous analysis of the metaphor itself and the poetic ways in which

Dickens sees it operating in the fictional world he is creating as a counterpart to and commentary on the real Victorian world is, it seems to me, an exciting and original contribution, not only in terms of the interpretation of the novel he provides, but also, most interestingly, for the investigative model he provides. Sylvère Monod's study of some of the linguistic devices in *A Tale of Two Cities* is, as all readers of his *Dickens romancier* would expect, a lucid, perceptive analysis of the linguistic and rhetorical devices he finds most important in that novel. So tightly woven is this essay that it is impossible to summarize without writing at great length, but perhaps I might quote what I think is his most central point: "When the revolutionary disruption of style is combined with other devices (rhetoric, imagery, cumulative vocabulary, and repetition), . . . genuine prose poems can be the result of their association, . . . remarkable pieces of elaborate and, on the whole, felicitous writing." A most happy way of expressing the basic theme of this whole volume!

In a way, then, the editor and authors of this book are reiterating the criticisms and eulogies expressed a century ago on the death of Charles Dickens, with the inevitable refinements of analytical techniques and increased knowledges that derive from long attention to the same subject. We too find Dickens a great man well deserving careful study; we too find that he was an artist and poet, for perhaps more justifiable reasons than those brought forward by our Victorian predecessors. We therefore offer this work in honor of the centenary of the death of The Inimitable, and in the hope that the essays included will contribute to the greater understanding of Dickens as a craftsman, an artist, a poet of the novel.

Carbondale, Illinois   *Robert B. Partlow, Jr.*
26 June 1969

NOTES ON CONTRIBUTORS

A. W. BRICE is a post-graduate research student in the Department of English Literature, University of Edinburgh. He is working under Professor Fielding on contemporary criticism of Victorian fiction, especially in *The Examiner*.

PHILIP COLLINS is Professor of Engish Literature and Chairman of the Victorian Studies Centre, University of Leicester. His major volumes are *Dickens and Crime* and *Dickens and Education;* forthcoming publications are *Dickens: the Critical Heritage* and *Dickens and Politics, and Other Studies*. He is also editing Dickens' letters and two of his novels.

RICHARD J. DUNN is an assistant professor at the University of Washington. He has published articles in the *English Journal, Dickens Studies, The Dickensian,* and *Studies in the Novel,* and is currently studying the influence of Carlyle on Dickens.

K. J. FIELDING is Saintsbury Professor of Modern English Literature at the University of Edinburgh; he is also on the advisory boards of *Victorian Studies* and the *Dickens Studies Annual*. A prolific writer, he is best known for his *Charles Dickens: A Critical Introduction* and for several important studies of *Bleak House* and *Hard Times*. He is currently working on Dickens' journalism.

JAMES R. KINCAID is an associate professor at Ohio State University. He has published articles on *Pickwick Papers, Oliver Twist,* and *David Copperfield,* and is now finishing a book to be titled *Dickens and the Rhetoric of Laughter*.

SYLVÈRE MONOD is Professor of English in the *Institut d'Études Anglaises* of the Sorbonne. He is best known for his *Dickens romancier,* recently translated into English and partly rewritten, and for his numerous articles. He is now at work on a history of English literature from Victoria to the present and is preparing an edition of *Bleak House.*

ROBERT L. PATTEN, assistant professor of English at Rice University, spent 1968–69 in England on a National Endowment for the Humanities Younger Scholar Fellowship, writing a book about the cost and sales of Dickens' novels. Author of several articles on Dickens' early novels, he is currently preparing an edition of *Pickwick Papers* for the Penguin English Library series.

RICHARD STANG is an associate professor of English at Washington University (St. Louis, Missouri). He is perhaps best known for his *Discussions of George Eliot* and his *Theory of the Novel in England, 1850–1870.* He will be in England for the 1969–70 academic year.

HARRY STONE, Professor of English at San Fernando State College, is the editor of *Charles Dickens' Uncollected Writings from "Household Words"* (*1850–1859*), a contributor to *Dickens 1812–1870,* and a member of the *Dickens Studies Annual* Advisory Board. He is currently at work on a book to be called *Dickens and the Fairy Tale.*

DICKENS THE CRAFTSMAN

THE LOVE PATTERN
IN DICKENS' NOVELS

Harry Stone

> Early unhappiness, a wound from a
> hand I loved and trusted, and a loss that
> nothing can replace . . .
> Thus . . . I bear within me a Sorrow
> and a Wrong. Thus I prey upon myself.
> —*The Haunted Man*

Reading through a writer's entire oeuvre one is often struck by repetitive patterns. These patterns—they can consist of recurrent images, situations, or attitudes; obsessive emphases, emotions, or responses—assume their full significance only as they emerge in work after work. Encountered in a single work, such patterns are likely to seem topical or idiosyncratic. Encountered in book after book, however, they suggest a deeper significance: they suggest that they embody the author's most profound hopes and fears. This is another way of saying that such repeated motifs are coterminous with the author's chief concerns and with his way of viewing the world; it also follows that such patterns can be used reflexively to provide fresh insights into his writings. With a pattern firmly in mind we can go back, reread a work, and assess it afresh. Sometimes we can do more: we can explain aberrations in constructions or responses or relationships that baffled us before.

I should like to trace one such pattern—the love pattern—in Dickens' writings, attempt an explanation of how it came into being, and then use the pattern to do two things: to rationalize one of Dickens' most extraordinary critical responses, and to account for the nature of many of his heroines. In other words, I should like to use the love pattern to solve a conundrum and to elucidate a type of characterization.

The conundrum has to do with Robert Browning, more precisely with the strangest and most important episode in Dickens' relationship with Browning. That relationship began early. In 1838, the year in which they most likely met, both were twenty-six. Browning was then virtually unknown; Dickens was already the most famous writer in England. This disparity did not keep them apart; they had many friends in common and were frequently meeting at salons, dinners, plays, and receptions. Chief among those common friends was John Forster, Dickens' lifelong consultant, confidant, and ultimately his biographer. Forster was also one of Browning's earliest appreciators and advocates, and was to help and serve him for many years. Another mutual friend was the turbulent actor-manager William Charles Macready, the most famous tragedian of his day. Through these and other men of the same circle, Dickens and Browning came to know one another well. They dined with one another in London, Paris, or wherever their lives crossed; they argued theater, acting styles, and dramatic performances together; and they joined one another in excursions, outings, entertainments, and the like. But that was the extent of it. Their friendship remained casual; it is verified today by the few stray notes and trivial jottings that have survived.

One of these jottings, however, is not trivial. I have in mind a letter that Dickens wrote Forster in November 1842 concerning Browning's play *A Blot in the 'Scutcheon*. The letter is a concatenation of mysteries. Its occasion is puzzling; its history is strange; and its message is so extravagant—almost hysterical—that it has never been satisfactorily explained. Here, in brief, are the facts. Sometime before 1842 Macready read and agreed to produce *A Blot*, but, when the time came to fulfill his promise, he hesitated. He had lost money on his last two productions and apparently feared that Browning's play would cause him to lose a great deal more. At this juncture Dickens was asked to read the play in manuscript and give his opinion. He did so, Macready produced the play the following year, and the accompanying recriminations shattered the Browning-Macready friendship.

But the recriminations and their consequences were still several months off. After Dickens read the play, he wrote excitedly to Forster

> Browning's play has thrown me into a perfect passion of sorrow. To say that there is anything in its subject save what is lovely, true, deeply affecting, full of the best emotion, the most earnest feeling, and the most true and tender source of interest, is to say that there is no light in the sun, and no heat in blood. It is full of genius, natural and great thoughts, profound and yet simple and beautiful in its vigour. I know nothing that is so affecting, nothing in any book I have ever read, as Mildred's recurrence to that "I was so young— I had no mother." I know no love like it, no passion like it, no moulding of a splendid thing after its conception, like it. And I swear it is a tragedy that *must* be played; and must be played, moreover, by Macready. There are some things I would have changed if I could (they are very slight, mostly broken lines); and I assuredly would have the old servant *begin his tale upon the scene;* and be taken by the throat, or drawn upon, by his master, in its commencement. But the tragedy I shall never forget, or less vividly remember than I do now. And if you tell Browning that I have seen it, tell him that I believe from my soul there is no man living (and not many dead) who could produce such a work.

One of the many puzzlements surrounding this dithyrambic praise of Browning and his play is that not one single echo of what Dickens wrote Forster reached Browning at this time. Browning first learned of the letter when Forster printed it in his biography of Dickens. Dickens was then in his grave, and the letter was more than thirty years old.

A Blot in the 'Scutcheon takes place in the eighteenth century. The chief protagonists are Mildred, a fourteen-year-old girl (she is the orphaned sister of Thorold, Earl Tresham), and Henry, Earl Mertoun, a young boy. In their innocence, almost in spite of themselves, the boy and girl become clandestine lovers. The play opens with Henry asking for Mildred's hand in marriage, a suit to which Thorold is happy to consent. But the next day, Thorold discovers that Mildred has been receiving a nightly visitor. When he confronts her with this fact, she confesses her guilt. Thorold demands to know the name of her lover, but she will not tell him. That night Thorold intercepts Henry on his way to a final tryst and mortally wounds him. As the boy lies dying, Thorold listens to him tell of his love, his hopes, his innocence—and he is filled with remorse. He goes to his sister and confesses what he has done. She upbraids but forgives him, and then, suddenly and inexplicably, dies in his arms. Thorold, having poisoned himself, dies a few moments later.

The play is trite and melodramatic. But Browning succeeds in one very difficult task: he makes us believe in the innocence and purity of his orphaned heroine. He also succeeds elsewhere: he creates memorable vignettes of childhood retrospect, moving threnodies of vain regret. Yet the play as a whole seems contrived. It lacks motivation and psychological verity; it contains characters and episodes that are insufficiently developed; it glorifies behavior that is stilted and shallow; and it fails to convey its meaning through action. Why, in view of all this, did Dickens heap such extravagant, such inordinate, praise on the play?

The answer, it seems to me, lies both in Dickens and the play. His response was triggered, I believe, by dramatic and rhetorical elements in the play that he found irresistible. In particular I am referring to the love relationship of the orphaned brother and sister and the fervent language which expresses it. That relationship is at the heart of the play. Macready even suggested that Browning rename the play "The Sister." Dickens, I believe, responded unconsciously to this emphasis. For Browning's rhapsodic rendition of the brother-sister theme touched sensitive nodes in Dickens' life.

Dickens was very close to his sister Fanny, who was one year older than he. As children they were inseparable —they seem to have constituted a separate group within the family group—and Dickens always looked upon this time of closeness as the happiest of his life. The period of closeness had begun in Dickens' second year and had flourished as a result of the great chasm which had then opened up in his life. That chasm had appeared when his mother transferred her primary attentions from him to her next born, a turning away which was compounded in the following years by a steady procession of new brothers and new sisters. Dickens never got over this early turning away, but its consequences were mitigated by Fanny's sisterly companionship. In the next few years Dickens and Fanny drew ever closer together. That sisterly closeness provided Dickens with a succoring substitute for what he took to be the inadequate concern and inadequate love of his parents. But the idyll of sisterly devotion, though lasting some eight years, proved to be as impermanent as the much briefer idyll of motherly devotion, and the dissolution of that second relationship helped shape Dickens' notion of felicity and his pursuit of it.

Abruptly, in 1822, when Dickens was ten, the family

moved from the comforts and green fields of Chatham to the evil times and brick warrens of London, and the days of innocent companionship and affection ended. Fanny, by her talent and good luck, escaped those evil times. She won admittance to the Royal Academy of Music and extended her education and social life. Dickens, for no cause that he could discern, was consigned by his parents, especially by his mother, to live by himself and become a veritable orphan, a "labouring hind" in a blacking warehouse—a "small Cain," as he later put it, outcast from life's feast. Whatever the compelling practical reasons for this arrangement, Dickens never reconciled himself emotionally to why this happened or to what he then went through. He blamed both his parents, but he blamed his mother most. Many years later he described the crucial struggle which took place after he had been sent home from the blacking warehouse. In that struggle, his father had opposed and his mother had favored his returning. Dickens' comment on the episode, made more than twenty years later, vibrates with undiminished emotion. "I never afterwards forgot," he wrote, "I never shall forget, I never can forget, that my mother was warm for my being sent back." But his resentment was not confined to his mother or even to his parents. Years later he also described how he felt upon emerging one Sunday from his week-long blacking-warehouse isolation and drudgery to watch Fanny receive a prize at the Royal Academy of Music. "I could not bear," he wrote, "to think of myself—beyond the reach of all such honourable emulation and success. The tears ran down my face. I felt as if my heart were rent. I prayed, when I went to bed that night, to be lifted out of the humiliation and neglect in which I was. I never had suffered so much before."

These abandonments and betrayals by the women he trusted and loved the most (I adopt here the exaggerated coloring that Dickens' wounded emotions gave to these events) magnified and reinforced, and were in turn magnified and reinforced by, all similar events that occurred later in his life: most notably his devastating rejection and betrayal by his first love, frivolous Maria Beadnell; and his sudden loss of Mary Hogarth, his adored seventeen-year-old sister-in-law who collapsed and died in his arms—the latter abandonment conjoined with the apotheosis of death. These losses, bereavements, and betrayals, which helped emotionalize the ubiquitous orphan figure in Dickens' writings, and which provided, as we shall shortly see, the pattern for heroes and heroines yet unborn, all occurred before he read *A Blot.*

But the crucial fall from grace, the fall which set the pattern for all later falls, occurred with his mother and with Fanny. How baffled, rejected and guilty he felt when his mother turned from him to her next born may be glimpsed in that autobiographical novel, *David Copperfield,* especially in the painful and yet beautiful scene in which David, still a child, returns from his cruel exile to find his mother singing softly and suckling a newborn brother. His mother's song stirs in David memories of his own babyhood, and he is moved almost to tears. His mother is startled to see him, but then, on an impulse, takes him to her breast. Emotion floods his heart. He is not abandoned and betrayed after all; his guilt slips from him. He feels so loved and purified that he yearns to die in that blissful instant. But David's alienation, as he will soon discover, cannot be assuaged by a momentary return to his mother's breast. His infant brother is an emblem of irreversible change, a sign that David has been permanently displaced; indeed, David has been doubly supplanted. For only his brother may rightfully remain at his mother's breast; and his brother is a child not of David's father, but of the usurper, the evil Mr. Murdstone.

Dickens' fate was less dire and less symbolic. The undivided love his mother could not give him, he received from his sister Fanny. How important that interlude of sisterly love was to him, how devastated he was by its abrupt end when Fanny entered the Royal Academy of Music, and how exalted the interlude appeared to him long after it had decayed and vanished may be seen in "A Child's Dream of a Star," an allegorical tribute to Fanny that he wrote many years later when she had been dead two years. In "A Child's Dream" he says nothing about Fanny as a girl or as a conservatory student or as a bride or as a wife or as a mother. Instead he goes back to the idyllic Chatham days, and in Biblical cadences tells how he and his sister loved and trusted and solaced one another as children. In his fantasy his sister never grows up, never changes, never leaves or betrays him; the idyll is terminated by her death in childhood. This end, of course, precludes a fall; it may also indicate that we witness a slaying as well as an ending. The boy does grow up, but he always yearns for the time when he can rejoin his sister. For then, in heaven, as children once more, they will resume their interrupted idyll.

In this, as in other parallels, Dickens idealizes the lost paradise, broods over its loss, and yearns for its return. Here we have one phase of Dickens: Dickens the eternal romantic looking before and after and pining for what is not. This yearning for an Edenlike purity, ideality, and permanence—especially for an adoring female who would never change and never turn away, who would undo and heal his past—helps crowd his writings, especially his early writings, with unrealities that do not betray the heart: with virginal heroines of unexampled virtue and steadfastness —heroines such as Rose Maylie, Kate Nickleby, Little Nell, Ruth Pinch, Little Dorrit, Lucie Manette, and all that angelic host. But there is another, more curious element in many of these portraits. Dickens often concentrates on the brother-sister rather than the lover relationship. He often exalts the heroine in her role as a loving sister, rather than in her part as a leading lover—witness Rose Maylie, Kate Nickleby, Ruth Pinch, and Louisa Gradgrind. In other instances—with Florence Dombey, Agnes Wickfield, Little Dorrit, and Estella—the brother-sister quality in the love between hero and heroine acts as a barrier or a deterrent to sexual love and fulfillment.

I am suggesting that Fanny, his parent substitute in childhood, who became the object of his love and then, so he thought, betrayed him, even as his mother had earlier, later became, along with his mother and his first love, the equally unsteadfast Maria Beadnell, his image of womanhood, an image which shaped his attitude toward love, his wife, and his heroines. What Dickens sought was a wife who would be a companion, a sexual partner, a bearer of children, but at the same time (and unlike his unforgiven mother or the inconstant Maria) be steadfast and innocent, untouched and untouchable, the matured and idealized image of his childhood sister. The very terms of his desire made it unattainable; for to find the paragon wife was to destroy the sister, and to preserve the immature sister was to have no wife at all.

Hence Dickens' curious domestic compromise, his anomalous household which from shortly after his marriage contained not only his wife, but his wife's sixteen-year-old sister, Mary Hogarth. And when adored Mary died in his arms at the age of seventeen, still budlike and perfect, and thus forever so, he was able to convince himself that he had rediscovered, though again in fleeting form, the all-loving sister he had idealized and then lost in childhood. Now more than ever, therefore, he sought to give actual form to his dream of a sister-wife fusion. Five years later, he brought fifteen-year-old Georgina, another Hogarth sister, into his household. And there Georgina remained, unmarried and sisterly, sisterly even after her sister, Dickens' wife, moved out of his home, sisterly until his death, clinging to that portion of her brother-in-law which had need of a worshiping sister surrogate such as she.

Yet what Dickens really wanted was not two women

in his house, a wife and an aging sister substitute, but one woman who would be both wife and ever-young, ever-adoring sister. His makeshift attempts to give his dream reality by means of resident sisters-in-law, infatuations with teenage girls (such as Christiana Weller), and finally, in his forties, by a liaison with an eighteen-year-old actress —these attempts and the will-o'-the-wisp dream which prompted them had much to do with his growing restlessness, his increasingly unsatisfactory marriage, and his latter-day unhappiness. For Dickens wanted to combine the uncombinable. His perfect female is at once passive and provocative, naïve and wise, innocent and experienced, girl and woman, sister and wife, virgin and mother. She does not exist and so cannot be found. To search for her is to search for disillusionment and anguish.

His need and the dream which embodied it also led to a host of female characters into whom he projected, and through whom he partly vicariously realized, the confused sister-wife ideal of his emotional yearning. In the early works the projection is usually an idealized blending of Fanny Dickens and Mary Hogarth, a combination of the perfect but vanished childhood sister companion and the doomed sister substitute: a figure who is most notably represented by Little Nell. Or more commonly, such female characters are sister-wife figures who are depicted both as perfect sisters and perfect wives. (One usually gets the feeling that the sister role is the important one, that happy wifehood is a vague status which comes late in the novel as a reward for loyal sisterhood.) In the typical case, the dutiful, loving sister, having proved her boundless devotion, is allowed to marry an impeccable but bloodless spouse: Rose Fleming, the foster-sister of Oliver, and his aunt, as it turns out, marries Harry Maylie, whose foster-sister—to compound the pattern—is the very same Rose; Kate Nickleby, the sister of Nicholas, marries Frank Cheeryble; Ruth Pinch, the sister of Tom, marries John Westlock. In each case the marriage occurs at the end of the book, and it is the sister relationship, not the lover relationship, which is important. Sometimes, as with Ruth Pinch, the sister perpetuates the brother-sister relationship after marriage by bringing the brother into, or next to, her new household; and in some cases, the sister never marries, but, as with Harriet Carker, sacrifices her chance for marriage and happiness—nobly and fittingly as Dickens makes clear—in loyalty to her brother.

If we look at three or four of the novels more closely we can see how central this pattern is and how intricately Dickens varies it. *Dombey and Son* is a good example, for in *Dombey and Son* the pattern is at the heart of the novel, and Dickens' workings and reworkings of the motif produce some of the novel's characteristic anomalies. Through much of *Dombey,* for example, Dickens unaccountably treats the love relationship between his hero and heroine, Walter and Florence, as a brother-sister relationship. It thus parallels the other central love relationship of the novel, the real brother-sister relationship of Paul and Florence. The latter relationship, in turn, is contrasted in ways that heighten its importance. Dickens counterpoises the brotherly-sisterly love which exists between Paul and Florence to the love which is lacking between the children and their father. In a very real sense Paul and Florence are orphans—Dickens himself uses the term to describe their condition. Indeed they are the most pitiful of orphans: they have a father but are fatherless. Driven in on themselves, they turn toward one another. They find in their brotherly-sisterly love a substitute for the parental love they need, the love that Dombey is incapable of giving them.

These relationships are similar to Dickens' early closeness to his sister Fanny and his turning to her for love in the face of what he took to be parental neglect and rejection. The peculiar importance of the brother-sister relationship for Dickens is accentuated when Dickens unaccountably gives Walter and Florence, despite their disparate positions, emerging sexuality, and predestined marriage, a strong brother-sister identification. In a most curious way, the sibling quality of their relationship is emphasized at the same time that the possibility of sexual love and marriage is also underscored. In this respect, Dickens is perpetuating through Walter and Florence, little Paul's equally curious yearning for his sister. "I mean," said Paul, "to put my money all together in one bank, never try to get any more, go away into the country with my darling Florence, have a beautiful garden, fields, and woods, and live there with her all my life!" And after Paul has died in Florence's sisterly arms (as Mary Hogarth died in Dickens' brotherly arms), Dickens goes out of his way to make Walter a surrogate of Paul, and to give the brother-sister relationship of Walter and Florence an almost legal status. The day before Walter voyages into shipwreck on the *Son and Heir,* Florence visits him and says, "If you'll be a brother to me, Walter, now that [Paul] is gone and I have none on earth, I'll be your sister all my life, and think of you like one wherever we may be!" Walter accepts the offer, the clock strikes, Florence gets into a waiting coach, says "You are my brother, dear!" and the coach drives off. But Walter is to be Florence's husband, not her brother, and years later when he returns and realizes that he loves her sexually, the pledge of brotherhood becomes a torment to him, forces him to avoid her, and is dissolved only when Florence confesses her unsisterly love for him.

In later works Dickens probes the nuances of brother-sister relationships with greater subtlety; he also presents his conflicting feelings with increasing insight and sophistication. Yet he never fully resolves what are, after all, irreconcilable yearnings. Even his later heroines—think, for instance, of Rosa Bud and Helena Landless in *Edwin Drood*—have a tendency to metamorphose into sisters or to waver uncertainly in the limbo of conflicting roles. But he is much more likely in his later works to make the antipodal roles of sister and lover thematic, often by separating and then counterpointing them. In *A Tale of Two Cities,* for example, through Sydney Carton and Charles Darnay (alter-ego twins, and two projections of Dickens, as Dickens himself recognized), he again depicts a love which combines sexual and brother-sister qualities. The pale married love of Lucie and Charles represents an idealized husband-wife relationship; the emotional Lucie-Sydney conjunction represents, as chapter 13 of book II makes clear, a forbidden sexual love which is repressed and finally sublimated into a precarious brotherly love. At the end of the book this brotherly love is purged of its remaining sexual taint when Sydney (Dickens as illicit lover-cum-brother) forgoes the possibility of marrying a widowed Lucie and saves Lucie's lawful sexual partner (Dickens as conventional lover-cum-husband) by sacrificing himself.

In *David Copperfield* the bifurcation of *A Tale of Two Cities* is reversed. David has two loves, one Dora, a provocative but immature lover and an unsatisfactory wife, the other Agnes, a sister figure whom he finally recognizes, after Dora's death, as his proper spouse. In *Copperfield* Dickens came close to accepting his dilemma and the impossibility of resolving it; for, though David at last marries Agnes, he does so in a curiously asexual way, realizing that her love, no matter how deep and pure, lacks something which his first love possessed. As Dickens later partly confessed, Agnes is a recrudescence of the sisterly Fanny-Mary-Georgina figure, while Dora is compounded of Maria and his wife, Catherine, that is, of his early sexual love and disillusionment.

Pip and Estella in *Great Expectations,* to cite only one more instance of this repeated pattern—the pattern is further varied and partly reversed by Pip and Biddy—also have an odd brother-sister-lover relationship. The brother-sister aspects of their relationship, built up by years of childhood association, make Pip a confidant, a person singled out for favorable treatment, a charmed being who is supposedly safe from a destructive sexual love for Estella. Yet his presumed immunity proves to be his curse, for his favored position causes him to love Estella all the more. He loves her as sister, as wife, and as ideal (as Estella, the unattainable star); he loves her though he knows he cannot, and for his well-being should not, win her. But knowledge, reason, conscience are powerless to restrain him; he pursues her, and thus he pursues his own misery.

Intellectually, Dickens understood the dangers of such a pursuit; he also recognized many of the factors which impelled him to the race. On more than one occasion he touched upon the causes and consequences of his dilemma. One of the most compressed of these analyses—an analysis which sheds further light on the love pattern in his novels —occurs in *The Haunted Man*, Dickens' Christmas book for 1848. *The Haunted Man* was written under special stress. In the summer of 1848, while Dickens was planning his Christmas book, his sister Fanny lay dying wretchedly of consumption. Dickens visited her very often during that summer, and, as he looked upon her worn and wasted body, and grieved over her early decay, his mind kept turning to the days when he and she had been children together. Fanny died on 2 September, and a month or so later Dickens began *The Haunted Man. The Haunted Man* is a dirge to memory. Dickens used his Christmas novelette to probe some of his most profound dissatisfactions, dissatisfactions which went back to the old Chatham days and earlier, dissatisfactions which had been stirred up and intensified by his sister's death.

The theme of *The Haunted Man* is quickly stated. A famous chemist named Redlaw, haunted by the injustices of his past, longs to purge his memory of early sorrows and wrongs. The relief he desires is granted him, but he soon discovers that sorrow and wrong are linked to love and goodness; if he banishes one he crushes the other, and loses his humanity. Dickens dramatizes Redlaw's darker broodings by objectifying them in an alter ego. The alter ego, Redlaw's dark Phantom or Spectre self, communes with Redlaw in the solitudes of the night and voices his most profound disappointments and resentments. Redlaw's psychological confrontation with his gloomier self—depicted as a colloquy between Redlaw and his Phantom—is a version of Dickens' similar confrontation with his own misgivings and unhappiness.

It is worth looking at that confrontation in some detail, for it is Dickens' fantasized version of his early affections and early wrongs. The fantasy makes the version all the more revealing. For though the passage is intensely autobiographical, it is untrammeled by literal fact; Dickens was free to heighten and modify reality as his emotions dictated. At the same time the passage is more succinct, more expository, and more self-consciously autobiographical than the love patterns in the novels. If one makes allowances for fictional license, Redlaw's history is Dickens' history. Emotionally there are no differences at all, for the biographical modifications—the blending of Fanny and Mary, for example, the compounding of sexual betrayal, the failure to postulate a wife, the wish-fulfilling steadfastness of the sister—intensify rather than reduce the emotional identification with Dickens. Through Redlaw and Redlaw's Spectre, Dickens summons up the shaping events of his own past:

> "Look upon me!" said the Spectre. "I am he, neglected in my youth, and miserably poor, who strove and suffered, and still strove and suffered, until I hewed out knowledge from the mine where it was buried, and made rugged steps thereof, for my worn feet to rest and rise on."
> "I *am* that man," returned the Chemist.
> "No mother's self-denying love," pursued the Phantom, "no father's counsel, aided *me*. A stranger

> came into my father's place when I was but a child,
> and I was early an alien from my mother's heart. My
> parents, at the best, were of that sort whose care soon
> ends, and whose duty is soon done; who cast their off-
> spring loose, early, as birds do theirs; and, if they do
> well, claim the merit; and, if ill, the pity."

> .   .   .   .

> "I had a sister" [the Phantom went on]. . . . "Such
> glimpses of the light of home as I had ever known,
> had streamed from her. How young she was, how fair,
> how loving! I took her to the first poor roof that I was
> master of, and made it rich. She came into the dark-
> ness of my life, and made it bright."

Redlaw's sister falls in love with his most trusted
friend. At the same time Redlaw, emulating Dickens with
Maria Beadnell, falls in love and then discovers that he is
too poor to bind the girl he adores "by any thread of
promise or entreaty." Again like Dickens, Redlaw strives to
rise so that he can be worthy of his beloved's love, while his
steadfast sister—"sweet companion!"—remains patiently
by his side. Redlaw works on. He believes in himself and
his friends; he has faith in their undying love. He also has
faith in the future. His great comfort is to picture that
wonderful future. He envisions himself married to his love,
his sister married to her love (his best friend), and all four
living on in "mellowed happiness," bound to the past by a
"radiant garland" of "golden links." But these comforting
visions of eternal closeness and happiness are delusions;
betrayal shatters his "frail universe." His trusted friend
marries the girl he is striving to win. In the wake of this
catastrophe only one thing survives, or seems to survive—
jilted sister cleaves to jilted brother.

> "My sister" [continued the Phantom], "doubly dear,
> doubly devoted, doubly cheerful in my home, lived on
> to see me famous, and my old ambition so rewarded
> when its spring was broken, and then——"

"Then died," he interposed. "Died, gentle as ever; happy; and with no concern but for her brother. Peace!"

The Phantom watched him silently.

"Remembered!" said the haunted man, after a pause. "Yes. So well remembered, that even now, when years have passed, and nothing is more idle or more visionary to me than the boyish love so long out-lived, I think of it with sympathy, as if it were a younger brother's or a son's. Sometimes I even wonder when her heart first inclined to him, and how it had been affected towards me.—Not lightly, once, I think.—But that is nothing. Early unhappiness, a wound from a hand I loved and trusted, and a loss that nothing can replace, outlive such fancies."

"Thus," said the Phantom, "I bear within me a Sorrow and a Wrong. Thus I prey upon myself. Thus, memory is my curse; and, if I could forget my sorrow and my wrong, I would!"

Dickens also yearned to forget his sorrow and his wrong, but found that he could not. Yet, like Redlaw, he too came, intellectually at least, to accept his burden as both curse and gift. He saw that his blacking-warehouse days, his mother's insensitivity to his suffering, and his own secret agonies of frustrated love were somehow at the heart of his great achievement. "I know," he wrote much later, discussing these afflictions, "how all these things have worked together to make me what I am."

When Dickens read *A Blot in the 'Scutcheon* he had already experienced all that was formative in the tangle of events and emotions I have been analyzing here, the tangle that lay behind the literary and personal consequences I have just been tracing. And when he read *A Blot,* the emotions that composed that tangle were stirred into pas-sionate response. It is easy to see why this was so. Or-phaned Mildred is loving companion and sole sister to young Thorold. Their relationship, close, idyllic, all-impor-tant, is summed up by Thorold when he says,

Mildred, I do believe a brother's love
For a sole sister must exceed them all.
For see now, only see! there's no alloy
Of earth that creeps into the perfect'st gold
Of other loves—no gratitude to claim;
You never gave her life, not even aught
That keeps life—never tended her, instructed,
Enriched her—so, your love can claim no right
O'er her save pure love's claim: that's what I call
Freedom from earthliness. You'll never hope
To be such friends, for instance, she and you,
As when you hunted cowslips in the woods
Or played together in the meadow hay.

One can imagine Dickens' response to this passage. It must have seemed like an account of his own childhood, his own feelings. He too had been "orphaned"; he too had known the saving grace of "a brother's love for a sole sister"; he too, accompanied by his sister, had hunted flowers in the woods and played in meadow hay; he too believed that no one could "hope to be such friends" again as he and his sister had been in that lost time. Browning emphasizes these and similar notions again and again—always in ways to stir Dickens' heart—as, for example, when Thorold says a little later "—I think, am sure, a brother's love exceeds / All the world's love in its unworldliness."

To these notes of perfect love and perfect childhood companionship, Browning adds a third note, betrayal. Thorold is tormented by the realization that this pure selfless love, this time of perfect felicity, is bartered in a moment for a lesser love, a love lavished on an interloper. This too must have spoken unconsciously to Dickens' heart. Had not his mother, had not Fanny, had not Maria rejected and replaced him? Had they not betrayed him in a moment for some new interest? But perhaps there was another, still deeper identification between his emotions and those portrayed in the play. What dark impulses motivated Thorold's

murderous assault on the usurper of his sister's love?—and
what unexamined forces of sympathy and horror struggled
in Dickens' mind as he read and enacted Thorold's vengeance? Thorold's murderous triumph over an intolerable
event in his past permitted Dickens to enact a similar, if
momentary, victory over a parallel event in his own past.
This profound parallelism, together with all the other affin-
ities in *A Blot,* must have stirred and agitated Dickens. But
there was one last affinity in the play, an affinity that had
the power to call up a more recent and more cataclysmic
loss in Dickens' life. That last affinity is simple and cogent,
and it is this: Mildred's sudden death in Thorold's brotherly
arms is a re-enactment of Mary Hogarth's sudden death in
Dickens' brotherly arms. Dickens could hardly have failed
to respond to this parallel. When he read *A Blot* he was
only five years away from Mary's tragic death and was still
tormented by it; he must have found this final similitude
unutterably painful and touching, and unutterably convincing and true.

Browning, unconsciously, had involved Dickens completely. He had created a heroine and a situation which
shadowed forth central aspects of Dickens' life, which
embodied losses and yearnings—especially brother-sister-
lover losses and yearnings—which Dickens had already
dwelt on in *Oliver Twist, Nicholas Nickleby,* and *The Old
Curiosity Shop,* and which touched chords Dickens would
subsequently sound more elaborately in almost all his later
works. The pattern Browning had evoked in *A Blot* was a
permutation of the Dickensian love pattern, a confused
pattern which had originated in Dickens' early childhood,
been confirmed and reconfirmed in adolescence and youth,
and become fixed by early manhood. One can toll the words
that epitomize that stressful pattern: orphan, sister, lover;
innocent, rejected, doomed—the conjunction echoed ach-
ingly in Dickens' heart. Remembering all this, one under-
stands why Dickens, to use his own words, was thrown

"into a perfect passion of sorrow" by *A Blot;* why he claimed that he had never found anything "in any book I have ever read" as affecting as Mildred's recurrence to, "I was so young—I had no mother"; why he said of the play, "I know no love like it, no passion like it, no moulding of a splendid thing after its conception, like it"; and why he also said, "the tragedy I shall never forget, or less vividly remember than I do now."

DICKENS' SELF-ESTIMATE: SOME NEW EVIDENCE

Philip Collins

"It is not for an author to describe his own books," Dickens
pronounced in the Address prefacing the Cheap Edition of
his works in 1847; "if they cannot speak for themselves, he
is likely to do little service by speaking for them." The
Address says nothing about the processes of his art, and
merely alludes, in the most generalized terms, to the "purpose and sympathy" expressed in the novels, "the spirit in
which they have been written, . . . the cheering-on of
very many thousands of my countrymen and country-
women, never more numerous and true to me than now."
For most of his novels Dickens wrote a preface, and sometimes a new or revised preface for a later edition, but they
rarely say anything substantial about the aims or methods
of his art. On occasion, indeed, he will confess that a
preface is provided "more because I am unwilling to depart
from any custom which has become endeared to me by
having prevailed between myself and my readers on former
occasions of the same kind, than because I have anything
particular to say" (1844 Preface to *Martin Chuzzlewit*). He
was no Henry James, no Wordsworth believing (with Coleridge) that every great and original writer must create the
taste by which he is to be relished, must teach the art by

which he is to be seen—or, to shift to a hackneyed but still suggestive comparison, he was in this respect more like Shakespeare (so silent on his art) than like Ben Jonson, always busily telling his audiences the why and wherefore of the play they were seeing or reading.

Shakespeare tells us nothing about the elements of his art which we discuss—his development, his blank verse, his imagery, and so on. How much more does Dickens tell us? How fully aware was he of the achievements and developments that seem evident to us? Dickens is of course much more fully documented in this matter than Shakespeare: at least we have those prefaces; we have the records by many people of conversations with a man who was, for over thirty years and in an age of publicity, the world's darling; and we have, or shall have, the twelve thousand surviving letters to be published in the Pilgrim Edition. On his art, these various forms of evidence tell us, I think, little that is not evident to the most cursory reader of the novels. Thus, for two of the novels about which we might most welcome extended comment from the author (*Hard Times* and *Great Expectations*) Dickens wrote no prefaces at all. There are of course some letters referring to them, but K. J. Fielding strikes one as just when he comments upon J. Hillis Miller's claim that one of these letters provides an "important sign" of the basic conception of *Great Expectations;* this, says Fielding,

> shows almost desperation in looking for a sign. . . . It is strange, in fact, how little Dickens's own remarks reveal about what *Great Expectations* must have meant to him. . . . We should recognise that, even for his own times, he was exceptionally close about his imaginative life; however little he may have examined himself, he must have understood more than he says. . . . But he hardly once looks out from under cover.[1]

If we turn to Dickens' other art, that of the actor and public reader, we find his numerous letters on those activities

similarly uninformative about his platform aims and techniques: he refers often to the evidences of "that particular
relation (personally affectionate and like no other man's)
which subsists between me and the public"[2] and to the
artistic and monetary success of reading after reading. On
the few occasions when a performance fell short of success, he generally blames the dullness of the audience.
Never does he make the self-analysis or express the self-
criticism that on finds in, say, the diaries of W. C.
Macready.

The prefaces to the novels, indeed, recur to three
topics: the particularly affectionate relationship which ex-
isted between himself and his readers, the problems and
difficulties of serialization, and the truth and reality of
what he had written. Remarks on the artistic aims and
intentions are few, brief, and vague, for example, the
Christmas books were "a whimsical kind of masque"; in
Bleak House "I have purposely dwelt upon the romantic
side of familiar things." Much the most interesting of
these preoccupations in the prefaces is the reiterated assertion (usually in reply to criticisms expressed while the
novel was being serialized) that such-and-such a person or
institution is, *pace* the critics, true-to-life. John Forster
records, helpfully,

> What I had indeed to notice in him, at the very out-
> set of his career, was his indifference to any praise of
> his performances on the merely literary side, compared
> with the higher recognition of them as bits of actual
> life, with the meaning and purpose on their part, and
> the responsibility on his, of realities rather than crea-
> tures of fancy.[3]

"Higher recognition" indeed!—so much for Aristotle and
for fiction's being "a higher and more philosophical thing
than history." Of course this won't do as an aesthetic, but
the insistence certainly tells us a part of what Dickens most
passionately thought he was doing.

Thus he defends Krook's death by spontaneous combustion, not in terms of symbolic rightness or its place in the pattern of *Bleak House*, but as a proved medical possibility. On more promising materials, the same protest and defense occurs repeatedly: Pickwick's change of character is credible; Nancy's devotion to the brutal Sikes may seem improbable or unnatural but "It is true" (later strengthened to "IT IS TRUE"); Mr. Dombey's character is credible— "the faculty (or the habit) of correctly observing the character of man, is a rare one" which Dickens asserts that he himself possesses and uses in creating Mr. Dombey, though some readers (and critics) don't have it and therefore wrongly fail to be convinced. More often, and more fully, it is his presentation of social fact that he defends. Jacob's Island *is* as he presents it in *Oliver Twist;* "Mr. Squeers and his school are faint and feeble pictures of an existing reality, purposely subdued and kept down lest they should be deemed impossible"; the American part of *Martin Chuzzlewit* "is in no other respect a caricature than it is an exhibition, for the most part, of the ludicrous side of the American character—of that side which is, from its very nature, the most obtrusive, and the most likely to be seen by such travellers as Young Martin and Mark Tapley"; and so on through assertions of the truthfulness of his presentation of the Chancery Courts in *Bleak House,* of the French Revolution in *A Tale of Two Cities,* of strange will cases and the operation of the Poor Law in *Our Mutual Friend.*

With what qualifications, and with what sense of their relevance, we would want to accept these assertions by Dickens, I am not now concerned: my subject is what Dickens thought about his work. Other forms of evidence, surveyed elsewhere,[4] are his letters and the articles touching on literary criticism which he wrote, or as an editor published, in his weekly magazines. Certainly, too, his selection of authors and contributions for his magazines is a useful exercise in practical criticism, an extended demonstration of his standards and taste, as I have briefly suggested elsewhere.[5]

Again, in my view nothing very remarkable emerges from these sources; Professors Engel and Stang try hard, in the books I have footnoted, but sound more uplifted by the result than most readers are likely to feel. Writing about his own novels, Dickens is usually making some obvious point about what hard work it all is (and needs to be), or he states the political, social, or moral intentions of his current novel and affirms his sense of the dignity and responsibility of popular fiction. Exceptionally, he remarks on a formal quality, for example, his own interesting comments on how Society, the Circumlocution Office, and Mr. Gowan "are of course three parts of one idea and design" in *Little Dorrit,* and how Miss Wade's History of a Self-Tormentor relates to the themes of that novel.[6] More nebulously, he discusses the operation of "fancy" in the style and structure of his writings.[7] In letters to or about his contributors, he is usually concerned, not with large artistic questions, but with humbler matters of craftsmanship and with how, at a very simple level, to please the reader. His editorial suggestions are sensible enough, though unremarkable: for instance, he writes, "You constantly hurry your narrative (and yet without getting on) *by telling it, in a sort of impetuous breathless way, in your own person, when the people should tell it and act it for themselves. . . .* I think your chapters should be shorter."[8] Or take this long letter to a beginner whose offered contribution, "A Wife's Story," much impressed him, although he returned it to her with suggestions for her to consider:

> I particularly entreat you to consider the catastrophe. You write to be read, of course. The close of the story is unnecessarily painful—will throw off numbers of persons who would otherwise read it, and who (as it stands) will be deterred by hearsay from so doing, and it is so tremendous a piece of severity, that it will

defeat your purpose. All my knowledge and experience, such as they are, lead me straight to the recommendation that you will do well to spare the life of the
husband, and of one of the children. Let her suppose
the former dead, from seeing him brought in wounded
and insensible—lose nothing of the progress of her
mental suffering when that doctor is in attendance
upon her—but bring her round at last to the blessed
surprise that her husband is still living, and that a
repentance which can be worked out, *in the way of
atonement for the misery she has occasioned to the
man whom she so ill repaid for his love, and made so
miserable*, lies before her. So will you soften the reader
whom you now as it were harden, and so you will
bring tears from many eyes, which can only have their
spring in affectionately and gently touched hearts. I
am perfectly certain that with this change, all the
previous part of your tale will tell for twenty times as
much as it can in its present condition. . . . I
observe some parts of the story which would be
strengthened, even in their psychological interest, by
condensation here and there. If you will leave that to
me, I will perform the task as conscientiously as if it
were my own.[9]

This letter expresses not only the views of Dickens as editor
of a family magazine, but also (rather depressingly) a not-
unimportant tenet of Dickens, the greatest of English novelists: that fiction should, in a very simple sense, please
and satisfy the customer. To cite two well-known incidents,
when he was revising his intentions: could Walter Gay
deteriorate in character "without making people angry"?
and, with the rewritten ending of *Great Expectations,* "I
have no doubt the story will be more acceptable."[10] In
neither case does he argue which development would be
more logical or "better." Not only or even primarily to get
their money, Dickens hated disappointing people; he had
an endearing desire to cheer them up, though he also was
willing to reject his readers' clamor that he should "save
Little Nell" and other apparently doomed victims when

moving toward a conventionally accepted dénouement of tender pathos. As his delight in giving public readings also reminds us, he saw his function as akin to the entertainment industry as much as to Art.[11] And much of the particular quality and the strength of his achievement springs from this view of his task—not only the weaknesses exemplified before. It was an aspect of his working, as Thomas Hood put it, "along the great human currents, and not against them"[12] that helped give his work its human centrality.

Few of these remarks, however, take us close to the detail of Dickens' achievement. On the direction of his development, for instance, so very striking to us, he has remarkably little to say. Except for frequent, but unspecific, comments on how much more carefully he is planning his novels, we are apt to get only such generalized and unhelpful comments as this, made while he was writing *David Copperfield:* "The world would not take another Pickwick from me now, but we can be merry and cheerful, I hope, notwithstanding, and with a little more purpose in us."[13]

"The advantage of doing one's praising for oneself," Samuel Butler sagely observed, "is that one can lay it on so thick and exactly in the right places."[14] As we have seen, Dickens was not his own severest critic; indeed, he was apt, like the Lord on the sixth day, to look back on all that he had made, and, behold, it was very good, but a modesty about saying so, and the reluctance to say very much except in the broadest terms about his aims and methods, make his self-praise disappointingly inexplicit. It is my contention, however, that there exists a substantial and apparently unused body of evidence about Dickens' self-awareness and self-estimation: John Forster's reviews of his works in the *Examiner*.

"Friendship is better than criticism, and I shall steadily hold my tongue"—the words are not Forster's, but Dickens', in a letter to him about the limitations of contemporary English painting, particularly the work of various close friends of theirs such as Stanfield, Frith, Egg, and Ward. So "of course" these animadversions would remain private, "between ourselves."[15] Forster probably also believed that his friendship with Dickens was more valuable than inopportune criticism which might offend him, and he was very well aware of his friend's "susceptivity almost feminine and . . . eager craving for sympathy."[16] Several times in the *Life* he reverts to this, tracing it back to the painful experience of Dickens' childhood. The savage review of *The Battle of Life* in the *Times* (2 January 1847) "momentarily touched what he too truly called his morbid susceptibility to exasperation"; he was "sensitive in a passionate degree to praise and blame, which yet he made it for the most part a point of pride to assume indifference to"; he "felt criticism, of whatever kind, with too sharp a relish for the indifference he assumed to it; but the secret was that he believed himself to be entitled to a higher tribute than he was always in the habit of receiving."[17] Despite their occasional tiffs and disagreements, particularly in later years, Dickens and Forster remained the closest of friends from their meeting in 1836 or 1837 until Dickens' death in 1870, and it surely is a reasonable hypothesis that, as Forster knew how easily Dickens was upset by adverse criticism, he took care not to disturb their friendship by saying anything in his reviews of the novels and stories from which Dickens would much dissent.

But Forster had of course enjoyed ample opportunity to criticize the novels in private, before they were published or, indeed, before they were even written. From late 1837 onward, as he says, he read all of Dickens' work either in manuscript or proof;[18] in the Dedication of the Library Edition (1858) he was publicly thanked for the "many patient hours he has devoted to the correction of the proof-sheets of the original editions" and for his counsel "during my whole literary life." Moreover, as dozens of pages in the

Life attest, Dickens constantly discussed with Forster the artistic problems he was facing in every successive book. There must indeed have been far more of such discussion than Forster records: in the *Life* he relies almost exclusively on documentary evidence (Dickens' letters to him), but it is clear that the letters only supplemented or substituted for (when Dickens was away from London) the usual prolonged conversational exchanges of opinion. (Thus, as has been remarked, *The Chimes* and *Dombey and Son* are unusually well documented, simply because Dickens was abroad when writing them.)[19] So Forster, besides having a strong motive for pleasing Dickens when reviewing him, had much fuller knowledge than anyone but the author himself of what was being attempted and how. He not only had reasons for laying the praise on thick, but he also knew exactly the right places.

Not that one should assume that his praise of Dickens was insincere: he certainly much admired his work, as well as loving the man and valuing the friendship. Before they had met, he was praising the early numbers of *Pickwick* as "beyond a doubt, the most original and amusing series of comic sketches that have been produced in our time" and their author as taking rank with the best comic writers in the language.[20] He was notoriously loyal to his friends and was often accused of log-rolling for them. In my judgment, however, he did pull his punches when reviewing Dickens —not expressing insincere praise so much as suppressing his reservations. Particularly over the later novels, from *Bleak House* onward, he felt less enthusiasm, I think, than his reviews suggested. I infer this from a comparison of the accounts of the novels in the *Examiner* with those in the *Life*. Possibly, of course, the verdicts in the *Life* represent more critical second thoughts, written as they were ten or twenty or thirty years later; but I doubt this, as the general structure of the argument tends to be similar in the review and in the *Life*, but with the *Life* adding qualifications and adverse criticism. If I am right, then, there is a strong case for regarding the original reviews as being pretty much an expression of what Dickens thought, and wanted others to think, of his latest work.

All this assumes that Forster is known, or can be proved, to have written the *Examiner* reviews. In the absence of any satisfactory biography and of Forster's collected correspondence, there is to my knowledge hardly any external evidence that he wrote these reviews of Dickens in the *Examiner*. Only once, I think, in the *Life* does he acknowledge having written a review of Dickens, but then (as he claims) he omitted from the *Life* much "matter concerning myself."[21] Certainly there is a prima facie probability that Forster would have written the *Examiner* reviews of Dickens, at least until he ceased editing that journal in 1855: he was its literary editor when Dickens began publishing (and met him soon afterwards) and was editor from 1847 to 1855. Even without his having a personal motive to review the latest Dickens, he was the obvious staff man for the job. Charles Kent, in the *Dictionary of National Biography* entry on Forster, states categorically that he never wrote a line for the *Examiner* after resigning from the editorship,[22] but it is clear that at least he continued reviewing Dickens (and it would be a foolish editor who failed to retain so well-qualified a reviewer of the leading novelist of the day, especially as the job would still be done anonymously). There is abundant evidence that Forster wrote the *Examiner* reviews of the novels after, as well as before, 1855.

When compiling the *Life,* Forster restricted himself to giving notices of the novels "which are rather biographical than critical,"[23] and certainly did not make scissors-and-paste insertions from his old reviews. But almost all the "notices" in the *Life,* however brief, echo phrases and lines of thought from the *Examiner* reviews. Indeed, either Forster had a very good verbal memory for his favorite phrases, written up to thirty-five years earlier, or (much more likely) he had kept, and now read over, a cuttings-book of his miscellaneous journalism. Moreover, the repetition of ideas from review to review, sometimes explicitly ("we dwelt upon" the same feature of Dickens' art, when reviewing *A Tale of Two Cities*, the review of *Great Expectations* remarks),[24] shows that many of the *Examiner* reviews were written by the same man. To sum this up, there is entirely convincing evidence that Forster wrote almost all of the *Examiner* reviews of Dickens, and I can see no reason to believe that he did not write every one of them except the review of *The Chimes*.[25] To present detailed evidence for the authorship of so many items would overburden this essay, so I relegate to the end a few specimens of the proofs I rely upon. I hope that readers will accept as proved what they would surely expect to be the case anyway: that so loyal a friend and so active a journalist as Forster did not neglect the opportunity to review, in the journal with which he was so closely associated, the works of his dear friend Dickens. The fiercely possessive manner he adopted toward Dickens in private life and the intense concern he showed for his well-being[26] surely did not desert him when there was a chance to praise his works in public—or puff them, as was said by their enemies, who made malicious jokes about Dickens' "Fostering friends" and about his being supported by "the *Examiner* clique."[27] The reviews of the earlier novels were, in fact, rather more critical than these jibes suggest. While praising the earlier novels highly—repeatedly claiming that the young Dickens was a novelist in the same class as the great eighteenth-century masters, duly recognizing these stories, as Dickens desired, "as bits of actual life, . . . realities rather than creatures of fancy,"[28] and particularly commending the pathos and sentiment—Forster reverted to two criticisms. He remarked about *Nicholas Nickleby*, "And with all these masterly requisites for his art, is Mr. Dickens a perfect novelist? By no means. He has yet to acquire the faculty of constructing a compact and effective story. . . . He has yet to subdue his tendencies to exaggeration. . . . In reserve for Mr. Dickens are still greater triumphs if he has the patience and perseverance to prepare himself by study and self-restraint, by the pursuit of art and the pruning of common-place exuberance."[29] These complaints cease with *Martin Chuzzlewit*, where Forster discerns "a management of the design more skillful . . . than in any former work of Mr. Dickens. . . . It seems to us that with no abatement of the power which gives out sharp and bold impressions of reality, we have more of the subtler requisites which satisfy imagination and reflection."[30]

Thereafter, indeed, not much is criticized, and then usually in general and decidedly forgiving tones. Thus, he says of *Our Mutual Friend*, "We may say, if we will, that here we like and there we don't like any character or passage, but far above desire to criticize by the small way of personal comparison between our individual tastes and opinions and those of our author is the keen enjoyment of his genius."[31] A rare instance of Forster's making a specific criticism of a later novel is this, on *Bleak House:* "The character of Esther Summerson has been much elaborated, and the early portions of her narrative are as charming as anything Mr. Dickens has ever written, . . . but we suspect that Mr. Dickens undertook more than any man could ever accomplish when he resolved to make her the naïve revealer of her own good qualities. . . . Yet the virtues and graces of Esther have won so many hearts that we do not care to dwell on our objection to his method of displaying them."[32] In both these cases, the *Life* is much more blunt: *Our Mutual Friend* "will never rank with his higher efforts. It wants freshness and natural development"; and to use Esther as a narrator "was a difficult enterprise, full of hazard in any case, not worth success, and certainly not successful. . . . Nor can this be said of Esther's narration without some general application to the book of which it forms so large a part."[33]

As we would expect, these reviews are fuller of praise than criticism, and the praise is the more interesting because it keeps reverting to three points which other contemporary reviewers made much less often and less insistently. These points—which I take to be very much Dickens', however sincerely they may have been accepted by Forster—are (1) an insistence, from *David Copperfield* onward, on the unity of every novel: every character and episode is relevant, and as the central organizing force there is an idea; (2) a repeated comparison of Dickens' art to that of a poet; and (3) a growing impatience with serialization, and an emphasis on the necessity of reading, or rereading, each novel as a whole in order to appreciate its finer points. These three points are indeed all different ways of stressing Dickens' artistic control of his material, of his imposing an imaginative unity upon it, and of defining the mode and nature of that unity ("the novel as dramatic poem," to cite a famous twentieth-century attempt at redefining some of the possibilities of prose fiction).

The insistence upon the formal unity of Dickens' later novels is part of the larger claim that, by now, he is "not only a writer of rare and original genius—when at his best, we say it most deliberately, the greatest master of the whimsical and the pathetic yet to be found in any age among the prose writers of Europe—but he has wrought himself into a novelist who is master of his art."[34] This claim for the perfection of his design is first enunciated (where we might demur against finding it so strongly evidenced) over *David Copperfield:* "Amid all the prodigal profusion of distinct and distinguishable figures, the gothic abundance of graceful and quaint details . . . there is yet a unity in the book which is always felt, both as to purpose and to aim. It has a profoundly studied aim. Without parade of moral maxims we are incessantly reminded . . .

of the duty of tolerance towards individuals, of charitable and kindly construction for all."[35] The unity of other later novels is more convincingly described and demonstrated,[36] and in the review of *Our Mutual Friend* Forster offers his fullest description of the peculiarly English form of unity which Dickens creates. He illustrates this mainly in reference to Shakespeare, naming the principle of unity in four of his plays, and then by referring to *Tom Jones*, before turning to the novel being reviewed: "Latinized races accuse English writers of a disregard for unity in works of art. . . . [But] although we recognise even more thoroughly than our neighbors the demand for unity of action, what we mean by that is not outward simplicity and singleness of plot, but a well-harmonized relation of all parts to one central thought, . . . a crystallization of thought about some one central idea. . . . Mr. Dickens invariably fulfills in his novels this condition of deep-seated unity which has always been recognised in English art."[37] Forster's definition of the "idea" which he discerns at the center of the successive later novels never comes close to exhausting the possibilities for critical discussion (any more than the notion of "selfishness" takes one far toward understanding *Chuzzlewit*),[38] but at least the repeated emphasis on this form of unifying the novels seems to be one of the points that Dickens most wanted Forster to make.

The comparison with poetry is another way of suggesting the unity of the novels, as well as defining other aspects of Dickens' art. "Novels as Mr. Dickens writes then rise to the dignity of poems"[39]—and not merely the dignity, but also the mode, of poetry, so that "much that the ordinary reader may pass carelessly in the book [*Dombey*], will seize upon the fancy alive to poetical expression and accustomed to poetical art."[40] Forster uses this comparison for several purposes: sometimes to draw attention to the texture, imagery, and symbolism of the writing. Thus, the descriptions in *Bleak House,* apart from having "great beauty in themselves," are "so employed as to bear always a subtle and thoughtful reference to the imaginative and romantic design of the story."[41] Or, in *Dombey,* "the recurrence of particular thoughts and phrases is an instance of the [poetical] kind, running like a leading colour through a picture, or the predominant phrase in a piece of music, because subtly connected with the emotion which it is the design of the story to create."[42] The notion of "poetry" also suggests Dickens' mode of characterization: "From other English novelists we think that Mr. Dickens may hereafter be distinguished as the one writing most habitually with the temper of a poet. This it is, in no slight degree, which gives their peculiarity to nearly all the characters he paints. They are personifications . . . to be taken rather as one of the elements of truth reduced to its pure state by the chemistry of genius than as the ordinary compound truth which enters into every-day life."[43] Or, again, the comparison with poetry helps Forster to explain his narrative devices. For instance, the use of the rainstorm in Soho in *A Tale of Two Cities* "to suggest the greater storm of which the first drops had then fallen . . . is artifice, but it is the artifice of a poet, and by like touches that are often flashed suddenly into a word or through a single line, the force of poetry is added to the book."[44] Other critics were referring to Dickens as "the poet of great cities" and suchlike, but no other critics, I think, so often or so suggestively used the analogy to define both the force and the nonnaturalistic mode of his art. And here perhaps was one of Forster's ways of offering him that "higher tribute than he was always in the habit of receiving," but to which he thought he was entitled: certainly it helped him to suggest the "immortal" qualities beneath his topicalities, as in the review when he said that Dickens' novels rise to the dignity of poems: "Upon this high ground we must stand if we would properly discuss *Bleak House.* . . . The world will grow wiser than it is, the abuses attacked by this greatest of humorists and kindliest of satirists will disappear—but the spirit in which he writes, and to which he appeals, is indestructible; and the emotions he awakens are not more fresh and true to us than they will be to future generations."[45]

Dickens had always been conscious (Forster wrote in the *Life*) of "the tendency of composing a story piecemeal to induce greater concern for the part than for the whole, . . . but I remember a remark also made by him to the effect that to read a story in parts had no less a tendency to prevent readers noticing how thoroughly a work so presented might be calculated for perusal as a whole."[46] Forster certainly did his best to force readers to notice this: Dickens' remark appears verbatim in his review of *Bleak House,* and the idea is repeated and expanded in every subsequent review of the novels.[47] "Read piecemeal [*Our Mutual Friend*] was satisfactory only to those who had faith in their author," and indeed the reader "sometimes may have rashly supposed that here [in the Boffin plot] the master's hand had lost its cunning"; but, read as a whole, all becomes clear and the "ingenious arrangement and skillful conduct of the story" are evident.[48] Forster's most emphatic statement of this point occurs in the *Great Expectations* review, which opens with the recommendation, "All who have read this story from week to week, as it appeared in the vigorous and entertaining pages of Mr. Dickens' popular journal, should join those who now read it for the first time as a finished work," and then makes the point twice again later: "It is worth any man's while, and the better the man the more it is worth his while, to read the tale twice—for the second time critically, in order to observe the exquisite art of passages that at the first reading influence, at the author's will with unsuspected subtlety, alike the cunning and the simple."[49] This emphasis was no doubt Forster's response to Dickens' letter to him, enclosing the chapters which open Stage III: "It is a pity that the third portion cannot be read all at once, because its purpose would be much more apparent; and the pity is the greater, because the general turn and tone of the working out and winding up, will be away from all such things as they conventionally go."[50]

It is also in the *Great Expectations* review that Forster makes his fullest statement (in the *Examiner*) of the nature of Dickens' development, protesting against those readers (particularly the older ones) who cling overmuch to the pleasures of the past, and see Dickens still as the author of *Pickwick:*

> Let it not be forgotten that to the sober middle-aged man who believes only in *Pickwick* and *Nicholas Nickleby*, those books were among the choicest delights of twenty years ago, when he read only for enjoyment, delighted openly and heartily in all that he enjoyed, and had a mind that he could deliver alive into the hands of his entertainer. Such power of enjoyment may be blunted now, but very sure are we that in the author of *Pickwick* the power of giving a true and high pleasure has been sharpened and refined. . . . In place of the old sketch books of adventure lengthened at will, and the pathetic or humorous personifications of life that were the spontaneous outpouring of an earnest mind and a swift fancy, we have now the same wit that has so vividly represented detached scenes, concentrated with its whole strength upon the construction of a plot that shall knit every fragment of its detail into one round and perfect whole.[51]

This stress upon the unity and total relevance of the later novels is, as we have seen, the main contention of Forster in these reviews; over *Great Expectations* he could express this praise with the fullest sincerity and the least sense of suppressing unpalatable criticisms, for (as the *Life* makes clear) *Great Expectations* was much his favorite among the later novels.

Forster's view of Dickens' development seems indeed akin to G. K. Chesterton's that the later books are less bad, but not better.[52] In the *Life* he notes how much more care Dickens was taking and how his constructional skill increases, but he does not repeat from the *Examiner* reviews those Coleridgean obeisances to wholeness and unity, nor the contention that Dickens was a poetic novelist. Rather, in the later work he finds strain and failure of spontaneity and too much that is "disagreeable" (a term that he uses very loosely, with the assumption that anything unpleasant is bad art). Thus, after delighting in the whimsicalities of Micawber, he uses this extraordinary argument: "It is a tribute to the generally healthful and manly tone of the story of *Copperfield* that such should be the outcome of the eccentricities of this leading personage in it; and the superiority in this respect of Micawber over Skimpole is one of the many indications of the inferiority of *Bleak House* to its predecessor." So, as he puts it in the *Life, Bleak House* "with a very restless dissatisfied moral . . . is too much brought about by agencies disagreeable and sordid" and has many characters "much too real to be pleasant"; *Hard Times* was undoubtedly below (not above, as Taine thought) his ordinary level as a writer; *Little Dorrit* used agencies "less agreeable even than in *Bleak House*" to bring about its catastrophe, and "it made no material addition to his reputation"; *A Tale of Two Cities* "was for him a hazardous, and can hardly be called an entirely successful, experiment"; *Our Mutual Friend* "will never rank with his higher efforts. . . . It has not the creative power which crowded his earlier pages." The novels following *Copperfield* were, for Forster, spoiled by "the underlying tone of bitterness"; the abuses which Dickens exposed "would not have been made less odious by the cheerier tones that had struck with much sharper effect" in the earlier novels, for "anger does not improve satire."[53] These fundamental reservations about the later novels are scarcely hinted at in the *Examiner* reviews, of course; hence my belief that these reviews represent what Dickens wanted to read rather than what Forster entirely thought.

Such, then, are the recurrent emphases of the *Examiner* reviews. Two other ways in which they are relevant to the study of Dickens (apart from their having much the same virtues of unexciting competence as a dozen other reviews of the same novel) are, I suggest, that they amplify our sense of the advice that Dickens was getting from his closest literary adviser, and that they offer an official spokesman's account of particular novels or of controversial elements in them. To illustrate these points briefly, by one example of each: recall that *Times* review of *The Battle of Life* which touched up the inimitable Boz with a blunt razor. The *Times* had indeed been excoriating: *The Battle* was *the very worst* of all the trashy Christmas books which Dickens' example had induced publishers to promote; Dickens was a genius, indeed, but here had not earned his remuneration; "the whole fabric is feeble in the extreme, false, artificial, worthless," and so on, demolishing at great length and in full detail the unhappy Christmas story.[54] Forster, on the other hand, wrote another favorable review in the *Examiner* (and was still, in the *Life*, warmly disposed toward the book).[55] *The Battle of Life* surely now seems so little defensible against the *Times* attack that one sees the element of justice in Carlyle's grumpy contention that "Dickens lived among a set of admirers who did him no good—Maclise the painter, Douglas Jerrold, John Forster, and the like."[56] Forster encouraged Dickens in more worthy enterprises than *The Battle*, and had in earlier reviews checked him for weaknesses that indeed Dickens later corrected (though whether *propter hoc* or *post hoc* is another question); but the large measure of uncritical adulation he received from Forster (much of it sincere, like the praise of *The Battle*) doubtless helped to arrest him at immaturities he might have outgrown more quickly.

The other point (that the reviews offer the "official"

comment on controversial matters) may be illustrated from the review of *Hard Times*, a novel for which, as was noted, no preface was written. Forster discusses the story's "purpose," arguing, as he does again in the *Life*, that fiction cannot prove a case, but may suggest a righteous sentiment. Then he comments on Dickens and "Facts":

> *Hard Times*, in fact, is not meant to be fought through, prosed over, conned laboriously, Blue Book in hand. If the heart is touched with a lively perception of the true thought which pervades the work from first to last—then the full moral purpose of it is attained. The very journal in which the novel appeared is itself a complete answer to any man, who, treating in a hard-fact spirit all the fanciful allusions of the novelist, should accuse Mr. Dickens of attacking this good movement and the other, or of opposing the search after statistical and other information by which only real light can be thrown on social questions. What is *Household Words* but a great magazine of facts? And what one is there, of all those useful matters of detail which the novelist has by some readers been supposed to treat with disrespect, which he has not, as conductor of that journal, carefully and fully urged upon the public notice? In his character of journalist Mr. Dickens has from the first especially laboured to cultivate the kindly affections and the fancy at the same time with the intellect, and that is simply what he asks men in "these times" to do. But because he knows that facts and figures will not be lost sight of by the world, he leaves them, when he speaks as a novelist, to take care of themselves, and writes his tale wholly in the interests of the affections and the fancy.[57]

A perusal of *Household Words* is indeed, as Forster suggests, a useful complement to *Hard Times* if we seek to understand Dickens' intention (not necessarily his achievement) in that novel, and not only in its Facts/Fancy element. And so broad a hint about Dickens' intention would certainly not have been made by Forster if he had thought that Dickens would reject it.

In these various ways, then, Forster's reviews of the novels tell us, usually in far more detail than the prefaces and letters, what Dickens valued in his work and how he thought his art operated. If my argument on this is found unconvincing, at least the reviews (together with the *Life*) still deserve special attention as the considered views of the colleague on whose literary advice, as well as practical sagacity, Dickens most fully and continuously relied.

Evidence for Forster's Authorship of the Examiner *Reviews*

There is usually some similarity between the *Examiner* reviews and the *Life* "notices" of Dickens' novels in terms of the nature and structure of the argument, and the selection of characters or episodes for special comment. To illustrate this would require too much space, so, instead, I shall quote a few phrases from *Examiner* reviews which reappear, verbatim or with modification, in the *Life*. To save space, I shall not transcribe the *Life* passage but refer to the page (in Ley's edition, 1928) where the phrase appears; as further aid, I add book and chapter references. Also to save space, I give examples from the reviews of every second novel. Evidence could also be cited for reviews of the Christmas writings.

OLIVER TWIST: "The scrupulous reader may make what deduction he pleases for the 'lowness' of the subject— the absolute truth and precision of its delineation are not to be disputed" (10 September 1837, p. 581; cf. *Life*, II, *iii*, 113).

MASTER HUMPHREY'S CLOCK: "*Barnaby Rudge* is Mr. Dickens' first attempt out of the actual life and manners of the day. The story is told with a purpose: the characteristic of all his later writings" (4 December 1841, p. 772; cf. *Life,* II, *ix,* 169–70).

DOMBEY AND SON: "What was said of it [the death of Paul] by the author of the *Two Old Men's Tales,* that it flung a nation into mourning, was hardly an exaggeration (28 October 1848, p. 692; cf. *Life,* VI, *ii,* 476–77).

BLEAK HOUSE: "Even the fits of the little law-stationer's servant aid directly in the chain of little things that lead indirectly to the catastrophe of Lady Dedlock's death" (8 October 1853, p. 644; cf. *Life,* VII, *i,* 560).

LITTLE DORRIT: "Its aim . . . is to show the beauty . . . of a simple, unaffected doing of all duties, great and little. . . . Through poverty and wealth the golden thread of Duty runs, ever the same" (13 June 1857, p. 372; cf. *Life,* VIII, *i,* 627).

GREAT EXPECTATIONS: The *Examiner* review presents no verbal, and few other, parallels to the *Life* notice, but is written by the same hand as the review of *A Tale of Two Cities* (see above, citing *Examiner,* 20 July 1861, p. 452); so I give evidence for Forster's review of the latter.

A TALE OF TWO CITIES: "This novel is remarkable for the rare skill with which all the powers of the author's genius are employed upon the conduct of the story. . . . The subtlety with which a private history is associated with a most vivid expression of the spirit of the days of the great French Revolution is but a part of its strength in this respect" (10 December 1859, p. 788; cf. *Life*, ix, *iii*, 732).

OUR MUTUAL FRIEND: "Little Miss Wren, with . . . her precocious wit sharpened by trouble, in which the spirit of childhood casts its golden threads across the dull woof of her life of care" (28 October 1865, p. 682; cf. *Life*, ix, *v*, 743).

"THE STORY-WEAVER AT HIS LOOM": DICKENS AND THE BEGINNING OF *THE OLD CURIOSITY SHOP*

Robert L. Patten

Unlike *Barnaby Rudge*, which, though it followed *The Old Curiosity Shop* in Dickens' three-penny weekly, *Master Humphrey's Clock*, gestated for almost five years, Little Nell's saga was an improvisation, Dickens' hasty, spirited response to a sharp and accelerating decline in sales. Edgar Johnson sets forth the standard account in his characteristically dramatic way.

> The public had flocked to *Master Humphrey* under the impression that it was another Dickens novel. With the second number the sales fell off alarmingly; by the third their decline was disastrous. There was a hasty editorial conference at Chapman and Hall's offices in the Strand. Dickens flung himself at once into the breach. He would expand *The Old Curiosity Shop* into a long serial, postponing the appearance of its first chapter from the third number to the fourth, where it would be announced as a continued story. Meanwhile Mr. Pickwick and Sam Weller would reappear in several intervening numbers and stem the tide while he was enlarging the plan of the story and getting it under way.[1]

Closer examination of the *Clock*, of Dickens' letters, and of the manuscript of *The Old Curiosity Shop* reveals in more detail what was involved in that sudden change of direction, in the wholesale abandonment of *Master Humphrey's Clock,* and the commencement, without advance preparation, of a new novel in weekly numbers. That examination also reveals the necessity of modifying both what Dickens said in his prefaces and elsewhere about his intentions concerning the *Clock* and the *Shop* and what Professor Johnson has reported of the novel's origin.

Dickens conveyed to John Forster his original conception for what was later to be called *Master Humphrey's Clock* in a long letter written from Petersham on 14 July 1839.[2] He was approaching the end of his *Nickleby* labors, and, apart from the agreement to furnish Bentley with *Barnaby Rudge* by the beginning of 1840, was thereafter free of major commitments. Desiring to share more largely in the profits of *Nickleby* (around fourteen thousand pounds), for which he was already to be paid three thousand pounds, he had Forster put before Chapman and Hall his "rough notes of proposals for the New Work" as further incentive for them to "do something handsome—even handsomer perhaps than they dreamt of doing" at the conclusion of *Nickleby* in October. The "new publication" was to be a weekly miscellany, "consisting entirely of original matter," with a club, like the Pickwick Club, whose "personal histories and proceedings" would be carried "through the work." Mr. Pickwick and Sam Weller would be reintroduced. There were to be "amusing essays on the various foibles of the day," a number of "Chapters on Chambers," "stories and descriptions of London as it was many years ago, as it is now, and as it will be many years hence," related by the London Guildhall giants Gog and Magog, and "a series of satirical papers purporting to be translated from some Savage Chronicles," but actually describing abuses of justice in town and country. For additional variety, Dickens planned to throw in "sketches, essays, tales, adventures, letters from imaginary correspondents and so forth, so as to diversify the contents as much as possible." In short, a main emphasis of the journal was to be social and political; like his avowed models the *Tatler,* the *Spectator,* and the *Bee,* Dickens intended to speak out on contemporary issues.

He certainly wanted to avoid writing another long novel. The consecutive, at times concurrent, production of *Pickwick, Twist,* and *Nickleby* had tired him; he feared another serial in monthly numbers might tire his readers; and he hoped, "by invention of a new mode as well as kind of serial publication," to lessen the "strain on his fancy."[3] Indeed, he anticipated a journal more like *Household Words,* a paper conducted by Dickens, but with contributions from other authors. "I must have assistance of course, . . . but I should stipulate that this assistance is chosen solely by me, and that the contents of every number are as much under my own control, and subject to as little interference, as those of a number of *Pickwick* or *Nickleby.*" Chapman and Hall concurred. The agreement, signed on 15 October 1839, provided that Dickens would receive half the profits, plus fifty pounds a week to "edit" the *Clock.*[4] It was mutually understood that out of that sum, after the first few weeks, he might employ others to help him, at a cost "which upon a liberal allowance may average £12 a week, but certainly not more."[5]

Six months after the Petersham letter, when the first number of the *Clock* was written, the social satire and essays on contemporary politics were no longer so prominent a feature of the work. Dickens' imagination had been fired by an "old file in the queer house," and by "his affection for an old quaint queer-cased clock";[6] on 13 January he wrote to George Cattermole asking him to make a sketch for a woodcut of "an old quaint room with antique Elizabethan furniture, and in the chimney-corner an extraordinary old clock." The fiction Dickens was developing, that Master Humphrey had stored odd manuscripts in the clockcase for years, which were now to be taken out and read to his assembled guests, was not congenial to accommodating "amusing essays on the various foibles of the day," but he was still experimenting with the content and arrangement of the numbers. Sending the manuscript of the greater portion of number II to Cattermole early in February 1840, Dickens remarked, "I am writing such things as occur to me without much regarding, for the present, the order in which they will appear, and thus you will receive in the course of the week another story."[7]

Because copies of the *Clock* were being sent to America and Germany, the numbers had to be printed "considerably in advance"; by the middle of February three numbers were in manuscript, and number I was in page proof.[8] In the remainder of the month, Dickens continued to work on number III, and to work also on the confession of a lieutenant in the army of Charles II, which was later inserted in it, for by 9 March Edward Chapman had read the tale and Cattermole had the manuscript. But he was harassed by Bentley's repeated announcements heralding the imminent publication of *Barnaby Rudge*, which, though due 1 January, had not progressed beyond a couple of chapters. On 21 February Dickens told Macready, "For today, the Vagabond has stopped my clock—and he knows that as well as I."[9]

Eight days later Dickens, accompanied by Forster, arrived in Bath to visit Walter Savage Landor at his lodgings, 35 St. James's Square. There, amidst the massed Italian paintings which covered every available surface, Dickens first spoke of his idea of the little child and her grandfather, what he was to call afterwards his "little child-story." The idea took hold powerfully: within a few days he was rearranging *Clock* material to fit it in. Dickens decided to take out of number III the "witch story" of John Podgers and his nephew Will Marks, displeased with its contrast to Master Humphrey. To fill up the gap, he told Forster, "I think of lengthening Humphrey, finishing the description of the [Clock] society, and closing with the little child-story, which is SURE to be effective, especially after the old man's quiet way."[10] At this stage the idea is still quite small, taking up less than a single number (twelve imperial octavo pages) of the *Clock*. Around the same time, Dickens wrote again to Forster, giving a list of alternative titles for the child-story, all stating that the tale is, unlike preceding ones, the personal adventure of one of the club, Master Humphrey himself.[11] Dickens thus reestablished one of the ideas contained in the Petersham proposals, that the "personal histories" of club members would be carried through the work.

Clearly, by Monday morning, 9 March, Dickens had decided not to include "Personal Adventures of Master Humphrey. *The Old Curiosity Shop*" in *Clock* III. On that day, he wrote to Cattermole to congratulate him for the way the woodcut of Master Humphrey's room had come out ("I had *not the faintest anticipation* of anything so good—taking into account the material and the dispatch"), and to inform him of his change of plans. The story of John Podgers is to stand over till a later number, and in its place in number III is to go, not the "little child-story," but rather the confession of the army lieutenant, for which he asks Cattermole to execute a subject as quickly as possible. Contrary to Professor Johnson's statement, this decision to postpone the appearance of *The Old Curiosity Shop* had nothing whatever to do with falling sales: the publication of *Clock* I was still almost a month away.

There is no definitive indication of when Dickens began the actual writing of the *Shop*. However, it seems from the manuscript, which is headed "MASTER HUMPHREY'S CLOCK—NO. IV)/MASTER HUMPHREY FROM HIS CLOCKSIDE IN THE CHIMNEY CORNER," that Dickens never actually *wrote* the "little child-story" for *Clock* III.[12] Under this heading, which is the same as that printed for *Clock*

III, except for the number, Dickens began the story, but after writing ten lines he discarded the opening, using the verso of the canceled slip later for the second page, and started anew on a clean slip, writing the same heading again. The manuscript contains no reference to the later title, which must have been supplied on the proof. This is a curious omission, since Forster says that Dickens' letter announcing "the following double title for the beginning of that little tale" was written on 9 March, and the tale itself could hardly have been started before Dickens returned from Bath on the 5th day. It is clear notwithstanding that Dickens probably began writing the story of Little Nell, for *Clock* IV, around 9 March, well before he had any concrete evidence that the public disliked his diversified miscellany.

We must therefore revise Professor Johnson's timetable, which is based on the somewhat unreliable accounts of Forster and Arthur Waugh. It is quite accurate to say, as he does, that the expansion of the *Shop* "from a short story to a full-length narrative was in part a result of the increasing hold it took upon Dickens's feelings. But even more it was a consequence of Dickens's ability to adapt himself to adverse circumstances"—that is, to the falling sales of the *Clock*.[13] However, Professor Johnson implies that the hasty editorial conference in the Strand was called *after* the reports on the sales of *Clock* III were received, and that *then* Dickens decided to postpone the appearance of the first chapter of the *Shop* from the third to the fourth number. This is patently impossible. In fact, with three numbers of the *Clock*, and the John Podgers story which would fill most of two others, finished by 9 March, Dickens evidently had time to complete the first chapter of the *Shop* and to arrange *Clock* IV in proof before the first number was issued.

Professor Johnson's phrase, "Dickens flung himself at once into the breach," is also misleading, in that it implies that Dickens was at that conference suddenly offering to do more than he had already contracted for. On the contrary, the decision that he would have to write all the *Clock* had been reached well before 22 March, when Dickens told Thomas Beard, "It has been for weeks quite clear to us that I must write it *all,* if we are to hope for that great success which we expect." In calling in Mr. Pickwick and Sam Weller to fill out the intervening numbers (V and VI) and "stem the tide" Dickens was following his original Petersham plan. That he had not changed his mind in the interval is indicated by the advertisement for the *Clock* issued by Chapman and Hall: Phiz's drawing shows Mr. Pickwick sitting at the base of the clockcase.[14] Indeed, all of *Clock* V and VI was probably in page proof, if not printed, before the third number went on sale 18 April.

What happened was probably less dramatic, and more defensible artistically, than Johnson's version. The first chapter of the *Shop* was quite certainly completed before Kate and Dickens left for Birmingham on Friday, 3 April, in accordance with his custom never to be in London on the first publishing day of a new venture. When Forster brought up the news that seventy thousand copies had been sold or ordered on that first Saturday, Dickens was jubilant. Bradbury and Evans had estimated a steady sale of fifty thousand over two years, but Dickens had been skeptical.[15] If the sales continued so strong, he might reap as much as ten thousand pounds annually in salary and profits.[16] As soon as he got back to London, Dickens wrote,

> The Clock goes gloriously indeed. What will the wise-acres say to weekly issues *now?* And what will they say to any of those ten thousand things we shall do together to make 'em wink, and stagger in their shoes? Thank God for this great hit. I always had a quiet confidence in it, but I never expected *this,* at first.[17]

Sales of the second number were not so great, but, as the second number of any serial was likely to sell fewer copies than the first, probably nobody was much disturbed. But when the decline continued, even intensified, with *Clock* III, Chapman and Hall may have held a conference, possibly on Tuesday, 21 April, when they dined with Dickens and Forster, ordered "to C. & H's per cab" then. There they may have asked Dickens what he thought should be done, and he in turn may have suggested elaborating the *Shop,* already set up for the next number, and eliminating most of the other *Clock* matter, thus giving up his recently-won freedom from the incessant labor of a continued story. In that sense, he was flinging himself into the breach. And the decision was of course a gamble: nobody knew whether the story would take with the general public, as nothing of it had as yet been issued. But Dickens' mind was full of possibilities, and the publishers no doubt agreed that a full-length novel would be preferable to the highly diversified contents of the miscellany.

If Dickens had managed to keep three to four weeks ahead of publication date, by this meeting he would have completed *Clock* VI. Returning to his desk after the conference, he would then have worked on *Clock* VII, in which *The Old Curiosity Shop* is resumed. The manuscript shows no sudden plunging into the novel at the expense of already composed *Clock* material: slips for number VII are regularly numbered, and the *Shop* begins on slip 12, the previous eleven (bound separately with the manuscript of the *Clock* portions) being filled with an account of a meeting of the Clock society. Nor was there panic in the Strand; Chapman and Hall had endured disappointing sales before. *Pickwick's* early circulation amounted to only a few hundreds; in comparison, the *Clock* had secured for itself an enormous audience. Nearly a month elapsed before, on 16 May, the second chapter of *The Old Curiosity Shop* was issued.

This being the case, it looks as if the "Personal Adventures of Master Humphrey. *The Old Curiosity Shop*" may have been originally conceived for a single number of the *Clock,* Dickens' fancy being of the little girl and her grandfather, amidst all the grotesque furnishings of the Shop—a sort of "Chapter on Chambers" partly inspired by Cattermole's studio at Clapham Rise, crammed with Byron's massive Albany furniture, tapestries, an elaborately carved escritoire, and suits of armor[18]—and especially of Nell, "alone in the midst of all this lumber and decay and ugly age, . . . smiling through her light and sunny dreams."[19] Master Humphrey's tale has at this point a finality about it, mixed with unresolved mysteries, rather like some of those which preceded it in the *Clock.* Moreover, despite Johnson's assertion that Dickens would announce the *Shop* "as a continued story," there is no indication in either the manuscript or *Clock* IV that this is only chapter one of a continuing tale: it is not headed "Chapter One" nor concluded with "To be continued." Instead, Dickens speaks in his letters of closing number III with the "little child-story" as if it were to be a brief, single installment; the decision to expand it almost certainly came after *Clock* IV was in proof, making it difficult to alter the text to indicate that the tale was to be extended.

On the other hand, Forster declares that Dickens decided, after writing "two or three chapters," that the subject was capable of "more extended treatment than he had at first proposed to give it . . . and he resolved to throw everything else aside, devoting himself to the one story only."[20] And Dickens evidently determined at proof stage that Master Humphrey would recur to this adventure "at intervals," for so he promises on the second page of his tale, a remark absent from the manuscript and deleted from the 1848 Cheap Edition text. Perhaps Dickens intended that the members of the Clock society would speculate on Nell's fate in the intervals between the miscellaneous papers. For surely the logical point of decision about expanding the tale is at the end of chapter 1: once

Dickens introduces Fred and Dick Swiveller in chapter 2, and Quilp in 3, he commits himself to a fairly extensive development, and moves decidedly toward writing a long novel.

This uncertainty about Master Humphrey's adventure —whether it was a tale for a single number, the first of several chapters of a short story, or the beginning of a long narrative, as the plural "Adventures" suggests—is reflected in the structure of the chapter itself, which underwent radical alteration in 1841. In the 1840 version, the final paragraphs seem designed to put an end to the "little child-story."

> "Stay here of course" the child had said in answer to my question, "I always do!" What could take him from home by night, and every night! I called up all the strange tales I had ever heard of dark and secret deeds committed in great towns and escaping detection for a long series of years; wild as many of these stories were, I could not find one adapted to this mystery, which only became the more impenetrable, in proportion as I sought to solve it.
>
> Occupied with such thoughts as these, and a crowd of others all tending to the same point, I continued to pace the street for two long hours; at length the rain began to descend heavily, and then overpowered by fatigue though no less interested than I had been at first, I engaged the nearest coach and so got home. A cheerful fire was blazing on the hearth, the lamp burnt brightly, my clock received me with its old familiar welcome; everything was quiet, warm and cheering, and in happy contrast to the gloom and darkness I had quitted.
>
> But all that night, waking or in my sleep, the same thoughts recurred and the same images retained possession of my brain. I had ever before me the old dark murky rooms—the gaunt suits of mail with their ghostly silent air—the faces all awry, grinning from wood and stone—the dust and rust and worm that lives in wood—and alone in the midst of all this

lumber and decay and ugly age, the beautiful child in her gentle slumber, smiling through her light and sunny dreams.

These paragraphs ring changes on the theme of contrast that has dominated the "Personal Adventures of Master Humphrey." They open and close with the little happy child, in contrast to the aura of gloom and mystery surrounding her grandfather and the Shop. The middle paragraph contrasts Master Humphrey's walk—the weather, the scenery, his thoughts—to the warmth of his clock-side in the chimney corner, to which he returns that night, and from which he reads aloud the story of that adventure. His thoughts have been on the Shop, with its grotesque lumber and decay and ugly age; his own home, by contrast, is cheerful and welcoming. Conversely, Nell, despite her surroundings, enjoys the pleasant warmth of "light and sunny dreams." And these, in turn, contrast to Master Humphrey's own troubled sleep.

In conception and execution, the paragraphs are cleverly constructed to close Master Humphrey's tale; the title of it, *The Old Curiosity Shop* (printed in Gothic type), draws attention to the juxtaposition of disparate curiosities that is the point of the story. By its strategy of presentation, the narrator's later observation is strikingly confirmed: "Everything in our lives, whether of good or evil, affects us most by contrast."[21] The whole story, indeed, is a static but effective composition of opposites, from Master Humphrey's opening walk through the city at night to his closing one, and from the feverish dreams of the sick man in Saint Martin's court, imagining himself dead, but conscious, in a noisy churchyard, to the dreams of Master Humphrey and Little Nell. There is no movement within this framework, and few lines are thrown out which are not tentatively resolved by the three closing paragraphs, with their almost chordlike repetition of contrasts.[22]

But this structure had necessarily to be changed when

Dickens decided to continue the story. Lines did have to be thrown out toward future complications and actions. How Dickens accomplished this in a part of the story already published displays his virtuosity and illustrates the complex evolution of his text.

The Old Curiosity Shop ended in *Master Humphrey's Clock* XLV, 6 February 1841. Dickens then had the sheets of the *Clock* containing the *Shop* bound up and sold as a separate entity in one volume. He told Miss Coutts on 20 April that he had instructed his binder "to weed out all the foreign matter that was mixed up with its earlier pages, in the Clock." As a result, "it will have some blank sides here and there, and will be regularly irregular in the numbers at the top of the leaves. But it will be all together, and free from interruptions, and will serve you, until it comes to be printed in a more convenient form some years hence." As Dickens explains, where *Clock* material was excised, there remained blank spaces. One of these occurs on page 47 (E6^r) of *Clock* IV, where a letter from an imaginary correspondent (one of the Petersham ideas) takes up all but the first paragraph of the page on which the opening chapter of the *Shop* is concluded. Here was a place where Dickens could extend the chapter in order to "foreshadow," in 1841, the subsequent developments not anticipated at the time of its original printing. So he took the opportunity, in place of the expunged *Clock* matter, to insert before the last paragraph four entirely new ones, which have since become a standard portion of the first chapter, but of which there is no trace either in the manuscript or in *Clock* IV.

> I sat down in my easy-chair; and falling back upon its ample cushions, pictured to myself the child in her bed: alone, unwatched, uncared for, (save by angels,) yet sleeping peacefully. So very young, so spiritual, so slight and fairy-like a creature passing the long dull nights in such an uncongenial place—I could not dismiss it from my thoughts.

We are so much in the habit of allowing impressions to be made upon us by external objects, which should be produced by reflection alone, but which, without such visible aids, often escape us; that I am not sure I should have been so thoroughly possessed by this one subject, but for the heaps of fantastic things I had seen huddled together in the curiosity-dealer's warehouse. These, crowding upon my mind, in connection with the child, and gathering round her, as it were, brought her condition palpably before me. I had her image, without any effort of imagination, surrounded and beset by everything that was foreign to its nature, and furthest removed from the sympathies of her sex and age. If these helps to my fancy had all been wanting, and I had been forced to imagine her in a common chamber, with nothing unusual or uncouth in its appearance, it is very probable that I should have been less impressed with her strange and solitary state. As it was, she seemed to exist in a kind of allegory; and having these shapes about her, claimed my interest so strongly, that (as I have already remarked) I could not dismiss her from my recollection, do what I would.

"It would be a curious speculation," said I, after some restless turns across and across the room, "to imagine her in her future life, holding her solitary way among a crowd of wild grotesque companions; the only pure, fresh, youthful object in the throng. It would be curious to find—"

I checked myself here, for the theme was carrying me along with it at a great pace, and I already saw before me a region on which I was little disposed to enter. I agreed with myself that this was idle musing, and resolved to go to bed, and court forgetfulness.

But all that night, waking or in my sleep. . . .[23]

These paragraphs substantially reinforce Dickens' later purposes; written after the novel was concluded and inserted at its beginning, they provide additional evidence of a design that grew more gradually and unconsciously than Forster could remember "in any other instance throughout [Dickens'] career."[24] The first paragraph emphasizes Nell's spiritual quality, her goodness, and her loneliness, "uncared for, (save by angels,) yet sleeping peacefully." Dickens thus prepares the reader slightly for her death, an event not in his mind at the time the first chapter was composed, and only imposed on the novel, at Forster's suggestion, months later, when he began to write the *Clock* numbers for October 1840.

The second paragraph points up the meaning of the Shop itself, and contains an important observation about the operation of fancy, further justifying Dickens' reliance on contrast. External objects, Master Humphrey remarks, often have the power of impressing our minds with truths which should be produced by reflection alone. Thus it was that the "heaps of fantastic things" in the Shop impressed him with how "surrounded and beset with everything foreign" to Nell and "furthest removed from the sympathies of her sex and age" she was. It was, according to Master Humphrey, as a result of this incongruity that he became "impressed with her strange and solitary state." She seemed, he concludes, "to exist in a kind of allegory."

The paragraph in general, and the last remark in particular, reflect an especially sympathetic appreciation of the first volume of the *Clock* written by Thomas Hood and published, anonymously, in the *Athenaeum* for 7 November 1840, over eight months after the "little child-story" was first conceived. While deploring the framework of the miscellany ("the main fault of the work is in its construction"), Hood praised the new story, and gave it the following interpretation:

> We do not know where we have met, in fiction, with a more striking and picturesque combination of images than is presented by the simple, childish figure of Little Nelly, amidst a chaos of such obsolete, grotesque, old-world commodities as form the stock in trade of the Old Curiosity Shop. Look at the Artist's picture of the Child, asleep in her little bed, sur-

rounded, or rather mobbed, by ancient armour and arms, antique furniture, and relics sacred or profane, hideous or grotesque:—it is like an Allegory of the peace and innocence of Childhood in the midst of Violence, Superstition, and all the hateful or hurtful Passions of the world. How sweet and fresh the youthful figure! how much sweeter and fresher for the rusty, musty, fusty atmosphere of such accessories and their associations! How soothing the moral, that Gentleness, Purity, and Truth, sometimes dormant but never dead, have survived, and will outlive, Fraud and Force, though backed by gold and encased in steel![25]

Hood's tribute to Dickens' conception, and Williams' execution, of Nell asleep in the Shop, impressed Dickens very favorably at the time, and led to a warm friendship that persisted through Hood's last years, dogged by misfortune and illness, until his death on 3 May 1845. Having heard privately in March of that year that the poet was "past all chance of recovery," Dickens eulogized him in a letter from Rome to Miss Coutts on the 18th:

He was (I have a sad presentiment that even now I may speak of him as something past) a man of great power—of prodigious force and genius as a poet— and not generally known perhaps, by his best credentials. Personally he had a most noble and generous spirit. When he was under the pressure of severe misfortune and illness, and I had never seen him, he went far out of his way to praise me; and wrote (in the Athenaeum) a paper on The Curiosity Shop; so full of enthusiasm and high appreciation, and so free from any taint of envy or reluctance to acknowledge me a young man far more fortunate than himself, that I can hardly bear to think of it.

Undoubtedly Dickens recalled Hood's essay when writing these four paragraphs in the spring of 1841, as he did again in 1848 when writing the preface to the Cheap Edition of the *Shop*.

I have a mournful pride in one recollection associated with "little Nell." While she was yet upon her wanderings, not then concluded, there appeared in a literary journal, an essay of which she was the principal theme, so earnestly, so eloquently, and tenderly appreciative of her, and of all her shadowy kith and kin, that it would have been insensibility in me, if I could have read it without an unusual glow of pleasure and encouragement. Long afterwards, and when I had come to know him well, and to see him, stout of heart, going slowly down into his grave, I knew the writer of that essay to be THOMAS HOOD.[26]

Having made explicit—probably more explicit than in his original conception—the function of the setting, Dickens in the third paragraph forecasts the action of Nell's story and relates it to the static "allegory" of her present environment: "It would be a curious speculation . . . to imagine her in her future life, holding her solitary way among a crowd of wild grotesque companions; the only pure, fresh, youthful object in the throng." Here is the essential connection that Dickens felt it imperative to insert between the "little child-story" and the expanded novel. But it cannot be said that because it was inserted after the novel's completion it is either simply Dickens' ex post facto rationale of his design, or merely an inspired use of what Hood had written the previous November. Rather, the character of this conception suggests a debt to Bunyan's treatment of Christian at Vanity Fair. And *Pilgrim's Progress,* which Dickens had known since childhood and already made use of in *Oliver Twist,* had become an explicit model for the *Shop* and its readers months before Hood's review appeared, when Nell, having escaped with her grandfather from the menacing squalor and commerce of London, sits down to rest in a pleasant field, and recalls Bunyan's hero: "I feel as if we were both Christian, and laid down on this grass all the cares and troubles we brought with us; never to take them up again."[27] As

Dickens asserted in the Cheap Edition preface: "I had it always in my fancy to surround the lonely figure of the child with grotesque and wild, but not impossible companions, and to gather about her innocent face and pure intentions, associates as strange and uncongenial as the grim objects that are about her bed when her history is first foreshadowed."

In the final paragraph of inserted material Master Humphrey interrupts his train of speculation and resolves to go to bed. Dickens, having thrown out the necessary lines to his later pilgrimage, in less than two sentences manages to return to the point at which the original narrative was interrupted. The transition is not smooth enough, however, to hide the scissors and paste; and though the paragraphs are transmitted *in toto* to subsequent editions of the novel, they are somewhat out of key with the tone and approach of the rest of the chapter. Still, they do emphasize the conceptual link with the continued story. Dickens, betrayed by his own awareness of how that story grew, felt called upon to insert them to justify the later action.

One other element of his original design was to plague him right to the end of the novel. The point of view he had chosen, that of the humpbacked Master Humphrey, was much too constraining for the longer story he now proposed to write. Humphrey was already proving difficult to manage in the *Clock* sections, and in number VII asked leave, "in treating of the club . . . to assume the historical style, and speak of myself in the third person."[28] At the close of chapter 3, therefore, Dickens cavalierly divested himself of the framework of a first-person narrative. Master Humphrey declares that he will, "for the convenience of the narrative detach myself from its further course, and leave those who have prominent and necessary parts in it to speak and act for themselves."[29] Abrupt and contrived though this announcement is, there is no indication in the manuscript that Dickens hesitated in writing it. Having determined on a full-length treatment of his "little child-story," he "set cheerfully about disentangling" himself from the *Clock* apparatus.[30]

But this particular point, that he had originally designed the *Shop* to be the "Personal Adventures of Master Humphrey," continued to cause trouble. When the first volume of the *Clock* (numbers I–XXVI) was issued in October 1841, Dickens tried in the preface to explain away the sudden abandonment of the Clock society:

> It was never the author's intention to make the Members of Master Humphrey's Clock, active agents in the stories they are supposed to relate. Having brought himself in the commencement of his undertaking to feel an interest in these quiet creatures, and to imagine them in their old chamber of meeting, eager listeners to all he had to tell, the author hoped—as authors will—to succeed in awakening some of his own emotions in the bosoms of his readers. Imagining Master Humphrey in his chimney-corner, resuming night after night, the narrative,—say, of the Old Curiosity Shop—picturing to himself the various sensations of his hearers—thinking how Jack Redburn might incline to poor Kit, and perhaps lean too favourably even towards the lighter vices of Mr. Richard Swiveller—how the deaf gentleman would have his favorite, and Mr. Miles his—and how all these gentle spirits would trace some faint reflection of their past lives in the varying current of the tale— he has insensibly fallen into the belief that they are present to his readers as they are to him, and has forgotten that like one whose vision is disordered he may be conjuring up bright figures where there is nothing but empty space.

Brilliant special pleading, of the kind Dickens frequently did in his prefaces, but hardly candid: he had thought originally of carrying the "personal histories and proceedings" of the Clock society through the work, and had committed himself to involving Master Humphrey in Nell's

life. To tie up this loose end, he wrote several paragraphs
intended to follow the last of the novel as we now know it:

> When Master Humphrey had finished the read-
> ing of this manuscript, and again deposited it within
> his clock, he returned to the table where his friends
> were seated, and adressed them thus:
> "Forgive me, if for the greater interest and con-
> venience of the narrative you have just heard, I
> opened it with a fictitious adventure of my own. I had
> my share in these transactions, but it was not that I
> feigned to have at first. The younger brother[,] the
> single gentleman—the nameless actor in this little
> drama—stands before you now!"
> Their emotion shewed that they had not expected
> this disclosure.
> "Yes my friends," said Master Humphrey, with a
> saddened but placid air. "I am he indeed. And this is
> the chief sorrow of my life!"

Wisely, Dickens decided to cut this out before publication, realizing that once the *Shop* was printed free of the
enveloping *Clock* material, the need for this revelation
would diminish.[31] But he still had to account to the *Clock*
readers, and so, in the pages that follow the conclusion in
Clock XLV, Master Humphrey, confessing himself uneasy
because he has had to disguise something in his story, takes
the opportunity to unburden himself when Mr. Miles, "a
gentleman of business habits, and of great exactness and
propriety in all his transactions," raises a timely question.
(The multiple facets of Dickens' artistic conscience are
here objectified in two different characters.)

> "I could have wished," my friend objected; "that
> we had been made acquainted with the single gentle-
> man's name. I don't like his withholding his name. It
> made me look upon him at first with suspicion, and
> caused me to doubt his moral character, I assure you.
> I am fully satisfied by this time of his being a worthy
> creature, but in this respect he certainly would not
> appear to have acted at all like a man of business."

"My friends," said I, drawing to the table at which they were by this time seated in their usual chairs, "do you remember that this story bore another title besides that one we have so often heard of late?"

Mr. Miles had his pocket-book out in an instant, and referring to an entry therein, rejoined "Certainly. Personal adventures of Master Humphrey. Here it is. I made a note of it at the time."

I was about to resume what I had to tell them, when the same Mr. Miles again interrupted me, observing that the narrative originated in a personal adventure of my own, and that was no doubt the reason for its being thus designated.

This led me to the point at once.

"You will one and all forgive me," I returned, "if, for the greater convenience of the story, and for its better introduction, that adventure was fictitious. I had my share indeed—no light or trivial one—in the pages we have read, but it was not the share I feigned to have at first. The younger brother, the single gentleman, the nameless actor in this little drama, stands before you now."

It was easy to see they had not expected this disclosure.

"Yes," I pursued. "I can look back upon my part in it with a calm, half-smiling pity for myself as for some other man. But I am he indeed; and now the chief sorrows of my life are yours."[32]

While revealing about Dickens' own creative processes, this elaborate confession, even longer in manuscript, is quite unconvincing: Master Humphrey, misshaped, deformed, a recluse, has nothing in common with the haphazardly energetic Single Gentleman. Nor do their portraits bear any resemblance. It is clear that Dickens, at the last minute, was straining his ingenuity beyond credible limits to provide some explanation of the novel's original title, and seized upon the hint contained in Master Humphrey's opening statement, that the old man sought solitude to heal an old wound and forget an old sorrow. Fortunately, Dickens removed this passage from the novel proper, so that *The Old Curiosity Shop* ends very effectively with the single sentence, echoing Psalm 90, that identifies Nell's passing with the passing of time and the passing of the story: "Such are the changes which a few years bring about, and so do things pass away, like a tale that is told!"

Even as he was writing it, Dickens was obviously of two minds about the opening installment of the *Shop*. On the one hand, the short story was an effective vignette, but on the other, possibilities for development pressed upon his imagination. What was Nell's grandfather doing at night? Is he a villain? Will Nell be wealthy?[33] Will she marry Kit? Is she really safe in that queer shop all night? Many questions, including those that vexed Master Humphrey, remained unanswered at the end of the "little child-story," and long before his readers could begin to ask them, they were agitating Dickens. The opportunities for extending the story were too numerous, and the pressures, both internal and from Chapman and Hall, too insistent for him to ignore. When *Clock* IV appeared, Dickens was already uneasy about "the desultory character of that work," and he believed his readers "thoroughly participated in the feeling. The commencement of a story was a great satisfaction to me, and I had reason to believe that my readers participated in this feeling too. Hence, being pledged to some interruptions and some pursuit of the original design, I set cheerfully about disentangling myself from those impediments as fast as I could."[34] Gathering up all the possible loose ends from the "little child-story," and giving his imagination free play to design the pattern, Dickens began weaving the vastly more complicated fabric of a full-length novel, inventing new characters, adding to the conception of old ones, subconsciously borrowing from the queer characters and quaint old chambers that fill the *Clock*, and extending the boundaries of the Old Curiosity Shop until it stretches as a metaphor to cover all of England.

LAUGHTER AND PATHOS:
THE OLD CURIOSITY SHOP

James R. Kincaid

Dick Swiveller steps into The Old Curiosity Shop for the
first time in order to introduce the logic of Mr. Pickwick:
"Why should a grandson and grandfather peg away at each
other with mutual wiolence when all might be bliss and
concord? Why not jine hands and forget it?" (chap. 2).
Why not indeed? It is just this argument which could settle
forever the friendly differences in *Pickwick;* it is a sane
argument and ought to have great force in a sane world.
But it has no relevance at all to the madhouse world of *The
Old Curiosity Shop,* and Dick Swiveller is funny precisely
because he is so incongruously sane. He sees, for instance,
that Nell's grandfather is really "the jolly old grandfather"
and Fred "the wild young grandson" of the comic theater
and that everything ought to come out "all right and comfortable." But no one will play these reasonable roles; "the
old dotard," as Quilp not unfairly calls him, becomes a type
of demonic selfishness, and Fred sinks in lurid degradation.
Dick suggests that they all pack up and go to Dingley Dell.
But there is no room for the bright simplicity of Dingley
Dell in this novel; it is both too dark and too complex.
There is, for instance, an awful and subtle irony in the
narrative structure,[1] and for all the "quietness"[2] Dickens

worked for—and achieved—in the atmosphere, there is an underlying bitterness and a dominant motif of retribution which make this quietness much more sinister and dark than soft and sad.

But soft and sad we continue to think it, and complexity is about the last quality ordinarily granted to *The Old Curiosity Shop*. More than any other Dickens' novel, this one has tended to be rewritten in critical mythology and has become grossly oversimplified in the process. For many, in fact, the novel has been distilled into the climactic page and a half, of which the following is a fair example.

> She was dead. Dear, gentle, patient, noble Nell was dead. Her little bird—a poor slight thing the pressure of a finger would have crushed—was stirring nimbly in its cage; and the strong heart of its child-mistress was mute and motionless for ever (chap. 71).

Perhaps even this is not representative, for the bitterness reflected in this passage, the rather ugly vindictiveness suggested by the reference to the bird, and the strange urge to wallow not with Nell, I think, but with the worms are not part of the popular myth. *The Old Curiosity Shop* has often become "The Death of Nell," and even that episode has been simplified in this century to the impression of "ineptitude and vulgar sentimentality"[3] attending the awful iambs with which the two-headed monster[4] is slaughtered. The spectacular contrasts between the Victorian response to Nell and our own have been often discussed and variously explained.[5] Obviously more is involved in this reversal than can be discussed here, but one thing, at least, seems to me clear. Our rather hysterical rejection of Nell is at least as much a rejection of those crowds on the docks in America, waiting for the ships from England and calling out, "Is Nell dead?" as it is of the novel itself. We strongly resist identifying ourselves with that group and that society, partly, I suppose, out of the snobbery which makes us believe in the progress of taste and which allows us to sneer at the Victorians; but surely more important is the inability to respond to or even admit the existence of the extraordinarily intimate appeals in that novel. We may laugh at the boorishness of those who could admire such unsophisticated art, but there is something challenging and therefore frightening about the openness with which they invested so much of themselves in Nell.

There is the same threat and challenge in the novel itself. When Dickens speaks in the Preface of "the many friends it won me, and the many hearts it turned to me when they were full of private sorrow," he is talking about something more than a novel, and he is asking for something more than a conventional response. *The Old Curiosity Shop,* for all its hatred of Little Bethel, uses evangelical rhetoric and clearly expects something like a religious conversion to Nellyism. In this expectation, then, the novel is clearly antagonistic, implying that a failure of respose is not an aesthetic but a spiritual failure.

And the proof of responsiveness is very simple and very extreme—tears. *The Old Curiosity Shop* is alone among Dickens' novels in being so emphatically centered on the dominant emotion of pathos, the most horrifying and deceptive of appeals. As Northrop Frye says, "Pathos, though it seems a gentler and more relaxed mood than tragedy, is even more terrifying. Its basis is the exclusion of an individual from a group, hence it attacks the deepest fear in ourselves that we possess."[6] The intimacy demanded by the novel, then, is an intimacy with desolation and death. We tend to escape these extremities, paradoxically, by concentrating on Nell alone; for even though she is the central figure of the pathos, the weight of the rhetorical burden is carried by other figures. While it is certainly true that Nell can, by herself, support very little meaning or emotion, she does receive enormous reflexive strength from her surroundings. Dickens' decision to surround Nell with the "grotesque and wild" (Preface, p. xii) was made not simply to gain picturesqueness but also to provide complexity and strength to the central figure and the central emotion. To a very large extent, Nell is made possible by Quilp and by Dick Swiveller, and the pathos is guaranteed by the humor. I want here to investigate the contribution made to these interconnected relationships by laughter.

For it was laughter that moved those dock crowds as well as tears, and laughter is primarily important in fixing our relationship to the central figure. In fact, for all its celebration of the grave, *The Old Curiosity Shop* is rooted in a comic impulse. Certainly the impulse is perverted and narrow, but it is there nonetheless. Since Dick cannot carry everyone off to Dingley Dell, we all go to the churchyard; Nell is fed to the worms in lieu of a Christmas festival. The unconscious logic of this movement toward death is comic in the sense that it is so strongly dedicated to youth and so violently opposed to age: if youth and its attendant values can no longer win in this world, then they will turn to the greater victory in death, thereby defying the aged, who want them to adopt their corruption. The grave becomes almost sanctified. In the child's defiance of the parent and the protection of the pleasure-principle through suicide[7] the novel suggests the last desperately ingenious defense of the comic spirit.

But this description puts rather too grossly what is in the novel a subtle and submerged tendency. It is also true that this suicidal tendency is disguised by the existence of its opposite: the glorification of the grave is matched by a repulsion to it. At one point Dickens says that to mourn the death of children is to forget the "bright and happy existence [to which] those who die young are born, and how in death they lose the pain of seeing others die around them" (chap. 26). This, it must be admitted, is not an indication of subtlety; it is mere confusion. Death is seen both as a victory and as an escape from the pain which somehow comes from seeing others attain that victory. Dickens' ambivalence toward death neutralizes any meaning. The ambivalence is understandable, of course, but it does tend to weaken the novel by dissolving many of its ironies. The perverse comedy of Nell cannot ultimately be sustained because the grave cannot be sanctified for the young. The old die too.

But, because of the conflicting attitudes toward death, the comedy can be maintained for long periods, primarily through a relentless underground attack on the old. At the funeral of Nell, the narrator makes this attack explicit by arguing that these old horrors are more dead than Nell.

> Old men were there, whose eyes were dim and senses failing—grandmothers, who might have died ten years ago, and still been old—the deaf, the blind, the lame, the palsied, the living dead in many shapes and forms, to see the closing of that early grave. What was the death it would shut in, to that which still could crawl and creep above it! (chap. 72).

Notice that these ancient vermin "crawl and creep," quite a change from old Wardle, old Brownlow, and the old Cheerybles. Usually, however, Dickens' attack is much more subtle and uses the mask of laughter. Even Dick Swiveller contributes to this warfare.

> "These old people—there's no trusting 'em, Fred. There's an aunt of mine down in Dorsetshire that was going to die when I was eight years old, and hasn't kept her word yet. They're so aggravating, so unprincipled, so spiteful—unless there's apoplexy in the family, Fred, you can't calculate upon 'em, and even then they deceive you just as often as not" (chap. 7).

The light tone and the physical absence of Dick's aunt provide the disguise for the aggression, but the tendency of the joke is serious indeed.

The central symbol for this attack is, of course, Nell's grandfather. Directly responsible for her death by removing her from every point of safety and kindness, he, it is clear, is much closer even than Quilp to being the chief villain. He serves as the archetypal parental butt, the object of the comic if vicious revenge of the child on the adult. He is allowed none of the conventional superiorities of age; he is simply a "hollow mockery" of "childishness," an adult ludicrously attempting to be a child, but justly (according to the comic logic) denied "the gaiety," "the light and life," "the hope," and "the joys" of childhood. Instead, he is to childhood what "death is [to] sleep" (chap. 12). The key joke against him is, significantly, made by children who run along beside Mrs. Jarley's caravan, "fully impressed with the belief that [Nell's] grandfather was a cunning device in wax" (chap. 28). The point of the joke is certainly clear, and it coalesces with many others to reinforce the secret dream wish: that the old might be annihilated.

Our laughter here, as in *Pickwick*, rejects the stuffy and pompous formulas of the old for the freshness of youth. The rejection in *The Old Curiosity Shop*, however, is much more desperately violent, and the alternative turns out not to be freshness but youthful death. In this basic way, then, laughter pushes us toward the ultimate terror of pathos invested in the solitary child.

And it is certainly Nell who is at the center of the novel and who makes the primary demands for our responsiveness. But the dominant critical error is to separate Nell from her surroundings. Despite her central importance, she is defined and made effective by the figures around her. I think we can, therefore, best understand Nell and the pathos she represents by dealing with the major forces exterior to her, primarily those represented by Dick Swiveller and by Daniel Quilp. In this most dreamlike of novels,[8] the connection of the important motifs exists almost entirely beneath the conscious level of the narrative.

The major figures and attitudes are involved with one another, but the involvement is scarcely explained at all by the logic of the plot. Instead, we have a conflict of basic tendencies, or, as Gabriel Pearson says, "fields of force,"[9] arranged in patterns of opposition and contrast often tangential to the plot itself. On one hand, there is the movement of Nell, her grandfather, Kit and the Garlands, Witherden the Notary, and those associated with this group, toward peace, sanctity, the expected, acquiescence, and stasis. Diametrically opposed is the force of Quilp, mostly isolated but echoed to some extent in Sally Brass and Tom Scott, toward energy, violence, surprise, rebellion, and continual motion. Paradoxically, these extreme forces tend to draw so far apart from each other by their mutual repulsion that they meet in common self-extermination. Despite Quilp's continual and brilliant parody of the Nelly-group, he ends in the same position exactly. As Pearson points out, this opposition of forces creates a more and more apparent vacuum in the center, which becomes filled, more and more adequately, by Dick Swiveller and the Marchioness.[10] Dick is not, I, think, primarily a parody on either group but a sane alternative made possible by their extreme and self-destructive antipathy. One can easily see this pattern as a simple extension of the one in *Oliver Twist*. Rose Maylie is pushed happily into the grave she is yearning toward and Fagin is made specifically subterranean. By carrying these tendencies to their logical conclusions, one could argue, there is room for a middle position in Dick, not possible when the split is as tenuous as in *Oliver Twist*. At any rate, the unity of *The Old Curiosity Shop* and its elemental force are determined by these three groups and the ways in which they reflect on one another.

The novel is not, however, really kaleidoscopic, nor is the pattern quite this neat. The determining reflections come from outside into Nell, and there is relatively little interplay in the other direction. The main problems, then, have to do with Nell and with the pathos she is meant to generate. In my opinion, the laughter which is exterior but thematically relevant to Nell makes that pathos possible and effective. Providing for the pathetic is, in fact, one of the two main rhetorical functions of laughter in this novel. The other is to provide for the final comic solution centered in Dick and the Marchioness. Dickens, by our laughter, leads us to the grave and back again, provides us with tears and with joy. But the tears are unquestionably dominant for a large part of the novel and even help make possible by reaction the final joy. The main issue, then, is the relationship in the novel between laughter and pathos.

Laughter provides for pathos primarily through its aggressive component. Like the humor of direct attack, it awakens the aggression necessary for laughter,[11] and then exposes that aggression by removing the original disguise. Both types of humor also utilize the guilt made possible by this exposure of the reader's callousness. The differences are mainly of intensity and distance. In *Oliver Twist* the backlash is immediate and the laughter immediately turned back on us;[12] in *The Old Curiosity Shop* there is vital distance between the laughter and the serious reversal, so that the guilt is less felt and less insisted upon, and may therefore be transferred to pity or tears. In the latter case, the guilt is a medium, not a final goal, and we are not so much attacked as softened. To be more specific, in this novel laughter at the Quilp and Swiveller forces and at the people Nell and her grandfather meet in their travels is used to heighten our response to Nell's sorrows and trials. A few examples should make this relationship of laughter and pathos clearer.

Probably the most basic relationship is rooted in the fact that the novel at once dedicates itself in Little Nell to all the feminine virtues and, at the same time, invites us to participate in vicious laughter at all women. The softness, humility, and gentle subservience of women is both

staunchly supported and ridiculed. For instance, there is
the brilliant humorous triumph of Daniel Quilp over all the
neighborhood women, gathered to sympathize with Mrs.
Quilp. Now Betsy Quilp is very nearly Nell's double, but we
are by no means invited to share in the cackling neighbors'
sympathy for her. We are, in fact, invited to laugh, first, at
the cowardice, blind egoism, and petty spitefulness of the
neighbors.

> "Ah! . . . I wish you'd give her a little of your
> advice, Mrs. Jiniwin. . . . Nobody knows better than
> you, ma'am, what us women owe to ourselves."
> "Owe indeed, ma'am!" replied Mrs. Jiniwin.
> "When my poor husband, her dear father, was alive, if
> he had ever ventur'd a cross word to *me,* I'd have—"
> the good old lady did not finish the sentence, but
> she twisted off the head of a shrimp with a vindictive-
> ness which seemed to imply that the action was in
> some degree a substitute for words (chap. 4).

Mrs. Quilp is urged to stand up for her superficial "rights"
as a woman, but she cuts through the chorus of self-deception with an admission that substantiates our aggressive
laughter: "It's very easy to talk, but I say again that I
know—that I'm sure—Quilp has such a way with him
when he likes, that the best-looking woman here couldn't
refuse him if I was dead, and she was free, and he chose to
make love to her. Come!" This provides the perfect comic
reversal and the perfect justification for our laughter.
Women, we are assured, are ludicrously inferior and their
pretenses to power are absurd simply because they have
been castrated. Their hilarious, snarling reactions to Betsy's
truth amount to confessions of impotence: "Before I'd
consent to stand in awe of a man as she does of him, I'd—
I'd kill myself, and write a letter first to say he did it!" So
when Quilp, the representative of pure male energy,
scatters the women merely by entering and inviting them to
supper, the comic triumph is complete. It is capped only by

the once-proud Mrs. Jiniwin being forced to go to bed (of all things) against her will. Mothers, wives, and daughters are all routed here in this vicious humor of expulsion.

Examples of humorous attacks on women could be extended indefinitely. Miss Monflathers and Sally Brass are flayed alive, and even Mrs. Nubbles comes in for attack on account of her religious stupidity. The existence of this recurrent impulse to attack women would seem to subvert the values associated with Nell and invest that figure with a strong irony, but I think not. There is a long distance between these attacks and Nell, and the very rejection of the feminine makes us, I think, all the more ready to respond to it when it is presented seriously. Again, this is a matter of distance and great tact; if Dickens brought the attack and the celebration close together, the result undoubtedly would be parody. But it seems clear that few have ever reacted to Nell as a parody figure, and we must remember that, while the defense of Nell's virtues is overt and explicit, the attack comes through laughter, which by its very nature hides its source. Thus, since the reader is given a breathing spell, the laughter is preparatory to pathos; our aggression against the feminine is activated again and again, but we are never forced to admit this aggression consciously. The aggression is therefore drained rather than focused, and any residual guilt is turned to a more intense pity for the threatened femininity of Nell.

Perhaps an even clearer example of the comic-pathetic connection is provided by the use made of jokes on loneliness to heighten our feelings for Nell's desolation. There are, for example, recurrent jokes specifically involving the confusion of friend and foe. First, there is the fixed notion of the business manager of the traveling Punch show: "Recollect the friend. Codlin's the friend, not Short. Short's very well as far as he goes, but the real friend is Codlin—not Short" (chap. 19). The dark point of this humor, we soon realize, is that neither is friendly and that both are willing to sell out Nell for the proper sum. The distinctions we are asked to make betwen the gruff and grim misanthrope, Codlin, and the jolly Short Trotters[13] break down; there is no play on the appearance-reality theme here except that under all appearances is the uniform bleak selfishness which causes everyone to be completely alone and friendless. This same point is made through humor several times by Quilp. A good deal of his success rides on just this confusion of friend and enemy, with the same awful point about human desolation being made. He traps Fred Trent, for instance, with just this ruse: "You little knew who was your friend, and who your foe; now did you?" (chap. 23). Ironically, Quilp is at least an enemy, and the existence of feeling, even of negative feeling, is better than the black indifference of Codlin and Short. Finally, in the case of the Marchioness, we have the most extensive humorous treatment of this theme of loneliness and a completion of the three-sided humorous pattern which reflects on Nell from each of the fields of force. The Marchioness is desperately lonely but combats this, at least partially, through the resources available to her through the keyhole. Though a very complex figure, she has a fund of protective humor at her disposal which makes it possible for us, at least at first, to conserve our pity and laugh at her. The Brasses treat her as a pure thing, a noise maker: "We have been moving chests of drawers over [the lodger's] head, we have knocked double knocks at the street-door, we have made the servant-girl fall down stairs several times, (she's a light weight, and it don't hurt her much,) but nothing wakes him" (chap. 35).

The laughter in all three areas of the novel prepares us for the pathos attending the central emotion, the awful isolation caused by the individual pursuit of selfish concerns. At the heart of the novel is this vision of alienation, of man lost in a purely atomistic society, "an atom, here, in a mountain-heap of misery" (chap. 44). Our previous laughter at the failure of human concern, at the absence of human friendship, prepares us for the heart of the pathos: "the two poor strangers, stunned and bewildered by the hurry they beheld but had no part in, looked mournfully on; feeling, amidst the crowd, a solitude which has no parallel but in the thirst of the shipwrecked mariner" (chap. 44). Even the parallel to Coleridge's poem (developed at some length in the passage) is ironic, for the loneliness here is the more awful loneliness "amidst the crowd," a crowd which emphatically does not hold out the possibility of grace or redemption, even if the commercial water-snakes are blessed. The jokes have been used as preparatory notes to establish in the reader a readiness for, really a susceptibility to, this appeal.

Though this three-part humorous support for serious or pathetic appeals occurs over and over again, a point-by-point treatment seems unnecessarily schematic and restrictive. Therefore, I propose to deal with each of the three sections separately: first, the Nell-force; second, its polar opposite, the Quilp-force; finally, the resultant intermediate Swiveller-force.

The approved goals of the Nell group are peace, serenity, sameness, and acquiescence—finally, of course, death. Nell is not alone in having these negative aspirations; she shares them with associated characters, like the Nubbleses and the Garlands. The Garlands, when hiring Kit, explain their extreme carefulness on the basis of being "very quiet regular folks." Because of this, they say, "It would be a sad thing if we made any kind of mistake, and found things different from what we hoped and expected" (chap. 21). The direction of this force is characterized very aptly by the sort of life described here: quiet and regular, without surprises. The whole group really distrusts change and excitement so much that its members are even unable to resist feeling guilty after the night at Astley's (chap. 40). All their energy and rebelliousness seem to have been transferred to the pony; the rest huddle desperately together in a pathetic search for safety.

It is this same search for safety which motivates the travels of Nell and her grandfather,[14] an attempt above all to elude the nightmare enemies, those who are "searching for me everywhere, and may come here, and steal upon us, even while we're talking" (chap. 24). The awful irony is that they are running from their avowed friends.[15] More horribly ironic still is the suggestion that they really don't go anywhere, that they simply move from death to death. Dickens makes this literally vicious circle symbolically clear by connecting the original Old Curiosity Shop with their final home provided by the schoolmaster. Both, of course, are connected with death, decay, and disuse, but the tie is made even more explicit. The shop contains "fantastic carvings brought from monkish cloisters" (chap. 1), and the final home "a pile of fragments of rich carving from old monkish stalls" (chap. 52), and they both have "strange furniture." Even the old church where Nell is so attracted to the dead contains rusty armor paralleled to the "rusty weapons" of the original shop. Finally, Nell's grandfather is described as simply returning home; at the original shop, Master Humphrey says, "The haggard aspect of the little old man was wonderfully suited to the place; he might have groped among old churches, and tombs, and deserted houses, and gathered all the spoils with his own hands. There was nothing in the whole collection but was in keeping with himself; nothing that looked older or more worn than he" (chap. 1). And just before his death the same association is made: "He, and the failing light and dying fire, the time-worn room, the solitude, the wasted life, and gloom, were all in fellowship. Ashes, and dust, and ruin!" (chap. 71). This circular structure insists that they have run desperately hard only to remain stationary—in the tomb where they began. And behind this structural circle of futility is a similar thematic one: Quilp is chasing the old man for the nonexistent gold the old man is also chasing; the dog is, indeed, chasing its tail and driving itself mad. The delusive and frustrating search for security in a commercial world ends in death.

For underneath all are those satanic mills and the system of life they have created. When Nell persuades her grandfather to leave London, she is clearly thinking of an escape from the commercial present. But it is equally clear that he cannot loosen himself from the premises of industrialism.

> "If we are beggars—!"
> "What if we are?" said the child boldly. "Let us be beggars, and be happy."
> "Beggars—and happy!" said the old man. "Poor child!" (chap. 9).

At the heart of their problem is the fact that they are unable to be happy outside the commercial system. This suggests an imaginative failure (Dick Swiveller is certainly an alternative in this regard) but partly an inescapable fact. The most intensely imagined scene in the novel shows Nell and her grandfather alone in the midst of a seething business crowd:

> The throng of people hurried by, in two opposite streams, with no symptom of cessation or exhaustion; intent upon their own affairs; and undisturbed in their business speculations, by the roar of carts and waggons laden with clashing wares, the slipping of horses' feet upon the wet and greasy pavement, the rattling of the rain on windows and umbrella-tops, the jostling of the more impatient passengers, and all the noise and tumult of a crowded street in the high tide of its occupation (chap. 44).

Here is the root cause of the central isolation, the separation of man from man by the cash nexus.[16] Dickens' attack on the mercantile organization of life in this novel is more indirect than in later novels, but it is nonetheless powerful.

The novel is more than a "failed idyll";[17] it is an exploration of the defeat of the Romantic imagination, the disjunction of man from nature and from his fellows. Even the divine child of the Romantics and of the parable is distorted: "It was plain that she was thenceforth his guide and leader. The child felt it, but had no doubts or misgivings, and putting her hand in his, led him gently away" (chap. 12). And she leads him to loneliness, defeat, and death.

It is against this background that Dickens introduces the "grotesque and wild, but not impossible, companions" he intended as a counterpoint to "the lonely figure of the child" (Preface, p. xii). And it is through these companions that Dickens begins the humorous juxtaposition that controls the form of this novel and makes effective its pathos.

Codlin and Short, the first of these contrasts, act as an awful parody of comic existence and of warm affection. At the Jolly Sandboys they are joined by Mr. Grinder and his weird company, Vuffin and his Giant, the dogs—in short, a kind of circus of feasting and revelry. The economic attack, however, becomes more and more insistent as the talk turns to the marketability (Short would use this sort of jargon if he knew it) of giants. "Once get a giant shaky on his legs, and the public cares no more about him than they do for a dead cabbage-stalk" (chap. 19), says the experienced Vuffin. Economically obsolete giants, he explains, are protected, not because of kindness but because they must be kept scarce:

> "Once make a giant common and giants will never draw again. Look at wooden legs. If there was only one man with a wooden leg what a property *he*'d be!" (chap. 19).

The alternative to protection is suggested by the case of the giant who "took to carrying coach-bills about London, making himself as cheap as crossing-sweepers." "He died," Vuffin continues ominously; "I make no insinuations against anybody in particular . . . but he was ruining the trade;—and he died." Our laughter is a refusal of this system and this cruelty. In case we were inattentive, Dickens suddenly reminds us that Nell has never laughed at this group. With some guilt we realize that she has been utterly alone in this company of economic freaks. The presumed friends, Codlin and Short, then complete the reversal and turn the laughter back on us. We realize finally that they are also protecting Nell and her grandfather for economic reasons, and, when Short calls through the keyhole, then we see how sinister the note of friendship is and how deceptive the circus joy has been: "I only wanted to say that we must be off early to-morrow morning, my dear, because unless we get the start of the dogs and the conjurer, the villages won't be worth a penny" (chap. 19). The perfect burlesque of this sort of cruel economic life is surely the picture of an enterprise which is determined to "get the start of the dogs."

Nell and old Trent escape, however, and after a brief stop with the lugubrious schoolmaster, come on "a Christian lady, stout and comfortable to look on" (chap. 26), Mrs. Jarley, a figure paralleled to Dick Swiveller in her imaginative powers and her humorous strength. "Unquestionably Mrs. Jarley had an inventive genius" (chap. 29), and that genius offers a potential solution to all the problems Nell faces; it is, in fact, a foreshadowing of Mr. Sleary's circus in *Hard Times* and is an early alternative to the devastatingly rigid political economy. With Mrs. Jarley, even the taking of tea becomes a time for joy, and her use of the "suspicious bottle" is exactly like Mr. Pickwick's: to make everything and everyone comfortable. Comfort is what Mrs. Jarley exists for—in a sense what she is; she has "not only a peculiar relish for being comfortable herself, but for making everybody about her comfortable also" (chap. 29). Notice that this comfort is not, as with Short, either delusive or sinister, nor is it associated with the rest and escape Nell seeks. It offers not safety but joy, not escape but active and continual combat with all the deadening economic forces. Mrs. Jarley is, most centrally, a figure who is associated with comic and comfortable life at war with death. She strongly parodies calmness, low spirits, the commerical world, and, most of all, death.

> "I never saw any wax-work, ma'am," said Nell. "Is it funnier than Punch?"
>
> •   •   •   •   •   •   •   •   •   •   •
>
> "It isn't funny at all," [said] Mrs. Jarley. "It's calm and—what's that word again—critical?—no—classical, that's it—it is calm and classical. No low beatings and knockings about, no jokings and squeakings like your precious Punches, but always the same, with a constantly unchanging air of coldness and gentility; and so like life, that if wax-work only spoke and walked about, you'd hardly know the difference. I won't go so far as to say that, as it is, I've seen wax-work quite like life, but I've certainly seen some life that was exactly like wax-work" (chap. 27).

She hates Punch for being "low," "wulgar," but most significantly, "practical" (chap. 26). The perversion of all joy to ugly economic ends is suggested by this last adjective, and Mrs. Jarley's proper distaste for the practical is consonant with her parody of the deadly cold genteel. Her description of gentility contrasts so directly with her own life that our laughter is made to reject precisely what she pretends to promote: the death that imitates life.

This abundant life-force is terribly impatient with the querulous old man—"I should have thought you were old enough to take care of yourself, if you ever will be" (chap. 27)—and suggests the real alternative to economic captivation: a comic transcendence of the whole system and its retributive morality. Even her wax-works burlesque the suffocating maxims; probably the best is the cautionary one of "the old lady who died of dancing at a hundred and thirty-two" (chap. 28). Her methods of warfare are made explicit in her confrontation with that pillar of commercial life, Miss Monflathers. Grimaldi the clown simply becomes by pronouncement the grammarian Mr. Murray, and "a murderess of great renown" is made to do for Mrs. Hannah More. No wonder Miss Monflathers is repulsed; only a complete fool could miss the parody.

But Nell's infuriating grandfather is far too deeply infected with getting and spending to be touched by Mrs. Jarley's medicine, and he forces Nell to take him away. The symbolic battle between joy and economic despair has resulted in the defeat of joy, and from this point on the travelers have no chance. Mrs. Jarley was the last hope, but that hope is now subsumed by the pervasive commercial death. It is necessary to insist on the generality of the villain, for there is a tendency to blame everything on the old man. The inescapable temptation to use vituperative adjectives for him expresses this evasion, but the dodge will not ultimately work. The narrator demands that we regard him as a purified economic dupe, not interested in personal gain and, despite his hysterical statements to the contrary, certainly not interested in Nell. In the midst of gambling "the anxious child was quite forgotten" (chap. 20). It is the system that has caught him in its hypnotic power, and by allowing that system to operate through "games," Dickens suggests how sinister and insidious the disease is.

From this point on, the route to death is unimpeded, and our laughter no longer strives for alternatives. The jokes are by now clearly preparatory for death. When Nell faints and is carried to an inn, for instance, "everybody called for his or her favourite remedy, which nobody brought; each cried for more air, at the same time carefully excluding what air there was, by closing round the object of sympathy" (chap. 46). How loaded the term "object of sympathy" is! The joke about the limits of sympathy clashes with the real and pervasive indifference and makes the pathos possible. By the time Nell is ready to die, our laughter, oddly enough, moves us toward an acceptance, almost a welcoming, of death and of the impossibility of any escape for her. The old sexton, for instance, who is so resistant to death that he practices the most ludicrous evasions, stirs the darkest laughter in the novel. It is a laughter which, for once, yearns for the grave. The sexton avoids the reminder of death brought on by a woman who died at the early age of seventy-nine by deciding that she, like all women, lied about her age.

> "Call to mind how old she looked for many a long, long year, and say if she could be but seventy-nine at last—only our age," said the sexton.
> "Five year older at the very least!" cried the other.
> "Five!" retorted the sexton. "Ten. Good eighty-nine. I call to mind the time her daughter died. She was eighty-nine if she was a day, and tries to pass upon us now, for ten year younger. Oh! human vanity!" (chap. 54).

He and his helper, David, "seemed but boys to her!" By the time they leave, David chuckling to himself over the notion that the sexton is "failing very fast," our laughter has rejected this absurd self-preservation and has moved to an instinctive support of the appropriateness of the grave for the limited humanity of this extreme age. As a result, we are prepared for the climactic and inevitable pathos attendant on the ironic reversal: the preservation of the sexton and the death of Nell.

At the opposite pole to the Nell group is Daniel Quilp,[18] dedicated to life literally with a vengeance. Sensitive to all personal attacks, he makes his existence over into a brilliant retaliation in order to fight the dehumanizing enemy and protect his own being. A brilliant parodist, he has enormous capacity for delight in "the rich field of enjoyment and reprisal" (chap. 23) he creates around him. He is really a more elemental Alfred Jingle, whose wit was also hostile and defensive and who was likewise caught in the system by the continual necessity of defense. The system, in other words, is so powerful that it absorbs all reactions to it that use its own weapons; Quilp, like Jingle, is trapped by his very anger. Fighting bitterly against everything Nell suggests—the passive, the calm, and the dead—he meets the same end. Like Jingle he fails to see that it is the weapons which are really at fault; and he is finally destroyed by them.

Before his death, however, he provides an immensely important parody of the main plot. The humor of this parody, however, is qualified locally by Quilp's viciousness and finally by his death. That is, laughter is often made difficult in individual instances by Quilp's own demonic laughter or his cruelty,[19] and we finally recognize, as we see him caught in the same economic quagmire, that his parody has lacked the freedom and detachment necessary for success. His humor ultimately reinforces rather than undercuts the pathos of the main plot. Just as much as the old grandfather, he represents the brutal power of the economic mill, and nearly as much as Nell is he a victim of it. Our laughter at Quilp, then, is contributory to our tears for Nell.

He is, first of all, an outlet for much aggression, a safety valve for our hostility against purity, women, and pathos itself. Among other things, he purifies our reactions and makes possible an unqualified response to Nell. His witty sadism checks our possible impatience with gentleness and drains off our mischievous impulses: "I don't eat babies; I don't like 'em. It will be as well to stop that young screamer though, in case I should be tempted to do him a mischief" (chap. 21). Quilp is the deadly enemy of the stock sentiment, of babies and all little, presumably helpless, objects of easy tears. He hates the terrible meek and their grinding demands, and he loathes the falseness of the transference of sympathy to babies, little girls, or even

dumb animals. When Kit finds Nell's little bird and tear-
fully asks, "What's to be done with this?" Quilp, immediately and with a certain rightness, responds, "Wring its
neck" (chap. 13). Quilp allows our impulse to wring necks
an outlet in laughter, so that the counterimpulse to protect
and love the small and helpless might be expressed more
fully. He is a very functional enemy of sentimentality.

But he is more than that. His sarcasm amounts to an
insistence that life be met head on, without paralyzing
precautions. When accused of being in Little Bethel chapel
for insidious purposes, he responds with a wonderful burlesque of prudence:

> "Yes, I was at chapel. What then? I've read in books
> that pilgrims were used to go to chapel before they
> went on journeys, to put up petitions for their safe
> return. Wise men! journeys are very perilous—espe-
> cially outside the coach. Wheels come off, horses take
> fright, coachman drive too fast, coaches overturn. I
> always go to chapel before I start on journeys. It's the
> last thing I do on such occasions, indeed" (chap. 48).

The exaggerated politeness of his tone also suggests his
central attack on all insulating gentility and his affirmation
of a primary relation between human beings.

The primary relation with Quilp is, at times, strongly
sexual and is always extraordinarily physical. His most
constant threat, "I'll bite you!" is both frightening and
innocent in its purity; for we recognize it as basically a cry
from the nursery, the insistence of the child that he be
noticed. Quilp is the elemental naughty boy, protesting
with his very life against indifference. And it is the positive
nature of this rebellion and its attractiveness in this cold
novel that draw our laughter to this partly demonic figure,
to the sense of physical freedom and self-gratification of
the child. What other demon would choose to assert his
power by something as childish as staying up all night and
smoking, especially after the mother has been sent to bed?

Surely this is a childhood fantasy of the tables turned, both attractive in its simplicity and sad in its limitations. Quilp loves physical tricks that are both satanic and pure, that are, in fact, little more than an exaggerated "showing off": "he ate hard eggs, shell and all, devoured gigantic prawns with the heads and tails on, chewed tobacco and watercresses at the same time and with extraordinary greediness, drank boiling tea without winking, bit his fork and spoon till they bent again" (chap. 5), and performed other variations of sandbox tricks. He delights further in practical jokes, or, as Dickens calls them, "childish pranks" (chap. 11). Perhaps most central to Quilp's boyishness, however, is his extreme vulnerability to personal remarks. He obviously lives in dread of the pointing fingers of playground mockery. His chief reason for tormenting his mother-in-law is that she called him names: "I'm a little hunchy villain and a monster, am I, Mrs. Jiniwin? Oh!" (chap. 5). Most important, his primary motivation for revenge in the novel comes from Kit's remark that Quilp is "a uglier dwarf than can be seen anywheres for a penny" (chap. 6). And his greatest delight comes in reversing the terms: "Kit a thief! Kit a thief! Ha ha ha! Why, he's an uglier-looking thief than can be seen anywhere for a penny. Eh Kit—eh? Ha ha ha!" (chap. 60). Quilp is extremely sensitive with just the sensitivity of a child, and he lives to anticipate and reverse insults.

This life traps him in defensiveness, of course, and admittedly causes him to be extremely violent, but his sadism, pure as it is, is often neutralized by the fact that it usually is released in language only. It is in language that he excels, and in the language of parody only can he break out of the defensive trap he is in. He can find temporary release in his great and aggressive creative instinct, displayed nowhere so brilliantly as in his arrangement for Dick to enter employment with the Brasses. His parody of the legal life is devastating:

"With Miss Sally . . . and the beautiful fictions
of the law, his days will pass like minutes. Those
charming creations of the poet, John Doe and
Richard Roe, when they first dawn upon him, will
open a new world for the enlargement of his mind and
the improvement of his heart" (chap. 33).

We laugh at Quilp, then, because his hostility is necessary to allow for purity, his extreme energy for extreme
passiveness, but also because his "evil" is often merely
mischievousness. He is not the real enemy but an actual
victim. Though apparently in opposition to Nell, he is
really part of her; they form a continuum, and together
make up the child, both aggressive and compliant, pure
and vicious. Faced with the adult world, both try desperately to live, one by hiding, the other by attacking;
neither is allowed to survive.

The parallels between the two are numerous. Most
basic is the play of Nell's pathetic littleness against the
pugnacious and grotesque littleness of Quilp. Nell asks for
pity; pity Quilp and he punches you in the nose. They
suggest alternate responses, but they are continuous with
each other. Similarly, Nell's flight to the country is per-
versely echoed in Quilp's association with the truly primitive, the slop and the slime. Nell's prettified country
becomes Quilp's "wilderness" (chap. 23) and his "summer-
house" (chap. 21). On "the slimy banks of a great river,"
Quilp insists on the parody of the natural: "You're fond of
the beauties of nature . . . . Is this charming, Brass? Is it
unusual, unsophisticated, primitive?" (chap. 51). Primitive
it is exactly, and Quilp provides the earthquake to Nell's
rivulets and hills, the tiger to her lamb.

The most important connection, however, involves
Quilp's mock death and resurrection, the wonderful triumph of his belligerent life and honesty over the cold and
artificial mourning of the Brasses. The situation here
evokes our laughter specifically at the important thematic

issues of death, pretense, and cold indifference masking as love. The laughter is not really at the Brasses but at the abstract and unfeeling language they use and the death they mock.

> "Ah!" said Mr. Brass, breaking the silence, and raising his eyes to the ceiling with a sigh, "who knows but he may be looking down upon us now! Who knows but he may be surveying of us from—from somewhere or another, and contemplating us with a watchful eye! Oh Lor!" (chap. 49).

The dramatic irony is heavy but appropriate; Quilp's reappearance is a victory over the ghouls. And he times his entrance, with true artistic instinct, so as to insist on his physical reality.

> "Our faculties [said Mr. Brass] must not freeze with grief. I'll trouble you for a little more of that, ma'am. A question now arises, with relation to his nose."
> "Flat," said Mrs. Jiniwin.
> "Aquiline!" cried Quilp, thrusting in his head, and striking the feature with his fist. "Aquiline, you hag. Do you see it? Do you call this flat? Do you? Eh?" (chap. 49).

He dares us to ignore him, to think he could die and leave these terrors victorious; for it is not Quilp but the falsity he fights that is dangerous.

But his fight is doomed and he finally becomes more and more elemental. As Nell moves to purity, he regresses. From joyfully punishing Mrs. Jiniwin, he moves to kicking an idol, suggesting his primitiveness certainly, but also the horrible frustration he must endure. He finally is forced to retreat altogether and to adopt the last desperate defense of the unwanted child, imposed isolation. He is, at the last, "convivial" only by himself and will laugh only when he has no company in laughing (chap. 67). Like Nell, he is finally killed by shutting out help and dies while his rescuers are at hand. The opposites meet then in a willed death, and the child, even in this divided state, has been crushed by a hostile world.

But out of this death is born an adult, the regenerated and transformed Dick Swiveller. In the midst of the trapped and the frustrated there emerges the liberated comic spirit. It may be that the triumph of Dick and the Marchioness cannot eradicate the pessimism of the novel, but it does present a very movingly realized alternative. It is an alternative, moreover, supported throughout by our laughter. For the humor has had two main functions, as always: not only the aggressive function which here heightens the pathos of Nell, but a defensive protection of pleasure, a construction which serves as a refuge from darkness. Dick not only creates our laughter, then, but is in a very real sense created by it.

That Dick was Dickens' favorite character in this novel is not surprising,[20] for he is a dramatic artist very much like his creator, using protective humor to create appropriate roles for himself. Pain itself means very little if he can arrange it into a part for which he has apt quotations.[21] His hat, even, is rather an emblem of his protective and liberating humor; it is a "very limp hat, worn with the wrong side foremost, to hide a hole in the brim" (chap. 2). He is flexible in exactly this way and has the freedom the others lack to try out different poses and directions in order to hide the holes.

But Dick is not primarily a defensive character but an open and expansive one. The pleasure that we protect through him is certainly not thin or starved. He lives over a tobacconist's shop, which provides him with a perpetual snuffbox, and he is as comfortable as Mrs. Jarley. And, like Mrs. Jarley, whose comfort always included others', Dick's creative life of the imagination engenders by necessity a similar life in others.

> By a like pleasant fiction his single chamber was always mentioned in the plural number. In its disengaged times, the tobacconist had announced it in his window as "apartments" for a single gentleman, and Mr. Swiveller, following up the hint, never failed to speak of it as his rooms, his lodgings, or his chambers: conveying to his hearers a notion of indefinite space, and leaving their imaginations to wander through long suites of lofty halls, at pleasure (chap. 7).

"At pleasure" indeed! As the narrator says, "to be the friend of Swiveller you must reject all circumstantial evidence" (chap. 7). Perhaps it is more accurate to say that Dick's friendship *allows* one to transcend the trivially circumstantial and live in "the rosy," here, as in *Pickwick,* a sure provider of joy and amiable conviviality—even if it is only gin. Though Dick is, from the first, a serious and complex character, much more self-conscious than Mr. Pickwick, his seriousness is always gentle. Unlike Quilp, the novel's other important life force, Dick is never defensive nor sinister. Dickens makes the contrast clear in an important scene where Quilp, rushing out of the Curiosity Shop, crashes into a man, whom he instantly begins pummeling. He almost immediately finds himself on his back in the middle of the street, "with Mr. Richard Swiveller performing a kind of dance round him and requiring to know 'whether he wanted any more?'" (chap. 13). Dick's dance engenders a kind of joy, and he launches into an important parody both of the retribution and the commercial ethic which dominate the novel.

> "There's plenty more of it at the same shop," said Mr. Swiveller, by turns advancing and retreating in a threatening attitude, "a large and extensive assortment always on hand—country orders executed with promptitude and despatch—will you not have a little more, sir?—don't say no, if you'd rather not" (chap. 13).

The dance and the parody neutralize the violence, and our laughter rejects the entire basis of the main plot. We are left with gentleness and freedom, pure pleasure and pure play.

But the fact is that Dick is not strong enough to maintain this purity by himself. Even in this same scene we are given hints that he is somehow incomplete. Mrs. Quilp's screams and jerks resulting from her husband's pinches, for instance, do not bother him at all: "he did not remark on these appearances, and soon forgot them." There are areas of life, in other words, which he is not equipped to handle, and it is, ironically, Quilp who begins his moral education by sending him to the Brasses, who, in turn, bring him into contact with the Marchioness and to an eventual initiation into poverty, starvation, nothingness, and symbolic death—and, of course, his triumph over them.

Dick's initial comic position is, in fact, for all its freedom, too acquiescent. It smacks too much of the attitude of Nell.

> "No man knocks himself down; if his destiny knocks him down, his destiny must pick him up again. Then I'm very glad that mine has brought all this upon itself, and I shall be as careless as I can, and make myself quite at home to spite it. So go on, my buck," said Mr. Swiveller, taking his leave of the ceiling with a significant nod, "and let us see which of us will be tired first!" (chap. 34).

There is an un-Nellylike defiance here, certainly, and a welcome rejection of work, but it is still too passive and, more important, too callous: it ignores those who "have been at work from [their] cradle" (chap. 34), specifically the Marchioness. Carelessness, by itself, is not enough. It is not enough to sing "Away, Dull Care"; one must earn the right to dismiss it. Dick's announcement, then, that the situation at the Brasses' does not concern him is ironic; his decision to "have nothing whatever to do with it" back-fires—to his great advantage.

He soon begins to worry very much about the Marchioness. It bothers him that "nobody ever came to see her, nobody spoke of her, nobody cared about her" (chap. 36). He sees Sally beat her and must abandon his reliance on destiny and test himself in this lonely world of the Marchioness. He must come face to face with the nothingness symbolized by the Brasses' servant girl:

> "Where do you come from?" [Quilp] said after a long pause, stroking his chin.
> "I don't know."
> "What's your name?"
> "Nothing" (chap. 51).

The catechism is brilliant in its suggestiveness. All the Marchioness can do is repeat her pathetic plea for contact, "But please will you leave a card or message?" Dick begins by helping the small servant, of course, and the joyous cribbage games they play are the most important symbolic contrast to the sinister games for cash which alienate and kill Nell and her grandfather. Dick learns that the Marchioness is reduced to looking through the keyhole for company, and, though he is temporarily self-conscious at the thought of his own absurd pastimes that she must have witnessed, he leaves self-consciousness behind and instinctively responds to her loneliness. He brings food, drink, and, most helpful, his free imaginative re-creation of reality: "To make it seem more real and pleasant, I shall call you the Marchioness, do you hear?" (chap. 57). It *is*, in fact, more real. The reality of the imagination is played off against the reality of the grave, and our laughter begins to build a world of real joy.

It is a world made possible by the Marchioness' presence, though it still must be painfully created. Even now Dick reacts with a new sensitivity to others. When the

Marchioness uses a less-than-poetic idiom, he thinks about correcting her but decides against it when he considers that "it was evident that her tongue was loosened by the purl, and her opportunities for conversation were not so frequent as to render a momentary check of little consequence" (chap. 58). He responds to her absolute trust and to the demands she makes on him simply as a lonely and isolated human being. But his initiation demands something more extreme than sympathetic and imaginative identification with the Marchioness; it demands that he re-create her grievous experience through a symbolic death.

Though Dick does become something of a classic hero,[22] his illness is more than an archetypal purging; it is a rehearsal of death, a real brush with nonexistence. And it is the Marchioness whom he has saved who must eventually save him. He must face death and come back from it somehow made triumphant by his honesty and simple trust. When he regains consciousness after his illness and asks his nurse if he has been very ill, the Marchioness very simply explains his situation: "Dead, all but . . . . I never thought you'd get better. Thank heaven you have" (chap. 64). After this Dick is "silent for a long while." His response to her presence and her love displays a new style, almost stark in its clarity and simplicity:

> "The poor little Marchioness has been wearing herself to death!" cried Dick.
> "No I haven't," she returned, "not a bit of it. Don't you mind about me. I like sitting up, and I've often had a sleep, bless you, in one of them chairs. But if you could have seen how you tried to jump out o' winder, and if you could have heard how you used to keep on singing and making speeches, you wouldn't have believed it—I'm so glad you're better, Mr. Liverer."
> "Liverer indeed!" said Dick thoughfully. "It's well I *am* a liverer. I strongly suspect I should have died, Marchioness, but for you" (chap. 64).

This is the heart of the rejuvenated comic center, a "liverer" born out of nothing and fully deserving the delight given to it at the end. Out of hunger and servitude and loneliness they recapture a bit of joy. Perhaps it is not enough to counterbalance the central gloom, but there is an enormous amount of strength, supported by our laughter, invested in those "many hundred thousand games of cribbage" (chap. 73) they play together. In the midst of death there is still this small but powerful glimpse of immortality.

DAVID COPPERFIELD'S
CARLYLEAN RETAILORING

Richard J. Dunn

Both *Sartor Resartus* and *David Copperfield* focus on the anguish of self-discovery; both convincingly catalogue personal and social deterrents to self-fulfillment; both declare the possibility of individual moral regeneration; but *Copperfield* alone artistically incorporates both the process and the product of self-discovery. Although I do not here argue that *David Copperfield* owes a conscious debt to *Sartor Resartus* or that it has the philosophic intensity of Carlyle's work, comparison with *Sartor* does demonstrate that Dickens' views of the self in *David Copperfield* parallel Carlyle's and that Dickens' novelistic form permits an artistic completeness not possible by Carlyle's experimental technique.[1]

Speculatively, Diogenes Teufelsdröckh approaches with wonder and fear "that unanswerable question: Who am *I*; the thing that can say 'I'?"[2] At the end of long despair he finally learns

> the Ideal is in thyself, the impediment too is in thyself: thy Condition is but the stuff thou art to shape that same Ideal out of: what matters whether such stuff be of this sort or that, so the Form thou give it be heroic, be poetic? (II, *ix*)

By a combination of self-control and creative labor one may, according to Carlyle, achieve and retain the sort of spiritual self-awareness so hard-won by Teufelsdröckh. Carlyle's book attempts more than theoretical philosophy and religion; through its unorthodox form it seeks heroic and poetic stature. Its disregard for conventionality, its elaborately ironic narrative framework, its parody of fictional forms, and its serious prophetic tenor organically produce many structural tensions.[3] These tensions greatly increase the emotional turmoil of Teufelsdröckh's story and of the work as a whole, but they do not permit Carlyle to project effectively any image of his regenerated hero. *Sartor Resartus* is convincingly and often mystically affirmative in its account of one man's search for meaning, but it fails to attend artistically to the final product of this search, its redeemed central figure. Just when we wonder what he is doing, how he is practicing his belief in creative work, we learn that Teufelsdröckh has disappeared, possibly to join a revolution.

Carlyle's main problem was that not Diogenes Teufelsdröckh but a literal-minded Englishman shapes the "stuff" of *Sartor Resartus;* only the hero himself could provide a true account of his life and works in a way that would demonstrate organically the practical results of his conversion. Certainly it is ironic that the world cannot interpret Diogenes' vision, which comes to the English editor in chaotic fragments, but does not the formal chaos on the other hand endanger the credibility of his conversion?

Carlyle's contempt for fiction and his lack of talent for writing it are well known, and certainly Teufelsdröckh's disregard for the materials contributing to heroic form reflects Carlyle's attitude toward much fiction.[4] Even modern readers, sophisticated toward experimental modes which extend the scope of fiction, might share an early critic's impression that Teufelsdröckh had few convictions because his thoughts are "too irregular and are not formed into a proper series and sequence."[5] Close study of *Sartor's* structure and even cursory attention to Carlyle's other works acquit him and his character of insincerity or shallowness of conviction, but unquestionably the very technical genius of *Sartor,* particularly its ironic point of view, is at once its ideal and impediment. The more traditional fictional form of *David Copperfield* resolves this problem largely because its hero returns to us as artist, attending carefully to the "stuff" of his form—a body of material similar to that which Carlyle drew upon for *Sartor.* Because Dickens' novel shows the hero's artistic and social survival after attaining selfhood, *David Copperfield* may be read as both an echo of and a sequel to *Sartor Resartus.*

David opens his history with wonder and a boding sense of uncertainty; "Whether I shall turn out to be the hero of my own life, or whether that station will be held by anyone else, these pages must show."[6] Tentative like the undiscovered (and in this instance unborn) self, this query paradigmatically anticipates the course of David's growth. For a period it will seem that the station of hero will be held by someone else, but like Carlyle's Diogenes Teufelsdröckh he will attain a selfhood that is unselfish, an identity formed by contact with the world beyond the self. This is to be a difficult struggle, and although the brilliant characterization of minor figures at times obscures David, he does emerge as the hero.

The uncertainty of *Copperfield's* opening extends to nearly all of David's early memories. His first reflections are patently romantic, presenting the familiar pattern of destructive reality eroding childhood innocence. He first speaks of the unusual conditions of his birth. Born on a Friday, he was, according to superstition, destined to be lucky. Yet the history of his next few years suggests that luck is denied him. When it does come fortune actually does him more harm than good in attaining selfhood. We find a very specific suggestion of personal uncertainty in what David tells us of the auction of his caul. The caul, conventionally a talisman against drowning, immediately assumes more importance in his memory, for, recalling that it was disposed of by auction, David remembers feeling "quite uncomfortable and confused, at a part of myself being disposed of in that way" (chap. 1). The nonchronological positioning of this information in the book's fourth paragraph gives it more than incidental importance. David, unlike Pip in *Great Expectations*, does not describe earliest memories as "first impressions of self-awareness." Instead, he structures his story to suggest that his memories begin with a fragmentation of himself at public auction. The boyhood discomfort of watching the sale of the caul anticipates the greater pains he will feel with further fragmentation of his being.

For both David and Diogenes the sense of childhood alienation is increased by the loss of family. Teufelsdröckh is a foundling, but it is some years before he knows it. Born after his father's death, David is a posthumous child, who later loses his mother symbolically, through her remarriage, and then literally, through her death. David remembers contrasting his father's cold white tombstone in the churchyard with the warm and bright parlor, and he recalls that "the doors of our house were—almost cruelly, it seemed to me sometimes—bolted and locked" (chap. 1). This incident, following closely the detail of the auctioned caul, quickly establishes his growing sense of isolation, a feeling that intensifies when Murdstone courts and marries his mother. Events such as Betsey Trotwood's angry departure when David does not turn out to be the niece she expected further his alienation, denying him a frame of family identity. The deaths of his mother and half-brother complete the process of severing him from family. Revealing his tendency to associate symbolically with others at critical moments (a sign of the undifferentiated self),

David remarks that "the mother who lay in the grave was the mother of my infancy; the little creature in her arms, was myself, as I had once been, hushed forever on her bosom" (chap. 9).

Dickens' clear presentation of David's childhood sufferings, particularly of his loss of identity, is but half the story, for counterpointing it is the account of the beginnings of a new, delusionary self. The David we see reading the crocodile book with Peggotty, falling in love with Emily, and assisting the inarticulate Barkis in courtship is a David struggling to find a surrogate family and a secure social identity. These acts occupy David at crucial periods to divert him from his more tragic moments, but the relationships he forms make few demands upon the self. Diogenes Teufelsdröckh, on the other hand, finds no such conditional relief from his youthful despair. Obviously there are many differences between the young boy and the university-educated Teufelsdröckh, but the point is that if David is to progress in self-discovery, he must rely as much upon his inner resources as upon social relationships. As the novel progresses, events gradually reveal to him the impossibility of vicarious involvement. Peggotty, through the marriage David arranges, becomes physically distanced from him, and, although he hears from her occasionally, she has no vital part in his future. The Little Emily romance disintegrates, first through David's deference to Ham Peggotty and then through Emily's attraction to Steerforth. The distancing of David from the Peggotty group occurs very slowly, but before it even begins we see the growth of David's self-delusion. As early as the time of his mother's death he feels a false sense of importance that recalls Teufelsdröckh's attitude under similar circumstances. Although sincerely grief-stricken, David exaggerates his mourning before leaving school for the funeral. He feels distinguished, and looks more melancholy, and walks more slowly when other boys notice him (chap. 9). Teufelsdröckh, learning of his father's death, feels "a certain poetic elevation, yet also a corresponding civic depression, it naturally imparted: *I was like no other*." He cites this moment as "the first spring of tendencies" which he later regarded as very remarkable (II, *iii*). For both him and David the egoism, the self-indulgent emotionalism, is remarkable only because it calls attention to selves not yet noteworthy. Obviously neither Dickens nor Carlyle demands undemonstrative stoicism, but both see the danger of genuine emotion turning to self-glorification. Personally, both authors consistently view their past with strong emotion. Carlyle, nearly twenty years after writing *Sartor*, observes in his journal, "Words cannot express the love and sorrow of my old memories, chiefly out of boyhood, as they occasionally rise upon me, and I have now no voice for them at all."[7] Dickens, in a fragmentary autobiography, recalling the agony of his boyhood employment in the blacking warehouse, confesses that even in maturity "I often forget in my dreams that I have a dear wife and children; even that I am a man; and wander desolately back to that time of my life."[8] Though these attitudes no doubt profoundly motivate the sympathetic treatment Carlyle and Dickens give to their youthful heroes, sympathy does not cloud the implication that the threats to young David and Diogenes include threats to their essential selfhood as well as to their material happiness.

As they move toward manhood, Diogenes' and David's lives seem to complement more than closely parallel one another. Completing his schooling, falling in and out of love, wandering discontentedly, Teufelsdröckh turns more deeply inward and becomes more intellectually proud than David, who, following a roughly similar course of external experience, evades the issue of his being until he reaches an emotional crisis demanding self-evaluation. It seems that his movement from the time he leaves London for Dover accelerates the flight from his inner self.

David's journey to Dover, his adoption by his Aunt

Betsey, and his improved worldly condition provide an interlude of materialistic satisfaction not found in Teufels-dröckh's story. Yet this period of David's life seems Carlylean when he changes his working-boy's rags for new vestments. Selling his clothing to pay for the trip to Dover, he now sells a figurative part of himself (contrasting his earlier passive presence at the caul auction). Once he arrives at Betsey's he receives new clothes, an act implying not moral retailoring but simply an exchange of identities. With clothes comes a new name—henceforth he is to be Trotwood Copperfield, in honor of the niece his eccentric aunt felt so unjustly deprived of. Yet toleration of Betsey's eccentricity cannot explain David's willing acceptance of the new identity. He remembers that his new life seemed a pleasant dream and that he "never thought of anything about myself, distinctly" (chap. 14). The greatest doubt he could have had, the question of whether he truly deserved and could utilize this new fortune, never occurred to him. Such self-consciousness came more naturally later and was hardly possible in the first moments of a new life.

It is at this point that the good luck predicted at David's birth seems to materialize, but in Carlylean perspective such luck may be more curse than boon. If the self is to discover its true nature, it cannot be deluded by the semblance with which others adorn it. A person must, as *Sartor Resartus* demands, renounce the selfish ego, deny imposture, and define his character by diligent work that aims at noble ends. Such is the pattern for moral and spiritual retailoring. In David's case the issue is complicated, not resolved, by good fortune. He has gone through the motions of seeking identity and has learned not renunciation and certitude but tactics of evasion. Though kindly intended, Betsey Trotwood's benevolence becomes in effect David's summons to join what Carlyle called the "Dandiacal Body," those whose "existence consists in the wearing of clothes" (III, x).

David unthinkingly accepts the new self and almost

immediately seeks approval of it. But he continues to seek vicarious existence just as he had when he was with the Peggottys. It is the relationship with Steerforth that most clearly indicates David's willingness to abandon himself to a false guide who leads him away from self-knowledge. He consistently describes his attraction to the older boy as an enchantment. Whether we go so far as to regard the relationship as one of latent homosexuality or simply as another instance of the Dickensian double, clearly the enchantment David feels endangers his potential for self-realization, because he sacrifices perception to passive idolatry. He admits enjoying the dashing way Steerforth had of treating him like a plaything. "It relieved me," he recalls, "of any uneasiness I might have felt, in comparing my merits with his" (chap. 21). To be a thing, not a person, in the hands of another and to fear comparison of individual merits clearly indicates his negation of self and suggests that his continuing problem is one of willful self-delusion. The only real difference between David's self-abnegation at this point and Uriah Heep's odious humility is that, besides being hypocritical, Heep's humility is maliciously excessive whereas David's self-abasement before Steerforth is not. David's behavior is sincere, and it is satisfying to him because it permits the luxury of vicarious indulgence, without guilt, in Steerforth's pleasures.

Interestingly, the relationship between Teufelsdröckh and Herr Towgood in *Sartor* resembles the David-Steerforth friendship. Like Steerforth, Towgood proves to be a false friend, coming between Teufelsdröckh and his beloved Blumine just as Steerforth does between David and Emily. With more bitterness than Copperfield ever seems capable of, Diogenes comments on the friendship in terms that apply also to David and Steerforth:

> Towards this young warmhearted, strongheaded and wrongheaded Herr Towgood I was even near experiencing the now obsolete sentiment of Friendship. Yes,

> foolish Heathen that I was, I felt that, under certain
> conditions, I could have loved this man, and taken him
> to my bosom, and been his brother once and always
> (II, *iii*).

The conditions necessary for friendship would for Carlyle
undoubtedly include a demand that each person bring a
clearly defined individuality to the relationship and that
neither be unduly submissive to the other. The trouble with
David's regard for Steerforth is that it is a blind attraction;
young David, who cannot yet interpret his own nature, is in
no position to evaluate others.

The mature David, the retrospective author, clearly
recognizes Steerforth's weaknesses of character, particularly the lack of earnestness and firmness of purpose that
Betsey had sought to impress upon David. But as Mario
Praz, in a rare comparison of *Sartor* with *Copperfield,* observes, Steerforth represents the Byron half of the Carlylean mandate, "Close thy Byron, Open thy Goethe."[9] The
comparison is particularly apt if we qualify it by remembering that even to the mature David, who may figuratively
have opened his Goethe, the closed Byron remains as an
attractive fantasy.

Just as it suggests the difficulties of true friendship so
does *Sartor Resartus* suggest that for the speculative man
there can be no lasting comfort in romantic or domestic
love. Diogenes Teufelsdröckh, though converted to sympathy with others, himself remains solitary. His infatuation
with Blumine prior to his conversion reveals an inner
vacancy that neither he nor Copperfield will fill with romantic love.

> Disbelieving all things, the poor youth had never
> learned to believe in himself. Withdrawn, in proud
> timidity, within his own fastnesses; solitary from men,
> yet baited by night-spectres enough, he saw himself,
> with a sad indignation, constrained to renounce the
> fairest hopes of existence. And now, O now! (II, *v*)

Now he falls in love with Blumine; for a period he relies on feeling; but soon he realizes that no "yet known religion of young hearts [will] keep the human kitchen warm"(II, *v*). Both Carlyle and Dickens agree that love must be undertaken maturely and wisely, but Dickens recognizes it as more practically possible than does Carlyle. The self must be defined and disciplined for such a love; if one's self-awareness is illusionary, one's concept of romantic and domestic love also is illusionary. Even worse, romantic love can often further distance one from self-discovery. David, when first seeing Dora, is not so consciously despairing as was Teufelsdröckh when discovering Blumine, but he too is in a solitary condition, living alone in London, engaged in work which has little interest or meaning for him.

It is at the time of his courtship, a period when he seems most hopelessly self-deluded, that his real discovery of self begins. Though yet a "young spooney," he now begins to confront external circumstances that demand a self-assertion that he has never before exercised (chap. 36). On the one hand, in his most private self, he is drawn from reality by romantic silliness, but at the same time, in his public character, he must face the challenges of actuality. His social identity as Trotwood Copperfield, rising young proctor, depends directly upon the allowance he receives from his aunt. When she loses her money (at the time of his courtship of Dora), David must for the first time actively apply himself and work for his living. He recalls, as he perceptively details the pains with which he began his new life, what a great sacrifice it seemed to sell several of his handsome waistcoats. From a Carlylean perspective, he is beginning to retailor his character, but because the delusion of romantic love persists, the process is most difficult. But the fact that in his public actions (his work) he is able to exert the perseverance, earnestness, and diligence that have long been latent in his nature promises that privately, in the inner self, delusion is now being challenged.

Finding that he has to work for a living, David recognizes the need for turning "the painful discipline of my younger days to account by going to work with a resolute and steady heart" (chap. 36). It was precisely this discipline, ironically exaggerated by the Murdstones and Creakle, that David so willingly forgot when he sought his aunt's protection at Dover. But now as he faces his new responsibilities he credits the early influences of past discipline with giving him strength. Retrospectively, he considers this difficult period as one in which his perseverance and energy began to mature as he developed "habits of punctuality, order, and diligence" (chap. 42). But at the same time he was continuing to worship Dora. His state of mind is best described by his chapter title "Enthusiasm," for, like the dog Diogenes Teufelsdröckh once saw chasing its tail, David goes on at a mighty rate, like "a Conquering Hero, to whom Fate . . . has malignly appended a tin-kettle of Ambition" (II, *iii*). With a different, but no less appropriate figure of speech, David remarks, "What I had to do, was to take my woodman's axe in hand, and clear my own way through the forest of difficulty, by cutting down the trees until I came to Dora" (chap. 36). Here he oversimplifies by thinking that the mere application of energy and receipt of payment are in themselves sufficient. His is the error of any who might interpret the Carlylean mandate, "Produce! Produce!" too literally. Carlyle calls for engagement of the whole self; he views work as the fullest expression of self, the application of "the utmost thou hast in thee" (II, *ix*). In work, as in friendship and love, energy and enthusiasm must be controlled by a balanced, rational self, or they may be wasted. Outwardly David develops strength and a new firmness, but he yet lacks the moral firmness, the will of his own that his aunt had earlier

remarked as necessary to develop the "strength of character . . . not to be influenced, except on good reason, by
anybody or anything" (chap. 39).

Despite his pride in his work, despite his successful
courtship, David finds a vague unhappiness that he comes
to analyze after his marriage. Unwilling yet to face directly
the problems in his own household, he sees in the Strong's
home analogies to his own. He is bothered particularly by
the phrase, "the first mistaken impulse of an undisciplined
heart," which Annie Strong uses to describe her former
attraction to another man (chap. 48). The "undisciplined
heart motif" becomes, as Gwendolyn Needham has observed, central to David's history.[10] Here we need to consider it as closely resembling Carlyle's ideas about control-
ling emotion, for nowhere in nineteenth-century literature
is the disciplining of heart more obvious than in Carlyle's
writing. Again and again he works to translate feeling into
thought and action,[11] and *Sartor* particularly demonstrates
this process. With Dickens we indeed frequently find much
feeling and much action but too little thought. But *Copperfield,* like *Sartor Resartus* and in a more conventional
manner, presents the rare artistic synthesis of feeling,
action, and thought—a combination possible from a self
fully alive.

Speaking early in the novel, Clara Peggotty tells David
that "a loving heart [is] better and stronger than wisdom"
(chap. 1), but much of *David Copperfield* seems directed to
prove her wrong. In instance after instance, involving
David's mother, aunt, Little Emily, and others we see that
loving hearts bring their owners little happiness and wisdom and lead often to imprudent acts. Nonetheless, the
loving heart, the capacity for emotion, is absolutely necessary (consider the Murdstones' heartlessness), and it must
be controlled by a self intellectually and morally awake.
Feeling must not be a self-conscious but a conscious act. As
Carlyle in his essay on biography put it, "A loving Heart is

the beginning of all Knowledge. That is, it opens the whole mind, quickens every faculty of the intellect to do its fit work, that of *knowing*; and therefrom . . . of *vividly uttering-forth*."[12] Feeling, then, is the prerequisite for action. The capacity for feeling, more than the firmness and discipline of the early years, is what David preserves through all his childhood and adolescent delusions. The very writing of his history, finally, is the uttering-forth Carlyle speaks of, although less prophetic and more explicit than Carlyle's own *Sartor Resartus*.

The finished product, the novel *David Copperfield*, was not artistically possible until David experienced the self-awakening he describes in its final chapters. Compared with the clarity of the section of *Sartor Resartus* that traces Teufelsdröckh's progress from the Everlasting No through the Center of Indifference to the Everlasting Yea, the process of David's conversion is not so obvious as his need for it or as the result of it. Also, it is easy to misinterpret the source of the change in David if we have not paid close attention to his earlier stages of self-awareness. For if we permitted other characters to dominate our attention during the years of David's rather passive adolescence, we are likely to have overlooked the complexity of his delusions and thereby too willingly to have attributed the source of his conversion to some force external to the self. Such a reading opens *Copperfield*'s final chapters to what I believe is an unjust charge of superficiality. Agnes Wickfield and/or external nature might be misunderstood as sources of David's regeneration, but I think that Dickens uses David's attitudes toward Agnes and nature to demonstrate rather than motivate the conversion. Certainly David finds new comfort in Agnes' love, but his comfort comes not merely from her but from within himself. Similarly, his related and more generalized response to nature originates within himself.

First, consider the Agnes problem. In the course of his

adventures David meets many people, both good and evil, having little in common except that most of them are eccentrics. Their eccentricities seem to isolate them not only from one another, preventing the formation of a harmonious social group, but also from nature. We hear of Betsey Trotwood's "green," but even animals are barred from it, and except for the Peggottys' relationship with the sea (more the symbol of stern external justice than of nature close to man), few of the people David meets seem to exist in nature. Young David himself, except for several uneasy nights in haystacks while traveling to Dover, seems rather insensitive to nature. Yet Agnes, the girl he describes as sister-spirit, good angel, and finally soul-partner, lives harmoniously with nature, that, although not pastoral, is persistently and calmly good—particularly when contrasted with the tempestuous nature which destroys Steerforth, David's "bad-angel." As early as the thirty-ninth chapter, when the disappointed David returns to Canterbury, he specifically associates the natural environment with Agnes and feels a sober pleasure calming his spirits and easing his heart.

> Strange to say, that quiet influence which was inseparable in my mind from Agnes, seemed to pervade even the city where she dwelt. The venerable cathedral towers, and the old jackdaws and rooks whose airy voices made them more retired than perfect silence would have done; the battered gateways; . . . the still nooks, where the ivied growth of centuries crept over gabled ends and ruined walls; the ancient houses, the pastoral landscape of field, orchard, and garden; everywhere—on everything—I felt the same serener air, the same calm, thoughtful, softening spirit.

David is not yet ready to receive any permanent solace in such an atmosphere; he has not yet sufficiently discovered the self and disciplined his responses. At this stage of his life he is an observer resembling Teufelsdröckh in the Center of Indifference when

> Towns also and Cities, especially the ancient, I failed not to look upon with interest. How beautiful to see thereby, as through a long vista, into the remote Time; to have as it were, an actual section of almost the earliest Past brought safe into the Present, and set before your eyes! (II, *viii*)

This kind of vision can be brought "safely" into the present because it demands little from the observer; it asks no application to present problems as did the vision Carlyle was to project later in *Past and Present*. Diogenes and David can pause, see a beautiful wholeness and calmness in reminders of nature and the past, and then return virtually unchanged to their present delusive lives. To put it another way, both young men are still spectators; like the outsiders to Hardy's Wessex, they move through an organic nature but are not yet part of it. In *Copperfield* only Agnes consistently is a part of a living external world, which for the greater part of David's early life seems dead.

As for external nature, both David and Diogenes seek in it a completeness and order absent from their own lives, but for neither of them is nature a personal ordering force. Though possessing an order of its own, external nature, like the self, is a strange mixture of elements, neither always wildly active nor calmly static. To trace the growth of David's sensitivity to nature is to clarify our recognition of his growth in self-knowledge.

Contrasted with the aggressive Teufelsdröckh who throws down the gauntlet of the Everlasting No and romantically endures in "a Universe seemingly void of Purpose" (II, *vii*), David seems pathetically passive when he flees England after the deaths of his wife and Steerforth. But an important thing is happening; he is growing conscious of the world beyond the self, and in mourning for Dora he demonstrates none of the vanity that had marked

his mourning for his mother years earlier. With Steerforth's death, coming soon after Dora's, David finds that
external nature is capable of great disorder; like the self
it can be destructive. How perfectly and intimately his
description of the storm reveals his need for self-definition.
The chaos he sees in nature does not so much reflect
here his own state of mind as demand discovery of a self
that has an order of its own. Never has David been so
alone as when he views "flying clouds tossed up into most
remarkable heaps . . . through which the wild moon
seemed to plunge headlong, as if, in a dread disturbance of
the laws of nature, she had lost her way and were
frightened" (chap. 55). Melodramatic though this tempest
chapter is if removed from the context of self-discovery,
David's reactions here demonstrate the need for inner
growth, and from this moment he responds, without indulgence, honestly and sincerely to the needs of the self.
David now is reaching the healthy condition that Carlyle
discerned in Goethe, the ability to think and to feel without
the wasteful processes of thinking *about Thinking*" or
feeling *about Feeling*."[13] When he leaves England he is
but vaguely conscious of his problem. He sees himself "as a
man upon a field [who] will receive a mortal hurt, and
scarcely know that he is struck, so I, when I was left alone
with my undisciplined heart, had no conception of the
wound with which it had to strive" (chap. 58). For the first
time in his life he is completely alone, and if in this isolation he were to attempt nothing more than recapitulation
of his previous experience the isolation would be produc-
tive. But in the course of time and solitude he achieves a
tempered sensibility, a new calmness, manifesting itself in
his new response to external nature. The terms of the
response, an apocalyptic alpine vision, approach cliché, for
they are commonplace in nineteenth-century poetry and
fiction. Just as Carlyle in the "Sorrows of Teufelsdröckh"
chapter of *Sartor* shows Teufelsdröckh gazing over "a hun-

dred savage peaks in the last light of Day" and learning
that nature "was One, that she was his Mother and divine"
(II, *vi*), so does Dickens present David descending an
alpine path at sunset and finding "some long-unwonted
sense of beauty and tranquillity, some softening influence"
(chap. 58). Even more directly than Diogenes, he feels "all
at once, in this serenity, great Nature spoke to me; and
soothed me to lay down my weary head upon the grass, and
weep as I had not wept yet, since Dora died!" Has the discovery of self been a cliché, a commonplace recognition of
sentimental weakness, a melting of strength into tearful
pathos? Such is not the case if we remember the contexts
of both Teufelsdröckh's and Copperfield's visions, for both
come before spiritual regeneration is complete, and neither
vision in itself causes regeneration. Teufelsdröckh's experience closely precedes his most negative period, for the
mountain view is interrupted by his sight of Blumine and
his rival, Towgood, passing in a barouche. By the time he
endures the pains of negation and indifference and reaches
the affirmation of the Everlasting Yea, he continues to
regard nature as organic and essentially spiritual, but he,
the viewer, is changed. He is now ready to act, not simply
watch; he will love God and the Godlike in nature and man;
"Conviction, were it never so excellent, is worthless till it
convert itself into Conduct" (II, *ix*). The Everlasting Yea is
not the reverberation of all nature's beneficence; it is the
cry for dutiful participation in life. Though Dickens is
certainly less explicit than Carlyle about the spiritual significance of his hero's rededication, I think he implies the
same theories as Carlyle. David breaks into tears before
nature after passing through a period of self-deception and
grief, and in the final chapters of his history commits
himself to what from a Carlylean viewpoint is the first
moral act in the regenerative process—renunciation of the
self (that is, renunciation of selfishness). Prostrate before
organic nature David begins his own organic life. Renun-

ciation of the former self here involves purging himself of delusions, and David's major delusion has been his faulty self-consciousness. From the time of his mountain vision, David proceeds as a writer. He begins redefining himself through his work, much of which we never see (he tells briefly of books he had written before the present one) but which is implicit in the entirety of *David Copperfield*.

Part of the reason that David's conversion may be misunderstood or simply discounted as shallow cliché may spring from the technical problem Dickens had with point of view in the late chapters. During the early parts of the novel narrative distancing was possible because of the attention he gave to minor characters and because of the time gap between the action and the narrator's recollection of it. But in these last chapters David is necessarily alone and must now describe his most intimate experiences with a directness that cannot easily permit the gentle irony and nostalgia of the earlier chapters. Moreover, for plot purposes Agnes must stay in the story. As far as Agnes is concerned, he does little here in the way of effective characterization. We learn that she has been busy teaching children and caring for her father, and that one of her preoccupations was her pleasure "in keeping everything as it used to be when we were children" (chap. 60). At such moments she seems a very unsatisfactory opposite to Dora, the child-wife, for like her she seems unwilling to live in present reality. But we should note that the Agnes we see is constantly presented through the narrator's clouded sentiment. There is another Agnes—there has to be if David's marriage to her is all he claims it to be—whom we never see. This unseen Agnes withstands sorrow, humiliation, and the advances of the odious Heep, but we see only the Agnes who has survived, the essentially passive being who waits for David to discover himself and his love for her. She permits David to act for himself and advises him (like a female Carlyle) to develop self-sufficiency through work and suffering.

The timing of David's recollection of Agnes' role in his life is very important to an understanding of his awakening. Less than a page after describing his conduct on the mountain path (here we see the telescoping of time), he recalls the message of Agnes' letters. This is a meaningful influence not because it came from the good, patient Agnes, but because her statements described what he was in fact discovering on his own.

> She gave me no advice; she urged no duty on me; she only told me, in her fervent manner, what her trust in me was . . . . She knew that in me, sorrow could not be weakness, but must be strength. As the endurance of my childish days had done its part to make me what I was, so greater calamities would nerve me on, to be yet better than I was (chap. 63).

It cannot be stressed too much that David's strength is more affirmed and described than prescribed by Agnes. On the Continent he is remote from her; the letters supply the technical narrative perspective for presenting topics which call for some modest reluctance even on the part of the most self-conscious narrator. All his life David has had ample advice and examples of conduct—from Dan Peggotty, Aunt Betsey, the Strongs, and Agnes herself. That he now awakens when remote from these influences can hardly be cited as a direct result of them. Rather, he has reached the degree of self-knowledge which, even in the despair of unending negation, Carlyle saw as possible, for "our Works are the mirror wherein the spirit first sees its natural lineaments. Hence, too, the folly of that impossible Precept, *Know Thyself*; till it be translated into this partially possible one, *Know what thou canst work at*" (II, *vii*). It is this truth, more than any other, toward which the disciplined heart aspires. David's material rewards are great, but creature comforts are not his sole end, emphasize them though Dickens may. David's physical wants were amply supplied at several stages in his career—first by

Betsey's providence, later by his own enthusiastic labors. But finally he brings a purged spirit to his work and engages his whole being, not with an illusionary end that might be approached with a metaphorical woodman's axe, but with healthy involvement in the work at hand. The best evidence of the disciplined heart, of the real self David has discovered, lies in the novel we read. The "end" of *David Copperfield* thus is implicit from its opening page. From this standpoint, a remark like E. K. Brown's that David's major ethical insight is that it is "God's way to cast down the mighty and raise the humble" is beside the point.[14] David's discovery, the one underlying principle necessary for creative work, is that man must struggle for self-definition, overcome all threats to it, and then assert selfhood in his labors. Humility may be rewarded and the sham-mighty may be cast down—but even in Dickens' works there is no consistent guarantee of it.

What is most ironic about *Sartor Resartus* and *David Copperfield* is that the former, while so intensely prophetic, hesitates to prophesy a practically unified self. Teufelsdröckh himself disappears, and his works survive only in fragments. But *David Copperfield*, less prophetic in tone, implies a working process that completes itself and presents a hero who finds both spiritual and material comfort. Despite all its transcendental optimism, *Sartor Resartus* is at best only an anti-novel, admitting the impossibility of total self-realization. But *Copperfield*, despite its bourgeois materialism, has an artistic completeness indicative of wholeness for the individual who brings a loving heart and knowing self together.

BLEAK HOUSE AND
THE GRAVEYARD

K. J. Fielding and A. W. Brice

One of the most striking aspects of Dickens' technique as a novelist is the way in which he used topical issues in order to lead himself and his readers into the heart of the imaginary world of his fiction. It is remarkable because almost any examination of it leads to two different, though not irreconcilable, conclusions. One is that this topicality is such a marked feature of the novels that it plays an important part in the author's communication with his readers, is even part of his language, and is bound up with both the form and substance of his work. The other is that, in spite of this, it happens that any good reader of the novels, who is sensitive to their tone and aware of their fictional implications, ought certainly to be able to dispense with the detailed knowledge that Dickens' contemporaries possessed, and that few students may even now have.

This has been observed before. Not only this, but it is an inescapable inference from some critical opinions dating from the last century, which attempted to write Dickens down because of this very topicality. One can see it, for instance, in the positively convinced observations of Mowbray Morris, writing in the *Fortnightly Review* just twelve years after Dickens' death.[1] He begins his retrospective review of Dickens' popularity with the assurance that it is "out of the question" that "posterity will regard Dickens as he was regarded in his lifetime, or even as we now regard him"; and he means by this that he has no doubt that its "censure" will be more "severe." He is clear that one reason for this is that "fictions which paint the manners and features of contemporary life . . . must inevitably lose, for an age which cannot recognise the truth of the painting"; and he is certain that the qualities of his writing will attract posterity no more than many of his chosen subjects. Especially, Morris says,

> Our descendants will have, we may be very sure, too frequent and too real claims upon their compassion to let them spare many tears for those rather theatrical personages which Dickens too often employed to point his moral. Harsh though it may seem to say, whatever his writings may actually have done to reduce the sum of human suffering, will tell against rather than for them. It will always be so with those who employ fiction for the purpose of some social or political reformation; for the wrongs they help to remove . . . will seem . . . unreal in the pages of fiction, because they have so long ceased to form a part of actual existence.

Now, two or three observations follow. One is that Morris' assured prophecy has *not* been fulfilled: Dickens is as popular as ever and even more respected as a writer. Another is that either reformist fiction sometimes evidently does not suffer from its success in setting the world right or (if this be not so) that reformism and topicality were not relatively important in Dickens' novels. Yet, perhaps it may be allowed that mere reformist fiction which achieves its demands, or which is overtaken by their fulfillment, does lose something of its appeal. If so, then it may remain a matter of interest how far Dickens' novels were really topical, and, if they were, why this has not diminished their interest for us today.

A full account of how the novels appeared to their first readers no doubt demands a great deal of detailed knowledge. But it happens that *Bleak House* has already been particularly well examined in relation to its times before: in his chapter on "The Topicality of *Bleak House*" in *Dickens at Work* John Butt has already pointed out how, though the "fable" of the novel has been "frequently interpreted," what had hitherto been overlooked was "the topicality of Dickens's particularization."[2] This is shown to be in religious affairs, the question of legal reform, the behavior of Parliament, feminism, philanthropy, and even some of the activities of Inspector Field, the army, and the ironmasters. It is shown how some of these matters were also dealt with in *Household Words*, how many of them came from Dickens' reading of the *Times*, and (in the matter of Mrs. Jellyby and Borrioboola-Gha) how there is also a link with a lengthy review-article that Dickens wrote for the *Examiner*.[3] In spite of the fact, therefore, that Dickens effectively distanced the action of the story to some time about 1830, there is no doubt that *Bleak House* did begin, as John Butt concludes, as "a tract for the times." What is suggested now is, at first, only an extension of his conclusions: not only was it begun this way, but one aspect of it at least can now be depicted more fully, and it can also be shown that Dickens was more alive to the issue of public health than has been supposed, that he played an even more active part for the cause through his journalism than has been known before, and that it was certainly persistently in mind both in the conception and the composition of *Bleak House*.

Yet it may well seem strange that Dickens should have been interested in sanitary reform, which in the late forties and early fifties was most concerned with the sewerage of London and the supply of clean water. Even Humphry House rather oversimplified when he remarked in *The Dickens World* that "in *Pickwick* a bad smell was a bad smell" and that it is only in *Our Mutual Friend* that "it is a problem." Dickens himself was nearer the truth when he dated his interest in public health to the very beginning of his career as a novelist.[4] Certainly the great sanitary reformer, Edwin Chadwick,[5] sought Dickens' support as early as 1842, as he was finishing *American Notes,* writing that "Mr. Dickens will have the ear not only of America but of Europe, and whatever he may say on the importance of a better scientific attention to the structural arrangements for promoting the health and pleasure and moral improvement of the population cannot fail to produce extensively beneficial effects."[6] It may appear bizarre, yet Dickens again (in the preface to the Cheap Edition of *Martin Chuzzlewit,* November 1849) expresses the hope that in *all his writing* he had taken "every possible opportunity of showing the want of sanitary improvements in the neglected dwellings of the poor."[7] Of course, many of the reasons for this are clear, and best expressed in his speeches on the subject in 1849 and 1851.[8] The health of London was clearly indivisible, and such reforms were fundamental: "even Education and Religion can do nothing where they are most needed, until the way is paved for their ministrations by Cleanliness and Decency."[9] Opposed to reform lay vested interests in property, and resentment of legislation which might affect its possession. Urban sanitation was also a topic of great interest as an enormous practical problem for which everyone had his own solution; but, even more, it affected every man's life in an inescapable manner, and concerned how he was born, what he ate, what he drank, where he lived, how he died, and the grave in which he would be buried. So, in some ways, it might be seen as a theme or subject above all others for a novelist.

As well as being topical, therefore, an interest in public health was intrinsic for the novelist. No less, there was a powerful extrinsic reason for his concern as well. For among Dickens' closest friends was his brother-in-law, Henry Austin, who had married Dickens' sister, Letitia

Mary, in 1837.[10] It was to Austin that Edwin Chadwick had written in 1842, asking him to enlist Dickens' help, and taking the opportunity to ask Austin to present him with a copy of his *Report . . . from the Poor Law Commissioners, on an Inquiry into the Sanitary Condition of the Labouring Population of Great Britain . . . July 1842.* Austin, himself, had written a section of the report, for he had first become interested in public health when employed in surveying one of the new railways, when he had been appalled by seeing the miserable conditions of the working-class homes through which it was to pass. He had been convinced that they must be improved, and had been active in forming the Association for promoting the Improvement of the Dwellings of the Labouring Classes. Then, in 1848, he was appointed Secretary to the newly-established General Board of Health.

Quite how much Dickens owed to Austin, it is hard to say. It happens that many of his letters to Austin survive, but their evidence is obviously incomplete. Many of them are about work Austin did for Dickens as an architect, in advising on house-buying and making improvements; others show the active interest Dickens had in helping Austin's career. Clearly they met too frequently to write much, but when we find that two years (1845 and 1846) are missing from the main collection of letters which is in the Pierpont Morgan Library, it is impossible to infer that correspondence was simply broken off for a while. Yet enough remains in these letters to show how closely they often worked together for sanitary reform, and even how they occasionally collaborated in writing.[11]

The clearest sure evidence for this comes after the spring of 1850, when Dickens began his own journal, *Household Words*. The earliest indications are in connection with contributions which it is now suggested that Dickens probably wrote, with Austin's help, for the weekly periodical, the *Examiner*.

It is rather complicated to outline all the proofs that

support the suggestion that Dickens wrote part of these articles on sanitary reform for the *Examiner*. The proofs depend on establishing that Dickens was a more regular contributor than previously supposed, and this has been shown elsewhere; they rely on showing how, in many ways, Dickens used his work for the *Examiner* as a try-out or training-ground for *Household Words;* and since it can certainly be proved that he and Austin collaborated directly he had his own periodical, it becomes a reasonable supposition that this began even earlier. The fullest possible details should be unnecessary, but what may be interesting is that it should be recognized that even before he had his own periodical, Dickens was active in anonymous journalism for the *Examiner* from 1847 to 1849. For the *Examiner* was the liberal or radical journal, founded by Leigh Hunt, then edited by Albany Fonblanque, and from 1847 under the editorial direction of Dickens' friend and ally, John Forster. Among previous editorial staff, in the early thirties, it had numbered Edwin Chadwick and John Stuart Mill. Contributors were anonymous, yet it has been known since 1908 (when B. W. Matz edited Dickens' uncollected journalism in the *Miscellaneous Papers*) that many of Dickens' contributions could be identified. Most of them, perhaps, were included in Matz's volume, but the list was closed too soon. It has recently been possible to show how much more frequent a contributor Dickens was than had been known before.[12]

Now, from Dickens' letters to Austin we can see that Austin had sent him the *Second Report* of the Metropolitan Sanitary Commission (February 1848) which argued vigorously for a central authority to deal with the sanitary problems of London. Dickens acknowledged it (25 February), writing, "Many thanks for the report. And as to that preposterous and idiotic band of humbugs called the Corporation, allow me to say in the words of a friend of mine (Captain Edward Cuttle) 'Hooroar my lad, Hooroar,

Hooroar!'" Some months later (18 October) he asked for
a second copy. He was obviously interested by it, and he
refers to it in passing in his critique of George Cruikshank's
"The Drunkard's Children," remarking that Hogarth's "Gin
Lane" was "worthy to be a Frontispiece to the late Report of
the Sanitary Commissioners" (*Examiner,* 8 July 1848,
known previously). This is just a small example of the way
in which Dickens, at this time, could write of an important
Report in private, in his journalism, and with reference to
his fiction, without one sensing that there is any deep
division about it in his sensibility.

In 1849 one finds Dickens making an appointment
with Austin for the first of their known conferences about
winning public support for the cause: on 15 May he writes,
"Both day and hour will suit me perfectly well. I have
booked myself accordingly." If this were all, perhaps the
conclusion would smack of Serjeant Buzfuz' deductions
from Pickwick's note on "Chops and Tomato sauce." Yet the
request for a meeting comes significantly close to Austin's
public clash with John Phillips over their conflicting plans
for the drainage of London.[13] This broke out early in June
1849, and we can surmise in the light of later letters that
Austin (realizing that he would have to present his case in
public) very naturally approached Dickens for advice. For
Dickens, as an experienced journalist and an influential
figure in the world of the liberal press, was the obvious
man to turn to. It is even possible that Chadwick, who
favored Austin's plan, suggested this step once again.
Dickens, of course, was glad to help Austin, for on 2 July
he wrote to make an immediate appointment, saying that
by the time of his arrival "I will have gone through all your
papers . . . and will be ready with the best advice it is in
my power to offer. It is necessary to explain, no doubt; but
beyond this, I do not see any cause for uneasiness in the
matter." Almost certainly an immediate result of this was a
letter to the *Times* about his plan, signed by Austin, which

appeared on 6 July 1849, page 8, dated 2 July, the evening of which he had met Dickens. On 6 July, Dickens wrote to Austin to say that he had seen Forster (as editor of the *Examiner*) "who had told me that he had anticipated your wish," though "the subject was too late for this week." He added that he hoped that a friend on the *Morning Herald* would assist them, and concluded, "I hope I need not say that any sort of help I can render you, I claim to be asked to give."

Next week, on the front page of the *Examiner*, there was an editorial attacking Phillips' plan for the drainage of London (14 July, page 233), entitled "Drainage and Health of the Metropolis." Now, it happens that in the few days before this Dickens had been ill, and had gone down to Broadstairs for a rest, so it is clear that that last paragraph (which includes an immediately topical reference) cannot have been his. Nor is it more than suggested that the main part of the article is likely to have been based on Austin's papers, revised by Dickens, and perhaps even subsequently modified by Forster. Yet the circumstances all come together. The first part is much in Dickens' fanciful style, which begins by drawing the reader's attention to the facts by mockery of the Commission of Sewers. Of course this very title for a government body would be dismissed as being as improbable as the "Circumlocution Office," if Dickens had merely invented it; but favorite references in the text, to Fielding's mock-heroic Tom Thumb, and the Upas tree are much in his manner, as is the sketch of how the Commission's survey was first conducted.

> "Crows' nests" appeared on the pinnacles of Westminster and above the cross of St. Paul's, to the consternation of many Chartist agitators, who thought them but a part of some gigantic machinery of espionage, by which the sleepless despots of the Home Office were to keep a bird's-eye watch over treason. "Dumpy levels," suspiciously resembling miniature

cannon, were planted in every street; and the nerves of elderly ladies were shaken by the apparition of non-commissioned officers of artillery.[14]

There is then another article, which is a continuation of this, which appeared in the *Examiner* (4 August 1849), entitled "The Sewers' Commission." Here again, Dickens' absence from town by the seaside precludes his having had the main part in this piece; perhaps he had none at all. But in a letter to Austin the week before (26 July) he refers to Phillips' rival scheme which is dealt with in detail in the article, mentioning that "I write to say that I shall be glad to hear when there is any change in the aspect of the 'Tunnel Scheme.'" Thus, even on holiday, at Bonchurch, Dickens was closely in touch. At the end of September, however, Austin resigned, and Dickens congratulated him, encouraging him to give his reasons for leaving in a letter which would be part of the record. Soon after, after the complete collapse of the Commission, he wrote again (19 October 1849): "As to the Commission that has superseded the first, I believe with you . . . [it is] as rotten at the bottom as the worst Sewer in London. I wish you could come and dine here. . . . I should like to talk over things Sanitary and insanitary—of which latter there seems to be a ripe harvest at present."

These two articles are, in fact, poor examples of Dickens' journalism; but they are interesting, firstly, because he possibly wrote part of them, then because they predate the interest he was to show in *Household Words*, and lastly because they help to show his involvement in a movement which actively engaged his imagination as well as his strong interest in administration. They belong with some sixteen other articles he wrote for the *Examiner* in 1849, mostly on public affairs; and, if taken in conjunction with the whole series of articles in the same journal on sanitary reform, they may well remind us how it was not only a picturesque turn of speech when Dickens said that the Public Health Act with London excluded from it was "like a performance of *Hamlet* with nothing but the grave-digger."[15] For at a graveyard in Portugal Street, only just around the corner from Forster's house in Lincoln Inn Fields, medical students were in the habit of buying fairly fresh human heads at the going rate of about seven shillings and sixpence each; there was "really no burial" there, it was said, as "the body deposited in the earth one day is soon disturbed, dismembered, and thrown to the surface again, to make room for other corpses."[16] The Jacobean or Gothic horrors of *Bleak House* were close neighbours to the everyday life of Victorian England. It may be that, in some ways, they are so at any time. Yet the connection for Dickens lay in the campaign for sanitary reform. For, when Austin presented him with the *Report on a General Scheme for Extra-mural Sepulture*, Dickens wrote to thank him, "Many thanks for the Report, which is extraordinarily interesting. I began to read it last night in bed—and dreamed of putrefaction generally" (27 February 1850). In May 1850, though "anxious to serve the cause," he had to excuse himself from helping for the moment, writing to Austin to explain that such matters were too powerful a disturbance to his imagination: "If I get fierce and antagonistic about burials, I can't go back to Copperfield for hours and hours. This is really the sort of condition on which I hold my inventive powers; and I can't get rid of it" (12 May). For, the death of Dora or the graveyard scenes at Blunderstone were of another order to those of *Bleak House,* even though at one point young David has the fear that "something . . . connected with the grave in the churchyard, and the raising of the dead, seemed to strike me like an unwholesome wind" (chap. 3). But Dickens' imagination may already be said to have been at work on one of the main themes of the next novel, the climax of which comes with Esther Summerson's discovery of her mother's corpse at the gate of the graveyard in which her father is buried, and in which Jo, Krook, Richard Carstone, Gridley, Tulkinghorn and Jenny's child are all overtaken by the darkness which pervades *Bleak House.*

Even so, there is a link between Dickens' earliest experience and the matters which Austin was continually bringing to his attention. We know, on the one hand, that the graveyard in *Bleak House* was an actual part of Dickens' boyhood experience. We also know that it was among the matters recalled to his awareness by the emphatic demands that were being made for the closure of the overfilled burial grounds of London. For Dickens wrote to an American correspondent, on 4 April 1868, fulfilling a promise made her during his voyage to America to explain precisely where it was. He made clear that it was near the corner of Drury Lane and Russell Street, being the burial ground of St. Martins-in-the-Fields, adding: "I do not remember that the graveyard is accessible from the street now, but when I was a boy it was to be got at by a low covered passage under a house, and was guarded by a rusty iron gate. In that churchyard I long afterwards buried the 'Nemo' of Bleak House."[17] Clearly, its use in the novel was bound up with his own direct experience. At the same time, the February *Report*, which left him dreaming of "putrefaction," specifically refers to the same graveyard (p. 59). Austin, himself, moreover, also wrote a second brief *Report to the General Board of Health on the Circumstances Attending the Revolting Practices that have been said to occur in the St. Giles's Cemetery, Situated in the Parish of St. Pancras* (dated June 1850), and this Dickens must certainly have been aware of. This pamphlet also refers to George Walker's *Lectures on the Conditions of Metropolitan Graveyards* (1846–49), a copy of which was in Dickens' library.[18] There is no point in accumulating evidence about Dickens' knowledge of the question; what is of some interest is the way in which we can trace his actual direct and indirect involvement.

Meanwhile, early in 1850, Dickens was again acknowledging official reports adding (in a letter of 26 January) "I hope I may be able to do the Sanitary cause good service in my new periodical [*Household Words*] by pressing *facts* upon the many-headed."[19] On 20 March he invited Austin to join an editorial meeting, at which they wanted his advice, and asked him to look over "the enclosed rough Proof and tell me whether there is anything challengeable in it." The next day, he wrote again, to urge him not to be too delicate in giving advice, since the subeditor Wills had been chosen just because he had good business qualities, but has "not the ghost of an idea in the imaginative way. . . . Whatever you know to be wrong . . . I shall oblige to be amended." He also said that he would show him the preface to the Cheap Edition of *Oliver Twist*, which turned on the same subject. Significant about this letter is that it assumed that Austin understood what was needed in collaboration: the only thing to be explained was that a third and fourth party were to be brought into conference. They must have worked together before. The collaboration went on after the first number of *Household Words* appeared, for on 12 May he repeated, "I am sincerely anxious to serve the cause, and am doing it all the good I can, by side blows in Household Words. . . . You will see next week, that I have turned a paper called 'The Begging Letter Writer' to sanitary purposes."[20] He wrote again, on 15 July, to offer Austin his help, and then persuasively added: "I should be very glad indeed if you could find leisure to write or suggest anything (the former the better) tending to promote the sanitary cause for the H.W. Shall we have another dinner there, after yours, and talk it over? Or a walk one day?" In fact, Austin never did write anything recorded under his name, but further letters leave no doubt of his close association.

More briefly, in November Dickens called Austin's attention to "something sanitary" in *Household Words*,[21] and mentioned other plans. On 22 January 1851 he asked for details about the Window Tax, on 30 January remarked that he would have liked to have joined him on an official deputation, and mentioned his, Dickens', article "Red Tape" (15 February 1851) and going to see abattoirs in Paris. In May, he spoke for the Metropolitan Sanitary Association, and wrote out the whole of his speech from memory for Austin, who was the unofficial secretary. On 25 July, he had to excuse himself from taking up the question of nationalizing the whole undertaking business (Chadwick's pet project) in a letter to the *Times*, because he regarded it as a lost cause, though he still offered every help through *Household Words*. Throughout 1852 Dickens continued to press Austin to work with him for *Household Words*, and Austin clearly responded. In July it was to ask him to take up a subject himself; and, if not, for it to be passed to Henry Morley (18 July). Then, on 4 October, Dickens wrote from Paris, and apparently asked Austin to see Wills and to help him arrange for a piece on funerals (evidently "Funerals in Paris," 27 November 1852) with the help of Morley. There is the clear indication that, certainly by this time, Austin would provide or check the information, Dickens would go over it with him, and together they would then put it into a popular form. But with *Bleak House* already in hand (it began in May) and Dickens being away from London, the "popularisation" had to be delegated to Morley through the subeditor Wills, although otherwise it was implied Dickens would have done it himself.

This journalism in the cause of public health was clearly by no means a mere task to him, nor was it a matter of such compelling interest that it would put fiction into second place. Nevertheless, Dickens obviously enjoyed it, and liked to think that men who were administratively in charge of affairs appreciated his part. So, on 21 November 1852, he wrote of an article ("Trading in Death," 27 November) occasioned by the state funeral of the Duke of

Wellington: "The enclosed . . . may have a good effect hereafter. I don't want it returned. As it will not be published 'till Wednesday, don't until then, shew it out of your office. But Chadwick, Southwood Smith and Lord Shaftesbury can see it (if you would like to show it to them) as soon as you like."[22] This letter happens to be the last that survives of those that Dickens wrote Austin about public affairs.

No doubt, after reading John Butt on "The Topicality of *Bleak House*," no one would question that when Dickens wrote the novel in 1852–53 he had experiences of the previous few years in mind as well as the period about 1830 in which it was set. Yet, with these new letters of Austin's to hand, it is thus possible to take up the single topic of public health and show how closely Dickens was concerned with it at the time and how this interest obviously foreshadowed scenes in the novel. More important than this, it can be seen that Dickens did not get his information merely by reading the *Times*, but helped to contribute to it. He did not just read the newspapers, but the official Reports as they were published. He was not only courted by Edwin Chadwick, but, as Secretary to the General Board of Health, Austin sought to make all the use of Dickens he could. He not only had access to the most important central authority on public health, on the sanitary problems brought by the great cities, and on measures to be taken against the dreaded visitation of cholera, but he was also enlisted as an ally and received help with his own writings in return. No less, as John Butt reminds us, he was also actively engaged about this time in leading Miss Burdett Coutts to effect actual housing reforms in Westminster, in studying projects for model buildings, and in persuading her to consult Austin and Dr. Southwood Smith about plans for new flats she was to build in Bethnal Green.[23] On another occasion about which we have written before, Dickens wrote a series of four remarkable papers for the *Examiner* on the Tooting Disaster, at the beginning of 1849, when over one hundred and fifty children died of cholera aggravated by neglect. On this occasion (though there are no letters to Austin about it) he was again in alliance with the General Board of Health, and the affair was remembered and referred to directly when he came to write *Bleak House*.[24]

Of course the question that must follow this concern with a mere topicality is—new as some of this is—what fresh light does this throw on Dickens as a novelist; and perhaps the first point to make is that it may help to establish that Dickens *was* a reformer after all. Even in his own day this was not infrequently questioned, as by the liberal Lord Denman for example (although he had special reasons), who wrote of Dickens as like Falstaff standing over Hotspur and claiming the victory for what had been won when he had played no part in achieving it.[25] More recent critics have sometimes implied much the same, and others have been so anxious to avoid the naïvety of taking a popular novelist too seriously that they too readily assumed that Dickens was imperfectly informed, that his sympathies were stronger than his understanding, and yet that he was sufficiently calculating to confine himself to winning causes. Yet to keep only to the present topic of public health: Henry Austin's plan for the drainage of London was not accepted, the General Board of Health was unpopular and was soon splintered by political disputes, and the campaign for sanitary reform was only too obviously one that could not gain its most limited objectives in less than a generation. Immediate success in this field, as in most reforms that Dickens took up, must have seemed as unlikely to him as the belief (which he certainly never held) that in his work for Miss Coutts's Home for Fallen Women he could settle the problem of London's prostitution singlehanded.

It may appear unsound to make this point first in

considering Dickens as a novelist. But any critical attempts to justify Dickens' novels as challenging a mature appreciation, which still leave it open to question whether he was naïve, ill-informed, and even intellectually dishonest, can hardly be satisfactory. The topicality of his outlook and his reforming energies were part of his quality as an artist which he had the extraordinary capacity of being able to reconcile with profounder and more permanent elements in his work. It is both impossible and undesirable, now, to expect of general reader, student, or teacher that he should fully recognize both aspects of Dickens as some of the best readers of his time and even of recent times must once have done. Even so, the general truth that they are vital parts of Dickens' novels needs to be accepted; the novels strongly insist that no one should withdraw his sympathies from the fictional world being presented, but this world is so clearly related to the actual world that we cannot divorce the two whatever distinctions we may rightly make. The imaginary world of fiction and the real world that appears to be about us are different, of course; but the general truths of man's nature, and his relations with others, are essentially the same in each of them. If Dickens were wilfully false in one, he must have been partly false within the other; and we can find no challenge in Dickens as a mature artist if he was unaware of what he was doing in activities that at this time in his life were obviously strenuous and demanding.

If that is accepted, there remains the question implied by the false prophecy of Mowbray Morris: if Dickens was so topical a writer, how is it that he is still so popular and respected? It is a question that to be treated fully demands another essay, and perhaps another writer; yet, in a most general way, it can also briefly be answered by referring to Dickens himself. For, when someone criticized him for being too fanciful, Dickens wrote to Forster: "It does not seem to be enough to say of any description that it is the exact truth. The exact truth must be there; but the merit or art in the narrator, is in the manner of stating the truth. As to which thing in literature, it always seems to me there is a world to be done."[26] In the form and substance of the novel so much depends on how it is told, and, among other ways, on the way in which the imaginary world of the novel is given a self-sustaining consistency which keeps it alive even after readers (as Mowbray Morris foresaw) are unable to recognize its external "fidelity." It may even be that, as such experience falls away from the reading public, the fictional truth becomes clearer.

So it might be found, for example, in this single aspect of the novel, which is so often seen as developed about the great theme of Chancery. For the opening of the book is in the High Court of Chancery, which was evidently chosen because the suit of *Jarndyce v. Jarndyce* is important to the plot: it brings the characters together in action; the court is a physical center on which they converge, and the imperceptible progress of the case is a measure of time. All the apparatus of the Law and its dramatic trappings are, moreover, especially useful to the novel's structure. Yet Chancery itself is also important because it is significant of something else within the novel, "the old ground of symbolism," as Edmund Wilson calls it, in which "the fog stands for Chancery, and Chancery stands for the whole web of clotted antiquated institutions in which England stifles and decays."[27] Their decay infects the whole novel from the world of fashion and the world of Chancery to the legal underworld dominated by "Lord Chancellor" Krook. And Krook's absurd death by spontaneous combustion is also symbolic of the outcome of injustice everywhere, which may be "inborn, inbred, engendered in the corrupted humours of the vicious body itself" (chap. 32).

Yet this way in which the cause of his death is described recalls another allied theme: it suggests that human relations or institutions are either living and natural, or decaying and corrupt. So we may remind ourselves of John Forster's remark that "the first intention was to have made Jo more prominent in the story, and its earliest title was taken from the tumbling tenements in Chancery, 'Tom-all-Alone's,' where he finds his wretched habitation: but this was abandoned."[28] The titles in fact, as first drafted, seem always to have combined Chancery and "Tom-all-Alone's,"[29] though it may well have been that a greater emphasis on "Tom" was wisely abandoned for the sake of the plot; but it may be argued that the dominant tone of the novel still remains in accord with the original conception.

For there are other signs which show that, although Dickens wrote at least chapters 1–4 (the first monthly number) meaning to emphasize Chancery, Jo probably reasserted his original importance as the story developed. The subject was too much a part of Dickens' experience, had taken too great a hold of him, and was too closely incorporated with his whole view of life to be subordinated. We may see this, for example, in the covers and title pages of successive editions. The original cover design for publication in monthly numbers is dominated by lawyers and Chancery, although the vignette on the title page (issued with the final number) is of Jo and the drover's dog (chap. 16). The vignette title page to the Library edition (1859), with just eight illustrations, has Lady Dedlock and Jo, whereas the strikingly illustrated cover for the People's edition (1866) prominently reproduces Phiz's illustration of Jo and Lady Dedlock at the iron gate, "Consecrated Ground." It would be very surprising, indeed, if these changes were not made with Dickens' sanction, if not expressly decided on by him.

For in Jo, Dickens had found a figure who had caught his imagination, and who also came to him through his journalism for the *Examiner,* although this is another story.[30] He had originated in the case of a boy who showed up the follies of the law when he was dismissed from **the** witness box at the Guildhall, one morning in January 1850, in the same way and for the same reasons that Jo's evidence is dispensed with in the coroner's court in chapter 11. As a crossing-sweeper, barefoot in the mud and ordure of the streets, Jo is the sole gesture (as seen in the novel) that London makes toward keeping its thoroughfares clean. He is also the victim of fever (or smallpox), a denizen of its worst slums, and an agent in the transmission of disease; so that, in all this, Jo, who might well have been made even more "more prominent" in the action, still helps to control the form of *Bleak House.* For it is Jo who embodies this other theme that pervades the novel: the way in which its scenes, tones and writing are so often concerned with public health (or public disease), corruption and death. Jo is the embodiment of "Tom-all-Alone's" which was certainly the key-phrase in Dickens' search for a title; and the slum which is his home has "bred a crowd of foul existence that crawls in and out of gaps in walls . . . sowing more evil in its every footprint" than the Coodles and Doodles can ever set right (chap. 16). Chancery breeds moral corruption; Tom-all-Alone's spreads physical corruption. For Tom "has his revenge. . . . There is not a drop of Tom's corrupted blood but propagates infection and contagion somewhere. . . . There is not an atom of Tom's slime, not a cubic inch of the pestilential gas in which he lives . . . but shall work its retribution through every order of society" (chap. 46).

Tom-all-Alone's is also linked with Chancery, because "this desirable property is in Chancery of course." Jo is thus linked with Chancery both through Tom-all-Alone's and his place in the plot—his meeting with Lady Dedlock and his acquaintance with Nemo. They both have the further link with Jo, and with the physical center of death in the novel, in the graveyard in which Nemo is buried, at the gate to which Lady Dedlock dies, and from which pestilence arises. All are corrupt. Nemo himself is sown "in corruption, to be

raised in corruption." The ghastly scene of his interment is
a parody of what it should have been (a travesty of the
Service for the Burial of the Dead), as the coroner and his
"pauper company" bear off "the body of our dear brother
here departed to a hemmed-in churchyard, pestiferous and
obscene, whence malignant diseases are communicated to
the bodies of our dear brothers and sisters who have not
departed, while our brothers and sisters who hang about
back-stairs—would to heaven they *had* departed!—are very
complacent and agreeable. Into a beastly scrap of ground
which a Turk would reject as a savage abomination and a
Caffre would shudder at, they bring our dear brother here
departed to receive Christian burial" (chap. 11).

So, although the form of *Bleak House* partly depends
on the way in which Chancery indirectly represents corruption and decay, it also depends on another network of
relationships which link up with still further patterns.
Through the figure of Jo, these are concerned with disease,
death and corruption. Nor do they depend only on the "old
ground of symbolism," but they are either shown directly or
sometimes by allusion. Stephen Gill has demonstrated in
his "Allusion in *Bleak House*: A Narrative Device"[31] how
highly developed was Dickens' skill in this way; and one of
his examples (already referred to) is the use of echoes
from the Prayer Book when Nemo is buried, which return
again when Richard is confronted by Vholes (chap. 39).
For when Vholes assures Richard of his reliability, and tells
him, "This desk is your rock, sir!" he then "gives it a rap,
and it sounds as hollow as a coffin." Then he raps it again,
"with a sound as if ashes were falling on ashes, and dust on
dust." Vholes is not only almost emblematical of death in
his appearance, in the hatchment over his office entrance,
and in "making hay of the grass which is flesh, for his three
daughters," but when he fetches Richard back to London
from the country, a sinister poetry is made of the scene by
Esther's description and allusions: "I have before me the

whole picture of the warm dark night, the summer lightning, the dusty track of road closed in by hedgerows and
high trees, the gaunt pale horse with his ears pricked up,
and the driving away at speed to Jarndyce and Jarndyce."
Of course, the whole force of the passage is enhanced by
recognition of the allusion to the Revelation of Saint John
the Divine, 6:8, "And I looked, and behold a pale horse;
and his name that sat on him was Death, and Hell followed
with him. And power was given unto them over the fourth
part of the earth, to kill with sword, and with hunger, and
with death, and with the beasts of the earth."

So, if with "Jo" we include everyone associated with
him and all that he stands for, he has a considerable part in
the novel even now. To have made it more prominent
would have been to have had *Hamlet* with a whole cast of
gravediggers. His own death is foreshadowed and closely
paralleled by Gridley's, who is mourned by Miss Flite as her
only fit companion in "all the living and the dead world."
Their language is constantly of death: Jo's sole oath is
"Wishermaydie." When he is ill, he is helped by Jenny (the
mother of the dead baby) who, when asked what can be
done with him, can only reply, "I know no more than the
dead" (chap. 22). Jo at first refuses to go with Esther and
Charley, but wants to "lay amongst the warm bricks."

> "But don't you know that people die there?" re-
> turned Charley.
> "They dies everywheres," said the boy. "They dies
> in their lodgings—she knows where; I showed her—
> and they dies down in Tom-all-Alone's in heaps. They
> dies more than they lives, according to what *I* see."

Jo's own death needs comment only because its treatment
is sometimes misunderstood. If it seems "sentimental," it is
scarcely Dickens' fault. It could not be clearer that the
process of saying the Lord's Prayer over a boy shown dying
because of man's neglect is as useless to him in his last
extremity as Snagsby's half-crowns. Dickens could hardly

have shown more forcibly that Jo cannot begin to understand what prayer means; he expressly does not know
where he will go "arter he's dead" (not "exactly"), he knows
nothing of the New Testament, he has less intellectual
grasp than the drover's dog.[32] Alan Woodcourt may relieve
his feelings, as Snagsby does, but any further sentiment is
mainly the reader's if he happens to enjoy it.

Those who live in Tom-all-Alone's are not beyond
hope, but they live almost out of the world, in chaos.
Chapter 46 begins ominously: "Darkness rests upon Tom-
all-Alone's. Dilating and dilating since the sun went down
last night until it fills every void in the place." It is like the
earth at creation before it was pronounced good. Jo himself
hardly appears human; his clothes "look, in colour and
substance, like a bundle of rank leaves of swampy growth
that rotted long ago." When he dies, at the end of the next
chapter, there is no suggestion that he benefits from beginning a prayer which is broken off before it gets as far as
asking for the will of God to be done on earth as in heaven.
The real pathos lies in his asking to be buried in the
hideous locked graveyard, beside his only friend.

"The production of pathos," wrote Fitzjames Stephen,
"is a simple operation. With a little practice and a good deal
of determination, it would really be as easy to harrow up
people's feelings as to poke the fire. . . . Every one knows,
for example, that death is a solemn and affecting thing.
. . . The pathetic power of the scene lies in the fact of the
death; and the artifice employed consists simply in enabling
the notion of death to be reiterated at short intervals by a
variety of irrelevant trifles. . . . The process is so simple
that it becomes, with practice, almost mechanical. . . .
Death—death—death—death—death, just as feeling of
another class might be worked upon by continually calling
a man a liar and a cheat."[33] Stephens was reviewing *A
Tale of Two Cities,* yet it is a subject even more to the fore
in *Bleak House,* though simple reiteration is not the way in

which Dickens shows his power. It is the question of what death means that overshadows the novel and which makes some scenes affecting.

Jo's death was written with his evidence at the inquest in mind, that he "can't exactly say" what will "be done to him arter he's dead." The inquest on Nemo follows the highly developed and yet directly written description of the discovery of his body by Tulkinghorn at the end of chapter 10, an expressive example of what Dickens meant that "the merit or art in the narrator, is in the manner of stating the truth," fully deserving analysis—if it were not that most readers can undertake it for themselves. It is certainly not done by "irrelevant trifles" or "by specifying all its details." Nemo's death is anticipated by that of Jenny's baby (chap. 8), at the brickmaker's, when, as Ada bends down to "touch its little face," all that we are told is in the sentence, "The child died." Its face is covered by Esther's handkerchief, the same handkerchief which she foresees, in telling the story (though only by oblique reference), is to be recovered by Lady Dedlock, discovered by Inspector Bucket, then to lead him on to his pursuit accompanied by Esther until at last they find her mother with one arm clasping a bar of the iron gate to the graveyard (chap. 59).

What meaning Dickens sees in death it is hardly possible to state satisfactorily outside the full context of the novel. It may be an end as bare as Jenny's child's; for the remarks about the "child's Angel" are peculiarly Esther's and hardly more marked than the father's immediate retirement to the drinking-house. It may be seen in "the darkness of the night" from Nemo's room, and in the two mere gaunt holes of the shutters "staring in." Equally it may lie in the response of the mother, the sympathy of Ada, Esther's faith, or Jo's affection for Nemo. But the value in men's lives is seen in their love and concern for others, and it is this which gives some importance to death. Ultimately Esther recognizes, in the confusion of discovering her mother (who has changed clothes with Jenny) at the iron gate, that it hardly matters who is dead—Lady Dedlock or the brickmaker's wife. It is the lesson taught by Dickens' analysis of society, too.

It is a general theme which could be traced at great length, and it would be greater still if some of those related to it were taken up. It is striking for example how, even in the more humorous passages in the novel, so many of the characters are shown as stunted, diseased, or unnatural. This is nothing at all like Captain Cuttle's hook, Squeers's one eye, or Wegg's wooden leg, which are appropriate but external and unrelated to the rest of the characters. There is an elaborate art in the introduction of Turveydrop, for example, culminating in: "He had a cane, he had rings, he had wristbands, he had everything but any touch of nature; he was not like youth, he was not like age, he was not like anything in the world but a model of deportment" (chap. 14). Similarly, in introducing Sir Leicester, who is crippled by gout, and who "would on the whole admit nature to be a good idea" but "a little low, perhaps, when not enclosed with a park-fence" (chap. 2). Also with Mr. Chadband who is so unnatural that he can only move "cumbrously," though he seems to have "a good deal of train oil in his system," and who converts "nutriment" into "oil" as he eats, like "a large factory" (chap. 19); while the paralytic family of Smallweeds are distinguished by having propagated themselves, without having had a child born to them, for generations (chap. 21).

On the other side, as it were, there are the figures of Esther, distinguished for her loving nature; Ada, who, from the first, is seen to have "a natural, captivating, winning manner"; Trooper George deliberately contrasted with the Smallweeds; Mrs. Bagnet, "healthy, wholesome, and bright-eyed"; Boythorn, of "warm heart" and "fresh blood"; Rosa, "fresh in her rosy and delicate bloom"; and Rouncewell, the ironmaster, "who has a perfectly natural and easy air."

Finally, there is Allan Woodcourt, hardly outstanding perhaps as a hero, but inevitably a doctor or surgeon, and at
last appointed as "medical attendant for the poor." Jarndyce finally brings Allan and Esther together in their new
home, saying, "My dearest, Allan Woodcourt stood beside
your father when he lay dead—stood beside your mother.
This is Bleak House." They then begin afresh. There is no
turning back to the corruption of legal system, city, or those
entrapped within them; no attempt to reform what is
already dying or dead. The story which began in the heart
of the city, which was conceived amid conflict to reform it,
and which was essentially topical to a degree that is hardly
recognizable now, turns away "to begin the world" afresh,
with a complete regeneration, recommending content with
an "ordinary level" of life, and the plain way of "usefulness
and good service."

LITTLE DORRIT: A WORLD IN REVERSE

Richard Stang

Little Dorrit is, as Lionel Trilling said, "one of the most profound of Dickens' novels";[1] it is also one of the best integrated to which almost every chapter, almost every scene, almost every image, makes a significant contribution. In order to demonstrate that assertion I would like to explore the use of a single metaphor. It occurs in book 1, chapter 20, "Moving in Society," in a scene linking the world of the Marshalsea, presided over by its degraded father, William Dorrit, and the world of high society, presided over by its high priestess, Mrs. Merdle, and it prefigures the connection by marriage between the two families. In this scene we see both Mr. Dorrit and Mrs. Merdle consciously acting out their roles, and so the scene we are focusing on is appropriately set in a theater, behind the scenes, where in some detail we witness rehearsals, people rushing about on errands, and strange personages like a man "so much in want of air that he had a blue mould upon him."[2]

The setting is doubly appropriate because during the scenes linked together we are, so to speak, behind the scenes while we are witnessing them, that is, we are painfully aware of Mr. Dorrit's degradation in playing the senti-

mental role of the injured father. Immediately after what
he considers a subtle rebuke to Amy for not leading John
Chivery on, he breaks down into maudlin self-pity, in the
worst tradition of melodrama: "Oh despise me, despise me!
Look away from me—don't listen to me, stop me—blush
for me, cry for me—even you, Amy! Do it, do it! I do it
myself! I am hardened now; I have sunk too low to care
long even for that." And the scene ends with little mother
soothing her father to sleep: "She sat by him in his sleep,
softly kissing him with suspended breath, and calling him
in a whisper by some endearing name" (1, *xix*, 246–49). In
the ensuing scene, Mrs. Merdle and Fanny recite their
prescribed lines to the obscene accompaniment of Mrs.
Merdle's parrot. But the important metaphor is in the
transitional scene:

> At last they came into a maze of dust, where a
> quantity of people were tumbling over one another,
> and where there was such a confusion of unaccount-
> able shapes of beams, bulkheads, brick walls, ropes,
> and rollers, and such a mixing of gaslight and day-
> light, that they seemed to have got on *the wrong side
> of the pattern of the universe* (1, *xx*, 253; italics
> mine).

The most immediate application one could make of
this extraordinary metaphor is, of course, to the immediately preceding scene, where a daughter becomes a mother
to her own father, as she has also done to the perpetually
ten-year-old Maggie. But the whole world of *Little Dorrit* is
on the wrong side of the pattern of the universe, and the
idea of reversal dominates the novel from its organization
into two books, "Poverty" and "Riches," to the ironic use of
many of the popular conventions of Victorian fiction. The
titles of books I and II are in themselves ironic in that there
is no essential difference in the Dorrit family's behavior,
rich or poor. The world is in a conspiracy to humiliate them
no matter where they are, and the family dignity must be

asserted at all cost. Mr. Dorrit's reversion to the Marshalsea at Mrs. Merdle's splendid dinner party only emphasizes what has always been apparent. Book 1 ends with the discovery that the Dorrits are heirs to a princely estate, one of the most popular novelistic dénouements of the period, an obvious cliché ending. As Pancks becomes more and more certain that the Dorrits are indeed the Dorrits of Dorsetshire, the tension mounts; and after the increasingly explicit hints of Pancks in his role as the gypsy fortuneteller, he finally becomes so excited that he plays leapfrog with Rugg in the Marshalsea yard. But Dickens has been arousing our expectations only to frustrate them, and, instead of ending at this point as a conventional novel would, *Little Dorrit* continues through its anticlimactic second half, which makes painfully clear that the prison in which the Dorrits were confined was not merely the Marshalsea and the Dorrits were not the only prisoners, but that all the world's a prison.

Dickens follows exactly the same method in the story of Pet Meagles' marriage. An aristocratic marriage for a middle-class girl with plenty of money, especially to a young and attractive aristocrat like Henry Gowan, allied to the best families of the country—even if he were in reduced circumstances—was, like inheriting a fortune, one of the most popular endings of conventional and even unconventional fiction (see *Pride and Prejudice* and *Jane Eyre*). Even Mr. and Mrs. Meagles, who have so opposed the match, are proud of their daughter's Barnacle connections. But again Dickens shows us the anticlimactic aftermath. Life reverses the pattern established by art, and Pet is one more sacrifice to her husband's sense of injured merit.

Rigaud, alias Blandois, a seemingly conventional villain, with his melodramatic swaggering, boasting, and very real cruelty, effects precisely nothing. There is no doubt about his evil nature, and the discussion at the inn, the

Break of Day, suggests strongly that, in spite of modern notions that all antisocial behavior is environmentally caused, there are still villains in life (not just on the stage), cases, as Herman Melville has it, of natural depravity, whose fundamental impulses are directed toward evil. According to the landlady, who certainly has the last word, Godwinian theories of "philosophical philanthropy" are worthless because they are not true to life, a nice reversal of the usual demand for mixed characters in the name of realism.

> But I know what I have seen, and what I have looked in the face, in this world here, where I find myself. And I tell you this, my friend, that there are people (men and women both, unfortunately) who have no good in them—none. That there are people whom it is necessary to detest without compromise. That there are people who must be dealt with as enemies of the human race. That there are people who have no human heart (I, *xi*, 137).

It is interesting that, in spite of the widespread commitment to liberal ideas like the social basis of all behavior, the much older counter-idea that certain men are innately good or evil, even mysteriously so, persists even in writers as enlightened as George Eliot. But, in spite of all Blandois's machination, the only evil deed he actually accomplishes in the novel is the poisoning of Gowan's dog. What he does do, however, is to make clear the code of values of society, one that is only implicit in many of the scenes of the book: "I sell anything that commands price. How do your lawyers live, your politicians, your intriguers, your men of the Exchange! . . . Society sells itself and sells me, and I sell Society" (II, *xxviii*, 812).

The same kind of reversals of ordinary expectations that pervade the structure of the book can be found in the smallest details. Whole families, for example, seem addicted to syntactical patterns that run backwards like a crab. "Sir," said Mrs. Chivery, "sure and certain as in this house I am. I see my son go out with my own eyes when in this house I was" (I, *xxii*, 278). Further on we find:

> "John Edward Nandy," said Mr. Plornish, addressing the old gentleman. "Sir. It's not too often that you see unpretending actions without a spark of pride, and therefore when you see them give grateful honour unto the same, being that if you don't and live to want 'em it follows serve you right."
>
> To which Mr. Nandy replied,—
>
> "I am heartily of your opinion, Thomas, and which your opinion is the same as mine, and therefore no more words, and not being backwards with that opinion, which opinion giving it as yes, Thomas, yes, is the opinion in which yourself and me must ever be unanimously joined by all, and where there is not difference of opinion there can be none but one opinion, which fully no, Thomas, Thomas, no!" (II, *xiii*, 624–25)

But the most extreme example of syntactical disorder in a novel full of such disorder is the ironically named Flora, the ripe peony, who "left half of herself at eighteen years of age behind, and grafted the rest on to the relict of the late Mr. F.; thus making a moral mermaid of herself, which her once boy-lover contemplated with feelings wherein his sense of the sorrowful and his sense of the comical were curiously blended." With Flora we reach the point where all pattern ceases, as does time itself and even space, and we float out on a sea of free association.

Flora's father, Mr. Casby, a rapacious though dim-witted slum landlord, is always referred to as the Patriarch, and his house is called "the patriarchal tent." His idea of a joke seems to conform to the pattern I have been pointing out. To Pancks, his efficient rent collector and chief subordinate, he says, "You are paid to squeeze, and you must squeeze to pay" (II, *xxxii*, 864). Mr. Casby keeps his long patriarchal locks and broad-brimmed hat until the final pages of the book when in exasperation Pancks shears him and reveals the real Casby underneath: "A goggle-eyed, big-headed, lumbering personage stood staring at him, not in the least impressive, not in the least venerable, who seemed to have started out of the earth to ask what was become of Casby" (II, *xxxii*, 870).

The fiercely energetic Pancks is ironically referred to as a tugboat though he meticulously carries out the orders of his superior, Casby. His great appetite for work is merely the result of inner emptiness, an important comment on the various Victorian gospels of work. One must distinguish carefully the motives behind the lives of Doyce, the inventor, and Pancks. Pancks' credo, like Blandois', helps to clarify the pattern of a world in reverse that is the world of this book: "Here am I. . . . What else do you suppose I think I am made for? Nothing. Rattle me out of bed early, set me going, keep me as short a time as you like to bolt my meals in, and keep me at it. Keep me always at it, you keep somebody else always at it. There you are with the Whole Duty of Man in a commercial country" (I, *xiii*, 173).

The reference to the Whole Duty of Man in a commercial country is part of a long series of religious references and images in which this pattern of reversal can be seen most starkly. These references begin at the opening of the book with the description of Marseilles, one of the entrances to the prison of Europe (book II opens with a parallel description of the Grande Chartreuse, which guards the passage from northern to southern Europe, and toward the end there is a parallel description of Calais), with its overtones of a world so completely estranged that it has become Hell: "A blazing sun upon a fierce August day. . . . The very dust was scorched brown, and something quivered in the atmosphere as if the air itself was panting" (I, *i*, 1–2).

Perhaps the most striking example of what I have been talking about is the portrait of Mrs. Clennam and the role she plays in the novel. Her religion, the polar opposite of Christianity, is a religion "veiled in gloom and darkness, with lightnings of cursing, vengeance, and destruction, flashing through the sable clouds. Forgive us our debts as we forgive our debtors was a prayer too poor in spirit for her. Smite thou my debtors, Lord, wither them, crush them; do Thou as I would do, and Thou shalt have my worship: this was the impious tower of stone she built up to scale Heaven" (I, v, 51). As Dickens makes clear in the chapter titled "Closing In," she "still abided by her old impiety—still reversed the order of Creation, and breathed her own breath into a clay image of her Creator" (II, xxx, 840). The story of the creation of man in Genesis has quite literally been reversed; as Flintwinch says in the same chapter—and he should know—"Call yourself whatever humble names you will, I call you a female Lucifer in appetite for power!" (848). Mrs. Clennam, who sees herself as a divine instrument, has significantly been guilty of one of the few actual crimes (in the legal sense of the word) committed in the book: she has suppressed a will, a nice irony since the letter of the law for her is all-important.[3] She has made life into death: "On a black bier-like sofa in this hollow, propped up behind with one great angular black bolster, like the block at a state execution . . . sat his mother in a widow's dress" (I, iii, 36). She is appropriately attended by Flintwinch, who replaces Arthur in the family business and who is described as a hanged man, reinforcing the pattern of life which has become death.

> His neck was so twisted that the knotted ends of his white cravat usually dangled under one ear; his natural acerbity and energy, always contending with a second nature of habitual repression, gave his features a swollen and suffused look; altogether he had a weird appearance of having hanged himself . . . and of having gone about ever since, halter and

all, exactly as some timely hand had cut him down (40–41).

Arthur Clennam, returning to London on a Sunday after twenty years of exile in China, perhaps best sums up his memories of childhood Sundays and his mother's bible of hell in the pictures that rise up of her sitting all day

> behind a Bible—bound, like her own construction of it, in the hardest, barest, and straitest boards, with one dinted ornament on the cover like the drag of a chain, and a wrathful sprinkling of red upon the edges of the leaves—as if it, of all books! were a fortification against sweetness of temper, natural affection, and gentle intercourse (32–33).

But in the world of the book Mrs. Clennam's kind of idolatry, her version of Calvinism, is a thing of the past. If it survives it survives only in a psychological form in the twisted worlds, in which we also participate rather fully since they are so fully rendered, of Miss Wade and Tattycoram, and Henry Gowan and his mother, and the various other victims of resentment and injured merit. The will to power is still there in these characters, but it now takes the form of paranoid (Tattycoram's refrain is "I am ill-used. I am ill-used") fantasies and perverse behavior, as Mr. Meagles makes clear after his consternation "in hearing his motives and actions [in relation to Tattycoram] so perverted": "I don't know what you are, but you don't hide, can't hide, what a dark spirit you have within you. If it should happen that you are a woman who, from whatever cause, has prevented delight in making a sister-woman as wretched as she is (I am old enough to have heard of such), I warn her against you, and I warn you against yourself" (I, *xxvii*, 357–58). At the end of this scene Dickens notes Miss Wade's smile, "a smile that is only seen on cruel faces" (358). Of course, this description is bound to recall the description of Mrs. Clennam's treatment of Arthur's mother and the peculiar luxury she feels in giving employment to Little Dorrit, whose legacy she has suppressed. Miss Wade also lives in a world of death. In London she lives in a "dingy house, apparently empty, with bills in the windows announcing that it was to let. The bills, as a variety in the funeral procession, almost amounted to a decoration" (I, *xxvii*, 353).

> And in Calais, she lives in a dead sort of house, with a dead wall over the way and a dead gateway at the side, where a pendent bell-handle produced two dead tinkles, and a knocker produced a dead, flat surface-tapping (II, *xx*, 707).

It is surely significant that the only real love affair she had, as she relates in her "History of a Self-Tormentor," should have been with Henry Gowan, whom she saw as "the dressed-up Death in the Dutch series: whatever figure he took upon his arm, whether it was youth or age, beauty or ugliness, whether he danced with it, sang with it, played with it, or prayed with it, he made it ghastly." After meeting Gowan she found everyone else tame. Only he knew "how to address me on equal terms, and how to anatomize the wretched people around us"(II, *xxi*, 725). It is interesting that Mrs. General, whom we will soon look at more closely, is referred to as a "Ghoul in gloves" (II, *xv*, 662).

But if Mrs. Clennam's fierce Calvinism is as much a thing of the past as is her old-fashioned way of doing business, idolatry is very much a part of the new world of vast financial speculations based on credit, and credit *is* the new faith. (Mrs. Clennam had insisted on seeing and authenticating Blandois's letter of credit before honoring it). The new idol, however, is no longer a clay image of one's creator into which one has breathed one's own breath, but literally a nobody, and a very muddy nobody at that, significantly named Merdle.

> Nobody knew that he had any capacity or utterance of any sort in him, which had ever thrown, for

any creature, the feeblest farthing-candle ray of light
on any path of duty or diversion, pain or pleasure,
toil or rest, fact or fancy, among the multiplicity of
paths in the labyrinth trodden by the sons of Adam;
nobody had the smallest reason for supposing the clay
of which this object of worship was made, to be other
than the commonest clay, with as clogged a wick
smouldering inside of it as ever kept an image of humanity from tumbling to pieces. All people knew (or
thought they knew) that he had made himself immensely rich; and, for that reason alone, prostrated
themselves before him, more degradedly and less ex-
cusably than the darkest savage creeps out of his hole
in the ground to propitiate, in some log or reptile, the
Deity of his benighted soul.[4]

Nay, the high priests of this worship had the
man before them as a protest against their meanness.
The multitude worshipped on trust (II, *xii*, 599–600).

Merdle himself during the dinner at which his son-in-law is
provided for by a government office, a scene in which
Dickens firmly connects the world of speculation and high
finance with that of government and aristocracy—the Circumlocution Office run by the Barnacles and Stiltstalkings
—"as usual, oozed sluggishly and muddily about his draw-
ing-room, saying never a word" (II, *xii*, 615). When the
official proclamation of Edmund Sparkler's appointment
as one of the Lords of the Circumlocution Office is issued,
"all true believers" hail it "as a graceful and gracious mark
of homage, rendered . . . to that commercial interest
which must ever in a great commercial country—and all
the rest of it, with a blast of trumpet" (615).

To make even clearer the parallel with Mrs. Clennam's creed and its reversal of authentic Christianity, Dickens inserted the following passage in chapter 16 of book II
called "Getting On," a title which echoes Carlyle's *Past and
Present.*

O ye sun, moon, and stars, the great man! The
rich man, who had in a manner revised the New
Testament, and already entered into the kingdom of
Heaven. . . . As he went up the stairs, people were

> already posted on the lower stairs, that his shadow
> might fall upon them when he came down. So were
> the sick brought out and laid in the track of the
> Apostle (664).

The heavy sarcasm as well as the idea itself is very much
like Kierkegaard's exactly contemporaneous *Attack upon
Christendom*. When one thinks of the thoroughgoingness
of Dickens' attack on the current establishment—the role
of Bishop of course comes to mind—the parallel between
the state of mind of the two writers is startling. Dickens
and Kierkegaard see their own worlds as the exact reverse
of what they profess to be; the standard for both writers is
the first five books of the New Testament.

The worship of Merdle—by the time of his suicide it
has explicitly become devil-worship ("every servile wor-
shipper of riches who had helped to set him on his pedestal
would have done better to worship the devil pointblank")
—has its own clergy. Mrs. Merdle speaks as a "Priestess of
Society," and its altar is her famous bosom, "not a bosom to
repose upon, but . . . a capital bosom to hang jewels
upon. . . . The bosom, moving in Society with the jewels
displayed upon it, attracted general admiration" (I, *xxi*,
267). It is the fame of this rich altar which spreads the
speculation fever, to use one of Dickens' own variations on
his metaphor for religious mania,[5] even to Bleeding Heart
Yard. The word about Mrs. Merdle rapidly spreads among
the poor tenants, how "his lady's dresses would fill three
wagons. That how she was as handsome a lady, ma'am, as
lived, no matter wheres, and a busk like marble itself" (II,
xiii, 617). It is this phase of "the progress of an epidemic"
(the chapter title of II, *xiii*), resulting from poor Sparkler's
appointment, that leads to Arthur Clennam's involving all
of the capital of Doyce and Clennam in the general collapse
following the Merdle suicide, leading further to Arthur's
imprisonment, subsequent disease (a sickness unto death),
his final despair of life and his miraculous rescue by Little
Dorrit—a perfectly just and appropriate sequence of ac-

tions since the disease Dickens describes is a moral one that defeats the will to live and has already been metaphorically equated to the worship of Merdle, who is mud, excrement, nobody, nothing, and the devil. We see at this point a particular appropriateness in one of the opening chapters' taking place in the quarantine room at Marseilles and in Arthur's returning from the East, "the country of the plague" (II, *xx*, 17). We also see how much more profound is Dickens' use of disease in this book than it was in the earlier *Bleak House*.

Mrs. General, as an educator of young ladies, plays a role parallel to that of Mrs. Merdle in making explicit the unexpressed assumptions of nineteenth-century society. " 'A truly refined mind will seem to be ignorant of the existence of anything that is not perfectly proper, placid, and pleasant.' Having delivered this exalted sentiment, Mrs. General made a sweeping obeisance" (II, *v*, 515). At the beginning of the second chapter of book II she is described as a kind of provincial goddess in a nice example of the kind of metaphoric energy and inventiveness now characteristic of Dickens' imagination, which almost forces individual metaphors to take on a life of their own.

> A stiff commissariat officer of sixty, famous as a martinet, had then become enamoured of the gravity with which she drove the proprieties four-in-hand through the cathedral town society, and had solicited to be taken beside her on the box of the cool coach of ceremony to which that team was harnessed. His proposal of marriage being accepted by the lady, the commissary took his seat behind the proprieties with great decorum, and Mrs. General drove until the commissary died. In the course of their united journey, they ran over several people who came in the way of the proprieties; but always in a high style, and with composure (II, *ii*, 482–83).

The way sound, rhythm, image, and theme all become inextricably united in this passage is typical of the style of the novel.

That Mrs. General is very much a part of the pattern of religious reference in the novel is obvious from the way she responds to Mr. Dorrit's alarming symptoms, which herald his final collapse. "On each recurrence of the symptom, she told her polite beads—Papa, Potatoes, Poultry, Prunes, and Prism—and, by dint of going through that infallible performance very slowly, appeared to finish her rosary at about the same time as Mr. Dorrit started from his sleep" (II, *xix*, 697). Their grotesque courtship scene which follows is conducted "much as some people may be seen to conduct themselves in church, and to perform their part in the service" (699), precisely what Mrs. General means by propriety. Earlier in the book the same point has been emphatically made by Mrs. Merdle in her complaint to Mr. Merdle when she tells him, "You really ought not to go into Society unless you can accommodate yourself to Society," and in answer to his angry expostulation on his sacrifices she tells him firmly, "You ought to make yourself fit for it by being more dégagé, and less preoccupied. . . . I don't want you to take any trouble upon yourself, or to try to be fascinating. I simply request you to care about nothing—or seem to care about nothing—as everybody else does" (I, *xxxiii*, 427–29). The word *nothing* is one of the most important words in the book.

Mrs. General in her capacity as educator follows this precept perfectly. She "had no opinions. Her way of forming a mind was to prevent it from forming opinions. She had a little circular set of mental grooves or rails on which she started little trains of other people's opinions, which never overtook one another, and never got anywhere" (II, *xx*, 486). The connection with the Circumlocution Office and also with the way so many people in the novel speak is obvious. That famous government office is evidently a satire not just on the English government but on the way people live their lives and the way they think and feel. We can even perceive in the heart of the good Mr. Meagles a

"microscopic portion of the mustard-seed that had sprung
up into the great tree of the Circumlocution Office" (I, xvi,
211) as we can indeed see his confusion of values in the
confusion, the lack of any meaningful pattern, in his apparently idyllic home. It contained such a "vast miscellany
that it was like the dwelling of an amiable Corsair. There
were antiquities from Central Italy; . . . bits of mummy
from Egypt (and perhaps Birmingham); model gondolas
from Venice; model villages from Switzerland; morsels of
tesselated pavement from Herculaneum and Pompeii, like
petrified minced veal; ashes out of tombs, and lava out of
Vesuvius; Spanish fans, Spezzian straw hats, Moorish slip-
pers" (I, xvi, 209). The list goes on for half a page. When
one remembers that Mr. Meagles can not understand a
word of the language of any of the countries he spends the
rest of his life visiting, the same kind of pattern of mean-
inglessness receives brilliant elaboration. (It is further
parodied in Mrs. Plornish's version of Italian: "muchaston-
isha padrona.")

As if to link Mrs. General's notions of propriety, the
world of prunes and prism, with the private story of Arthur
Clennam, Dickens uses the same candle metaphor for her
that he did for Arthur's announcement in quarantine of his
broken will: "If her eyes had no expression, it was probably
because they had nothing to express. If she had few
wrinkles, it was because her mind had never traced its
name or any other inscription on her face. A cool, waxy,
blown-out woman, who had never lighted well" (II, xx,
486–87). And, as any reader of the novel will remember,
she is always pictured as dipping "the smallest of brushes
into the largest of pots" and applying a coat of varnish to
"the surface of every object that came under consideration.
The more cracked it was, the more Mrs. General varnished
it" (487)—a clear anticipation of the society scenes of *Our
Mutual Friend*, especially those with Podsnap and the
Veneerings.

The sense of life lived completely on the surface is another of the themes announced in the two almost emblematic opening chapters in Marseilles. While waiting to be fed, Rigaud, with "much the expression of a wild beast," looks out of eyes that were "sharp rather than bright—pointed weapons with little surface to betray them. They had no depth or change" (11, *i*, 3–4), a clear anticipation of characters like Faulkner's Popeye, whose expression had the "depth and viciousness of stamped tin." It is precisely in Rigaud's lack of any imagination, any inner life, that his evil lies. He has become dehumanized and is usually described in animal terms in addition to being an avatar of the devil—but his diabolic nature has nothing metaphysical about it, for he has no strange powers. His evil nature is due to his lack of humanity, his almost complete bestiality: "His avaricious manner of collecting all the eatables about him, and devouring some with his eyes, while devouring others with his jaws, was the same manner. His utter disregard of other people, as shown in his way of tossing the little womanly toys of furniture about, flinging favourite cushions under his boots for a softer rest, and crushing delicate coverings with his big body and great black head, had the same brute selfishness at the bottom of it" (1, *xxx*, 381). If one thinks at this point of Mrs. Merdle's parrot and its viciousness—"he tore at a clawful of biscuit and spat it out, seemed to mock them with a pompous dance of his body without moving his feet, and suddenly turned himself upside down and trailed himself all over the outside of his golden cage, with the aid of his cruel beak and his black tongue" (1, *xx*, 262)—that is exactly what Dickens intended, with a clear parallel between the quality of Rigaud's life and Mrs. Merdle's and the insistence of both on their gentility.[6] Both are always playing a role—Rigaud's favorite line is "It's my character to be—," the blank to be filled in by whatever the particular scene demands—because, as Mrs. Merdle insists to Fanny and Amy Dorrit,

"We are not in a natural state. Much to be lamented, no doubt—particularly by myself, who am a child of nature if I could but show it—but so it is. [Dickens' use of her parrot, who does show what kind of nature she really is, is one of the best touches in the book.] Society suppresses us and dominates us—Bird, be quiet!" (II, *xx*, 259).

It is just this loss of selfhood, individuality, authenticity that forms the substance of Little Dorrit's vision of the English tourists in Rome. Note how this passage is dominated by the kind of religious imagery observed earlier and how this passage powerfully reinforces the theme of idolatry:

> Everybody was walking about St. Peter's and the Vatican on somebody else's cork legs, and straining every visible object through somebody else's sieve. Nobody said what anything was, but everybody said what the Mrs. Generals, Mr. Eustace, or somebody else said it was. The whole body of travellers seemed to be a collection of voluntary human sacrifices, bound hand and foot, and delivered over to Mr. Eustace and his attendants, to have the entrails of their intellects arranged according to the taste of that sacred priesthood. Through the rugged remains of temples and tombs, and palaces and senate halls . . . hosts of tongue-tied and blindfolded moderns were carefully feeling their way (II, *vii*, 522).

The very stylized, patterned quality of the prose and of the vision itself (it has the quality of one of Breughel's parables in its tendency to fall into a very clear design illustrative of its meaning), this quality, typical of so many of the descriptive passages which, like this one, tend to be the vision of a particular character, and typical also of the way the book itself is organized in its two contrasting halves, contrasting groups of characters and milieus and even contrasting chapters, powerfully reinforces the major theme of the novel as a whole: the weakening of the self, the tendency of somebody to become nobody, the loss of that energy that keeps a self a real self in the sense of a center of willing set up in opposition to one's milieu. The possibility suddenly crosses the reader's mind that the naturalistic novelists and philosophers may be right in their thesis that the individual is completely a product of his heredity and environment, determined by *la race, le moment, le milieu,* or at least nineteenth-century civilization is moving in such a direction that they will be right and Mrs. Merdle's statement that "society suppresses us and dominates us" will become the new gospel. Such a fear is surely at the heart of a good deal of the literature of the century, from the weary, bound figures of Blake's *Songs of Experience* to the defeated heroes of Thomas Hardy. Especially in the 1850's, the decade of *Little Dorrit,* it is what most of the work of the major poets—Tennyson, Browning, and Arnold—is really about, and two years after the publication of *Little Dorrit* this theme was to receive its classic formulation in the famous third chapter of Mill's *On Liberty.* The very possibility that Amy Dorrit represents and her "believability" as a creation will in the future become increasingly difficult for readers to accept. For Dickens, of course, she *is* the title figure: the book was not called "Nobody's Fault," as originally intended, and her importance in the design of the whole is clear in Arthur's retrospective musings in prison. "Looking back upon his own poor story, she was its vanishing-point. Everything in its perspective led to her innocent figure. He had travelled thousands of miles towards it; previous unquiet hopes and doubts had worked themselves out before it; it was the centre of the interest of his life" (II, *xxvii,* 795). In the same sense Cordelia could be considered the vanishing point in the design that is *King Lear.* It is worthy of note that here Dickens uses the language of realistic perspective painting as practiced since Piero della Francesca, painting that aimed to give the illusion of real space rather than the sort of highly stylized and grotesque vision of the preceding passage describing the English tourists.

The final stage in the process of dehumanization typical of the world of *Little Dorrit*—if we exclude characters like Edmund Sparkler, who is little more than an embodied repetition compulsion, and his father-in-law, who is nothing but an object of worship, nothing in himself—is most clearly represented by three characters. John Chivery, Amy Dorrit's permanently defeated suitor and a parodic version of Arthur in the role of Nobody, is perpetually writing his epitaph. Affery Flintwinch walks about with her apron over her head in a world where she is unable to distinguish dream from reality. One of her "dreams" is especially significant, that of Flintwinch face to face with his twin brother, which she perceives as a personality actually splitting before her eyes and talking to its own double.

> For Mr. Flintwinch awake was watching Mr. Flintwinch asleep. He sat on one side of a small table, looking keenly at himself on the other side with his chin sunk on his breast, snoring. The waking Flintwinch had his full front face presented to his wife; the sleeping Flintwinch was in profile. The waking Flintwinch was the old original; the sleeping Flintwinch was the double. Just as she might have distinguished between a tangible object and its reflection in a glass, Affery made out this difference with her head going round and round (I, *iv*, 46).

The idea of the double is further developed in Mr. Meagles' fancy about the dead twin sister of Pet's that he likes to think Arthur has fallen in love with—as Arthur has indeed fallen in love with the idea of death; and still further in the tortured relationship between Miss Wade and Tattycoram ("I have had Miss Wade before me all this time, as if it was my own self grown ripe" [II, *xxxiii*, 879]). And perhaps there is a further variation on the same theme in the connection between Rigaud and Henry Gowan. This sort of emphasis on the idea of the double stresses the underlying conception of the instability of the self—here it seems spontaneously to split in two before Mrs. Flintwinch's eyes.

The third and most extreme, perhaps one of the most extreme cases of dehumanization in literature, is one of the greatest of Dickens' inventions in a book full of inventiveness—Mr. F.'s Aunt:

> An amazing little old woman, with a face like a staring wooden doll too cheap for expression, and a stiff yellow wig perched unevenly on the top of her head, as if the child who owned the doll had driven a tack through it anywhere, so that it only got fastened on. Another remarkable thing in this little old woman was, that the same child seemed to have damaged her face in two or three places with some blunt instrument in the nature of a spoon, her countenance, and particularly the tip of her nose, presenting the phenomena of several dints, generally answering to the bowl of that article. A further remarkable thing in this little old woman was, that she had no name but Mr. F.'s Aunt (I, *viii*, 169).

Since she is only seen in company with Flora, one is tempted to see her as the dark underside of Flora's ampleness and efflorescence. Certainly her cryptic remarks (Lionel Trilling calls her "a fate") are often as much to the point as the comedy of Flora lies in her very pointlessness. On Arthur's sentimental visit to the Casbys in his hope against hope of recovering a lost past that never was, her comments are: "I hate a fool," and "What's he come there for then!" (I, *xiii*, 171). Arthur's moral collapse and drift toward death are sharply underlined by her "bring him for'ard and I'll chuck him out o' winder." It is one answer to the question he keeps asking himself: what to do with his life.

The word "*do*," like the word "*nobody*," is a key word in the novel, just as the possibility of an independent act of the will is the underlying idea. Can one act in a humanly intelligible fashion in a world almost literally on the wrong side of the pattern of the universe? For example, Fanny enters into her shameful marriage to Sparkler for a variety of motives not the least being self-punishment, along with the opportunities it will offer to torture her mother-in-law, who once condescended to her in an unforgiveable manner. To her father, though, it is clear that she marries to assert the family honor. She defends herself in a way we are now familiar with in the novel: "Other girls differently reared and differently circumstanced altogether, might wonder at what I say or may do. Let them. They are driven by their lives and characters; I am driven by mine" (II, *xiv*, 638–39). She apparently is not aware that there is any dramatic irony in the fact that she addresses this apologia to Amy, who was reared and circumstanced in the same way and does wonder and even disapprove. Fanny is thus the spokesman for all the driven and conditioned characters in the book—Miss Wade, Tattycoram, Mrs. Clennam, Mrs. Gowan, Henry Gowan, and possibly even the reader, but certainly not the author[7]—all acting out their particular fantasies, the particular version, most of which we are given, of their own inverted world. Miss Wade, for example, in a meeting with the Meagleses that was far from accidental—it was one she deliberately sought out—speaks in a similar fatalistic way: "In our course through life we shall meet the people who are coming to meet *us*, from many strange places and by many strange roads . . . and what it is set to us to do to them, and what it is set to them to do to us, will all be done" (I, *ii*, 28). And, of course, Mrs. Clennam, who more than anyone else deliberately plays the role of providence, is a believer in Calvinistic predestination. Self-imprisoned in her own room, she says, "The world has narrowed to these dimensions" (I, *iii*, 37), not "I have narrowed my world."

I have spoken earlier of Dickens' energy of invention in this novel, how metaphors seem to take on a life of their own and connect themselves with other metaphors until we get what seem to be systems of metaphors. Perhaps the most notable of these is the Circumlocution Office, which

begins its life in the book as "the most important Department under Government" (1, *x*, 111) and ends as government itself and suggests, by its connections with everything
else, the whole social system. Certainly for contemporary
readers the main purpose of the novel was satire and the
earliest discussions of it tended to center around the justice
and accuracy of Dickens' pictures of administrative in-
efficiency during the Crimean War.[8] For the twentieth-
century reader Dickens' picture of government seems to be
a striking anticipation of Kafka and so is read as a symbol
of man's metaphysical predicament.[9] From the point of
view of this particular paper it is above all one of the many
representations of a world in reverse, and so is related to
and is an example of the pattern of the whole novel. First
of all, the office is spoken of in religious terms, as if it were
the Church: "This glorious establishment had been early in
the field, when the one sublime principle involving the
difficult art of governing a country was first distinctly revealed to statesmen. It had been foremost to study that
bright revelation, and to carry its shining influence through
the whole of the official proceedings" (1, *x*, 111). When,
toward the end of the novel, Ferdinand, the sprightly
Barnacle, visits Arthur in prison, he tries to explain the
whole raison d'être of the office, an explanation Dickens
calls his "confession of faith," an explanation which clearly
relates Dickens' satiric invention to Carlyle's Gospel of
Mammonism, laissez-faire. (It is hard to imagine *Little
Dorrit*'s being written without the previous existence of
Past and Present.) Seen from the right point of view the
office is a perfect justification of the prevailing mood of the
country, spiritual sloth (recall Merdle and his muddy
Dantesque overtones: there is literally in the novel a worship of mud and excrement) and national paralysis. "It is
there with the express intention that everything shall be
left alone. That is what it means. That is what it is there
for. No doubt there's a certain form to be kept up that it's

for something else, but it's only a form. Why, good Heaven, we are nothing but forms!" (The relation again, to belabor a point, to Mrs. Merdle, Mrs. General, to the religious criticism throughout the book is obvious.) As young Barnacle concludes, he makes clear how far-reaching the idea of his office really is. "Everybody is ready to dislike and ridicule any invention. You have no idea how many people want to be left alone. You have no idea how the Genius of the country . . . tends to being left alone. . . . Our place is not a wicked Giant to be charged at full tilt, but only a windmill showing you, as it grinds immense quantities of chaff, which way the country wind blows" (ii, *xxviii*, 797–99). The reference to Cervantes, carrying the explicit idea of the death of all ideals, all possibility of transcending the given mud or chaff of the actual moment and the concomitant death of the spirit this implies is painfully evident, especially since this particular revelation is vouchsafed to Arthur in the Marshalsea in his particularly suicidal state of "unnatural peace" (xx, *xxvii*, 779), as he is slowly willing his own death because of the accumulation of guilt and the lack of an object to live for. The relation between this theme, as it is enacted within the person of Arthur Clennam, which is the main story line, and as it is explored in the entire world of the novel, is clearly connected with the same mood responsible for the vogue of the word *decadence* in the second half of the nineteenth century and the revival of Schopenhauer—the first essay on Schopenhauer appeared in England in the *Westminster Review* in 1852. For many thinkers the world was actually, even physically, in a decline, and entropy, the running down of energy, haunted more writers than Henry Adams.

After his disappointment at seeing the real Flora for the first time, so utterly unlike the figure his youthful imagination had created, Arthur "sat down before his dying fire, as he had stood at the window of his old room looking out upon the blackened forest of chimneys, and turned his

gaze back upon the gloomy vista by which he had come to
that stage in his existence. So long, so bare, so blank." At
forty he is an old man with nothing left to hope for.

> He looked at the fire from which the blaze de-
> parted, from which the after-glow subsided, in which
> the ashes turned grey, from which they dropped to
> dust, and thought, "How soon I too shall pass through
> such changes, and be gone!"
> To review his life was like descending a green
> tree in fruit and flower, and seeing all the branches
> wither and drop off one by one as he came down to-
> wards them (1, *xiii*, 177–78).

He then half-heartedly plays with the idea of marrying Pet
Meagles, but seems almost happy to renounce her to the
caddish Henry Gowan. Arthur in his own mind is a born
loser, really Nobody, and his mood is probed, as very few
states of mind ever were in Dickens, in the chapters called
"Nobody's Weakness," "Nobody's Rival," Nobody's State of
Mind," and "Nobody's Disappearance." That Arthur is a
representative figure so typical of the sad and defeated
young men of the 1840's and 1850's, from Tithonus to the
speaker of Arnold's Switzerland poems, becomes clear at
the end of 1, *xxviii*, in two paragraphs evocative of the
world of so much mid-Victorian poetry:

> When he had walked on the river's brink in the
> peaceful moonlight for some half an hour he put his
> hand in his breast and tenderly took out the handful
> of roses. Perhaps he put them to his heart, perhaps he
> put them to his lips, but certainly he bent down on the
> shore and gently launched them on the flowing river.
> Pale and unreal in the moonlight, the river floated
> them away.
> The lights were bright within doors when he
> entered, and the faces on which they shone . . . were
> soon quietly cheerful. They talked of many sub-
> jects . . . and so to bed and to sleep. While the
> flowers, pale and unreal in the moonlight, floated

away upon the river; and thus do greater things that once were in our breasts, and near our hearts, flow from us to the eternal seas (366–67).

Returning to the scene in which Arthur reviews his life and sees it all fall into a pattern as he sits before his dying fire, we hear him say just before the end of that scene: "From the unhappy suppression of my youngest days, through the rigid and unloving home that followed them . . . what have I found?" and we also hear the unexpected answer as the door softly opens: "Little Dorrit" (I, *xiii*, 179). This is the most important symbolic moment of the book and foreshadows the end, where the process is substantially repeated. The sudden opening of a door when Clennam seems imprisoned in his despairing state of mind, the possibility of grace in a fallen world, is dramatically rendered at the beginning of the next chapter with the shift in point of view to Little Dorrit. Her vision of Arthur's room is presented to us, also highly patterned, but with a different sort of pattern from Clennam's dying fire and withering tree. To her his dim room looks spacious and grandly furnished, and in one vision she brings back the possibility of a world full of color and interest, at the same time "courtly," "costly," "picturesque," "desolate," and, to use one of Dickens' favorite words, "teeming," all confused together. We think again of the English world of Martin Chuzzlewit, epitomized by Todgers', which stands juxtaposed to the gray world of death young Martin discovers in America and we realize that Arthur's condition is a further development of the sort of crisis that Martin had earlier gone through in Eden.

The often-quoted description of the sunset just before the symbolic collapse of the Clennam house is thus an intimate part of the total design of the novel. "From a radiant centre over the whole length and breadth of the tranquil firmament great shoots of light streamed among the early stars, like signs of the blessed covenant of peace

and hope that changed the crown of thorns into a glory"
(II, *xxxi*, 859). There is another kind of perspective possible on the world, which is represented by Amy Dorrit, and
to a lesser degree by the inventor Doyce, and which finds its
expression in Dickens' version of Christianity.[10] Pausing
for a moment on the steps of the church in which they are
married—the church that had earlier given Amy shelter
after her night out in the streets when she had ministered
to Clennam for the first time—Amy and Arthur look at the
"fresh perspective of the street in the autumn morning's
sun's bright rays" and then go down, taking part once more
in the world "inseparable and blessed" in their modest life
of usefulness and happiness (II, *xxxiv*, 826). The bright
rays of the sun they see are the same that Amy earlier saw
transfigure the black bars of the Marshalsea gate to stripes
of gold. "For aslant across the city, over its jumbled roofs,
and through the open tracery of its church towers, struck
the long bright rays, bars of the prison of this lower world"
(II, *xxx*, 826). Beyond this world, we are thus made aware
of a world of light, which can affect and irradiate this one
and bring things into proper perspective. A life of usefulness and happiness is possible after all, thus giving us some
meaningful alternative to the vision evoked by the bleak
words of Pancks, Mrs. Merdle, and Fanny Dorrit. At the
end of the book Arthur is more than a product of his up-
bringing and the society he lives in with its reversed pattern. He does "light 'em up again" and is not brought for'ard
and chucked out of winder.

SOME STYLISTIC DEVICES IN
A TALE OF TWO CITIES

Sylvère Monod

However intensely one may dislike many aspects of *A Tale of Two Cities*, however devoutly one would like to discuss its profounder significance, it must be recognized that the book possesses, first of all, the quality of superb and masterly writing. This has nothing to do with its extraordinary popularity,[1] which is both ambiguous and unquestionable.[2] Yet the artistry, or at any rate the craftsmanship, that went into the writing was entirely deliberate, and it conditions much of the effect, and nearly all the value, the novel achieves. Under almost every other count—ideas, history, characters, humor—*A Tale of Two Cities* has repeatedly and justifiably been found deficient. Rather than with the contemporary reviewer who claimed that "it would not, indeed, be matter of much difficulty to frame from such a book as the *Tale of Two Cities* regular recipes for grotesque and pathetic writing,"[3] I find myself in agreement with John Gross's view that "one goes to the book for qualities which are easier to praise than to illustrate or examine,"[4] or with Earle Davis' comment: "*A Tale of Two Cities* is the one book of Dickens in which the student can see his artistry in some detail."[5] At any rate, my purpose is to "illustrate and examine" in some detail the artistry of

Dickens in this novel, not to derive from it recipes for imitation. No one can hope to analyze all the details in a book of that size, but it is possible and perhaps not unprofitable to select a number of stylistic devices for accurate description and analysis, in the hope that such devices are representative and in the belief that they act as strategies of presentation. In other words, *A Tale of Two Cities* being, admittedly, a made thing, a contrived book, it remains to be seen as exactly as possible *how* it has been made and contrived by a highly conscious writer. After clearing the ground of a number of minor details, I shall concentrate on four specific devices: repetition, cumulative effects, imagery, and revolutionary style.

Dickens wrote the *Tale* under various influences which are comparatively easy to trace in his style. The Scriptural element, for instance, and the attendant religiosity, had seldom been so much in evidence. The fact that he was writing about the eighteenth century occasionally led the novelist to emulate the style of the period. On the other hand, he was influenced by having to deal with France and French-speaking characters. From that point of view, he did better than Carlyle, who, in his *The French Revolution*, hardly ventured beyond one or two consecutive words of French without betraying his imperfect knowledge of that exotic language by some ridiculous error.[6] Certainly the spelling "Ma'amselle Manette" (II, *xvi*) turns Defarge into a conventional stage-Frenchman. But the few actual French words used are accurate and the Anglo-French speech contrived for the French-speaking characters does provide the right amount of local color.

Dickens' familiarity with the works of Shakespeare is well known. It usually appears in the form of humorous allusions to the more famous scenes of the more famous plays. In *A Tale of Two Cities*, however, there is evidence of Shakespearian influence woven into the text itself. K. J. Fielding believes the first scene between Lucie Manette and

her father owes something to *King Lear*.[7] I seem to hear, in
the phrase "an hour and a half limped heavily away" (II,
iii), a faint echo from *Henry V:* "the cripple tardy-gaited
night, Who . . . doth limp so tediously away" (IV, *Pro-
logue*, 21–22). But the most Shakespearian character in
the novel is probably Madame Defarge, who reminds me
more than once of Lady Macbeth, for instance when she
tells her husband, "You are faint of heart tonight, my dear!"
(II, *xvi*) or at her most inspired moment when she expresses her resolution: "Then tell Wind and Fire where to
stop; but don't tell me" (III, *xii*).

   Yet if there is one writer with whose work Dickens
had become permeated when he wrote the *Tale*, that writer
was of course Thomas Carlyle—and it would be impossible
to name an English writer with a style more thoroughly
idiosyncratic or more inevitably infectious. (One of the
reasons for which I am grateful to Dickens and *A Tale of
Two Cities* is that they have sent me back again and again
to Carlyle's magnificent history.) Fortunately, the novelist
did not imitate all the irritating mannerisms of his friend's
style: he did not, for example, adopt the hideous double
adjectives and adverbs of Carlyle—his characters do not
fight "jesuitico-rhetorically," they do not look at posted-up
bills "authoritative-heraldic . . . or indeed almost magical-
thaumaturgic." On the whole, however, it is obvious that
The French Revolution exerted considerable influence on
the form as well as the substance of *A Tale of Two Cities*.
Dickens' "Bull's Eye of the Court" is his version of Carlyle's
Oeil de Boeuf; Dickens' narrative of the storming of the
Bastille (II, *xxi*) is both faithful to Carlyle's account and an
original piece of writing in its own right. But the clearest
consequence of Dickens' assiduous reading of *The French
Revolution* is the (no doubt largely unconscious) adoption
of several characteristic features of Carlylese.

   Dickens had never been above using occasional
archaisms, chiefly for humorous purposes. But when we

find in the same novel: "he was fain to" (I, *iii*), "what time, the mail coach" (I, *iii*), "and eke at the Sessions" (II, *v*), "besides these Dervishes, were other three" (II, *vii*), and "other seven faces there were" (II, *xxi*), "unlike any other that could have been holden" (II, *xiii*), "all adust and athirst" (II, *xv*), "all astir and a-buzz" (III, *ix*), "wending East" (II, *xxiii*), and "erst a mender of roads" (III, *xiii*)— then it becomes obvious that something has happened to him. Unmitigated Carlylese is not often to be encountered in the *Tale*, yet, I believe, it is patently and even blatantly recognizable in at least two passages: "in Wolf-procession" (II, *xxii*, with the characteristic capital W), and "a life-thirsting, cannibal-looking, bloody-minded juryman" (III, *ix*).

A great many of the stylistic characteristics of *A Tale of Two Cities* have their source in Dickens himself, whose own influence on his writing is to be felt in two ways. From the old or usual Dickens derive a number of devices, procedures, and mannerisms adopted, it would seem, because he could not do otherwise, because he was doomed to be forever, irrepressibly, himself. The new Dickens is the conscious artist, out to write an entirely new kind of book, with whom I shall be mainly concerned in this essay.

One of the great debates about *A Tale of Two Cities* is as to how far one finds the genuine Dickens in it. The touchstone of the genuine Dickens is comic characterization. The debate soon narrows down to the simpler question about Jerry Cruncher as a comic or even a humorous figure. I have been repeatedly charged with failing—probably because I am a Frenchman—to appreciate Jerry. But I derive some comfort from the company in which I find myself, a distinguished and by no means unduly Gallic group. Apart from Bernard Darwin (who, after nearly confessing that the *Tale* "is not quite the genuine Dickens," adds "but let us not forget Jerry Cruncher, who is the real thing"[8]), most of the critics have been in agreement on

that point, from John Forster[9] to John Gross,[10] and Edgar
Johnson, who finds much to admire in the *Tale* and has
written eloquently about it,[11] sees only "the smallest glints
of comedic exception" to the general seriousness of the
novel. It is only fair to add that, on being sent back to the
book with a guilty conscience, under the impression that I
had not done full justice to its merits or to its mirth, I again
found that its humor comes only in driblets, but that they
are more numerous and pleasurable than I had remembered. Darnay's English trial (ii, *iii*) is a great comic success. Stryver, in spite of his limited psychological range and
of the author's excessive dislike of him, provides excellent
opportunity for comedy and for grotesque exaggeration, for
example, in ii, *xii*, his bursting out of the Bank caused
"such a concussion of air on his passage through, that to
stand up against it, bowing behind two counters, required
the utmost remaining strength of the two ancient clerks."
Jerry himself, after all, achieves the very unusual feat of
being more funny after his conversion (iii, *ix*) than he was
as a rogue. His famous—or infamous—repetition of "flopping" to describe his wife's praying even makes good in the
end, since its being used in conversation with Miss Pross
leads to that lady's comment, "Whatever housekeeping arrangement that may be, . . . I have no doubt it is best
that Mrs. Cruncher should have it entirely under her own
superintendence" (iii, *xiv*). This is unsensational, this is
tame, and one may question the legitimacy of that kind of
built-in humor which rests on the use of esoteric phrases by
the characters. Miss Pross herself is in the tradition of
Dickens' large-hearted eccentrics, of his gruff diamonds,
like Miss Betsey of whom she is somewhat reminiscent (ii,
vi, "Hundreds of People"); such comparisons are, of course,
damning with faint praise, for it cannot be contended that
Miss Pross rises to the superb comic wealth of Miss Trotwood. However, one may penitently admit that humor in *A
Tale of Two Cities* is not non-existent, although irony, both

under Carlyle's influence and as an effect of Dickens' own polemical purpose here, is much more abundant.

Unfortunately, other usual Dickensian characteristics are also perceptibly present in the book. Pathos and unreality are indeed all too evident: the dying words of the Darnay's little son, spoken "with a radiant smile . . . in a halo on a pillow" (II, *xxi*), are more than most readers can take.[12] Lucie Manette's introduction to her father (I, *vi*) rings disastrously false and has all the usual features—such as exclamation, repetition, and capitalization—with which Em'ly's letters to her uncle had long ago familiarized Dickens' readers. Similar lapses into unreality are observable whenever edifying emotion is attempted; any comment on the stylistic devices in chapter *ii* of book III, for instance, is discouraged by the utter lack of verisimilitude in the words exchanged by the Darnays. The love-scenes (II, *x*, and II, *xiii*) are likewise drearily platitudinous, although the gestures are sometimes (in II, *xiii*, at any rate) less feeble than the speeches. As for theatricality and melodrama, two of the novelist's besetting sins, the ways in which they overshadow many passages of the *Tale* has often been denounced. The dramatic origin of the book, conceived while Dickens was acting in *The Frozen Deep,* has something to do with this, as also the fact that the *Tale* was the first novel written since the inception of the public readings.

Finally, the ordinary Dickens is present in the *Tale* in more satisfactory ways: a number of phrases are delightful because of their very Dickensianity, because no one but Dickens could have coined them. Such are the description of a picturesque horse at the beginning (I, *ii*), the reference to Stryver's "occasionally flirting with some lighter document" (II, *v*), verbal inventions like "three fellow-inscrutables" (I, *iii*), "wickedly, falsely, traitorously, and otherwise evil-adverbiously" (II, *ii*), "chocolate-sprites" (II, *vii*); the banking clerk's "surprised spectacles" (II, *ii*) are almost as

good as Mrs. Crupp's "Nankeen bosom" and quite as characteristic. And there are several palatable examples of
Dickens' habit of pouncing upon some current phrase and
exposing its inadequacy: "All the people within reach had
suspended their business, or their idleness" (I, *v*); Jerry's
arriving "circuitously at the understanding that the aforesaid, and over and over again aforesaid, Charles Darnay,
stood there . . . upon his trial" (II, *ii*); or, when Stryver
expresses his indignation at Mr. Lorry's having made a
preposterous statement, "Says it with his head on!" the
narrator adds, "Mr. Stryver remarked upon the peculiarity
as if it would have been infinitely less remarkable if he had
said it with his head off" (II, *xii*); even in the context of the
French Revolution, and with the guillotine looming in the
background, this comes fairly close to what Bernard Darwin called "the real thing" to the Dickens-addict.

So much for the old Dickens. With all his determination to do something new, he had not been able to
cancel himself out entirely. Yet, of course, with a man of
his fantastic energy, it was to be expected that the new
style he aimed at would be immeasurably more visible
throughout the book, as indeed it is.

Among the new devices most deliberately used by
Dickens in *A Tale of Two Cities* repetition clearly holds
pride of place. It is so obvious that it has sometimes been
mentioned by critics, but it has attracted little extended
comment. John Gross does notice "a tendency toward heavy
repetitions and parallelisms, brought out by chapter-head-
ings,"[13] but he seems to be referring to incidents rather
than to words; in any case it is not quite enough to say that
the repetitions are "heavy." It ought to be possible to find
out, through closer analysis of the text, what are the main
kinds of repetitions in the *Tale*, and what various purposes
they are meant to serve.

Repetition is only part of a general design to play with
symmetries and contrasts. Carton and Darnay are said to

be "so like each other in feature, so unlike each other in manner" (II, *iii*); the "shadows within" are opposed to the "shadows without" (III, *xiii*): at the beginning of the fateful interview between Miss Pross and Madame Defarge we are told that the latter "knew full well that Miss Pross was the family's devoted friend; Miss Pross knew full well that Madame Defarge was the family's malevolent enemy" (III, *xiv*).

Typical examples of repetitive processes are only too easy to encounter in the *Tale*. Almost at random, we come across "Hunger"—with the emphatic capital initial—repeated eight times in fifteen lines (I, *v*); "put to Death" nine times in eleven lines (II, *i*); "poor" ten times (plus "spare" once) within nine lines, followed by "tax" five times in two lines (II, *viii*); "stone" eight times (plus one "stony") in five lines (II, *ix*). Repetition can be used on a smaller scale, but also, characteristically, in "the gloomy tile-paved entry to the gloomy tile-paved staircase" (I, *v*), or "his heart grew heavier again, and grew yet heavier and heavier every day . . . with a heart growing heavier and heavier" (II, *xviii*).

In the above examples repetition is concentrated over a small number of lines. In other cases, words and phrases are repeated many times in a more spread-out way; they are not likely to have escaped the attention of any reader of the *Tale,* yet it may be suggestive to bring some of them together. Stryver's "shouldering"[14] and "delicacy," contrasted with Carton's "carelessness" and "no delicacy," and the "lion and jackal" contrast are tirelessly iterated by Dickens and emphasized by several chapter headings. When Mr. Lorry just as tirelessly (and rather tiresomely) describes himself as a "man of business" and Jerry Cruncher as an "honest tradesman"—together with his reference to his wife's pious "flopping" it is his most constant mannerism—the thought fleetingly occurs that Dickens may have intended to express his overall contempt for trade and finance by thus making both Lorry and Jerry advertize themselves in rather similar terms, especially as Jerry and his wife do at least once discuss his "business," not his trade (II, *xiv*). "Knitting" is another famous term in the novel: it suggests one or two observations. On the one hand, since Madame Defarge is forever knitting from the very beginning of her novelistic career (I, *vi*, where she knits sitting, standing, and even walking) and infects her friend with the habit, it is something of a mystery in such a poor country, where bread is so scarce and where wool has to come from the same source as even scarcer mutton: no knitted article of clothing is ever produced; knitting is a luxury, and it is thus in one sense gratuitous but in another, inevitably, expensive. Secondly, Dickens achieves through sheer repetition the remarkable result of turning the very word "knitting" from the name of a useful or at worst innocent pastime into something sinister, ominous, and even murderous: when we see Madame Defarge "pointing her knitting-needle at Little Lucie as if it were the finger of Fate" (III, *iii*), we realize that it is more like a sword or a dagger than anything else. And when Defarge is shown "speaking with knitted brows" (III, *i*), we protest that it is an awkward mistake, for his house is one in which, not brows, but Dooms, are being knitted. Finally, the words "footsteps," "echoes," and "corner" (in Soho) are played upon in an interesting variety of ways. All three occur throughout the book, sometimes in isolation, more often in association: "corner" and "echo" are linked in II, *vi* ("the corner has been mentioned as a wonderful corner for echoes"); "echoes" pass from symbolical narrative to historical realities and into the characters' speeches (II, *xxi*, a chapter titled "Echoing Footsteps"); and the three words are to be found together more than once (see II, *vi*, "the wonderful corner for echoes resounded with the echoes of footsteps").

It is consonant with Dickens' usual manner to employ

repetition for schematized characterization. A turn of phrase, a physical feature, a typical gesture is described once; whenever it is repeated, it points to the specific person to whom it has become attached. Many of the instances listed above—like Stryver's "shouldering" or Jerry's "honest tradesman" and "flopping"—belong in that category. But there are many additional examples in the *Tale*, "the thin straight lines of the setting of the eyes, and the thin straight lips, and the markings in the nose" (II, *ix*) place the Marquis before us; Carton drinks punch like clockwork (II, *xi*); Lucie's "old look of earnestness" (for example, in III, *ii*) identifies her unmistakably; the girl who dies with Carton cannot utter two consecutive sentences without describing herself as "a poor weak little creature"; "a croaking voice" (III, *xii, xiv*) is a surer sign of a certain revolutionist's identity than his name, which is merely given as Jacques Three.

In addition, Dickens' belief in the value of repetition is revealed in the scandalous use made of it in Dr. Manette's letter, in the chapter (III, *x*) rather optimistically called "The Substance of a Shadow." The only defense of this otherwise indefensible chapter lies in the Doctor's awareness that he ought to "abridge this narrative" and in his confession that he "cannot read" what he has written with "this gaunt hand." If he could read it, however, he would find, as we do, that the letter was written with a "rusty iron point . . . in scrapings of soot and charcoal from the chimney, mixed with blood," that is, under every encouragement to be sparing of words. One can condone his making the dying brother so repeatedly speak of himself as a "common dog" (that being so adequate an expression of the author's irrepressible sympathy with the underdog). But blood is surely too precious to be wasted on counting the strokes of the bell, one by one, up to twelve, or on reproducing the dying girl's ejaculations no fewer than four times; just before the fourth occasion, the Doctor had written, "I found her raving in precisely the same order and continuity," which was amply sufficient without the words themselves.

There are even in the *Tale* several comments on the uses of repetition. An implicit comment on its value is to be found in the fact that, the more eccentric a phrase is, the more certain it is to be repeated, like Jerry Cruncher's "I'll either catch hold of his throat and choke him for half-a-guinea" (III, *viii*), which is rather impudently flaunted on its second occasion: "Mr. Cruncher could not be restrained from making rather an ostentatious parade of his liberality —'I'd catch hold of your throat and choke you for half-a-guinea.'" Who could not be refrained, and who is making a rather ostentatious parade? Similarly, it would appear that Madame Defarge's superb phrase, "Then tell Wind and Fire where to stop; but don't tell me," was felt by Dickens too good to be used only once, so that the husband's interposed words "only elicited from his own wife a repetition of her last reply" (III, *xii*). Other comments are still more explicit. Miss Pross's repetition of the phrase (about Dr. Manette's "walking up and down" in II, *vi*) is curiously taken as testifying "to her possessing such a thing" as imagination. As for the opening sentence of II, *xxi*, "a wonderful corner for echoes, it has been remarked, that corner where the Doctor lived," it strikes the reader as superfluous and almost insolent—it could hardly have escaped his notice that the remark had been made before, more than once—unless it is meant to show that repetition is indeed deliberate and serves an artistic purpose and is therefore nothing to be ashamed of.

The "theme with variations" procedure glanced at in the preceding section is related to another noteworthy device which may be called the cumulative effect, an effect obtained by the accumulation of many words connected with one main idea. A study of the vocabulary used by Dickens in any random paragraph of *A Tale of Two Cities* is nearly always suggestive from that point of view. Some sections might serve (and have in fact been so employed) as lessons in English vocabulary. When Dr. Manette's recovered energy is described (II, *vi*), within some ten lines are to be found, not only the words "energy" (twice) and "energetic," but also the phrases "great firmness of purpose . . . strength of resolution . . . vigour of action"; and the reader is further told that the Doctor "sustained a great deal of fatigue with ease." This profusion of words, all of which are accurately distinguished, produces an impression of masterly and inexhaustible resourcefulness. Mr. Lorry's prospective visions of his impending encounter with Manette provide remarkable examples: "They differed principally in . . . the ghastliness of their worn and wasted state. Pride, contempt, defiance, stubbornness, submission, lamentation, succeeded one another; so did varieties of sunken cheek, cadaverous colour, emaciated hands and figures" (I, *iii*). The Defarges' staircase is not a pleasant place; its brilliant description contains the following words: "vile . . . foul . . . heaps of refuse . . . other refuse . . . uncontrollable and hopeless mass of decomposition . . . polluted the air . . . intangible impurities . . . bad sources . . . insupportable . . . a dark shaft of dirt and poison . . . corrupted . . . spoilt and sickly vapours" (I,*v*).

These examples show the nature of the device. But, like repetition, cumulative effects can be made to serve several distinct purposes. One of the most interesting is its use for conveying psychological observations. If the novelist's purpose is to show that Carton is careless, he will show him "leaning back, with his gown torn half off him, his untidy wig, . . . his eyes on the ceiling, . . . something especially reckless in his demeanour," and later, once more "careless . . . lounging . . . loitering" (II, *iii*). But Carton has altered at the end of the novel (III, *ix*) and this time, though the initial words strike the same keynote with "it was a reckless manner," the reader soon realizes that the vocabulary which piles up around him aims at creating the opposite impression: his manner now is not "more expressive of negligence than defiance"; the tables are turned at this point, and henceforth Carton's name is coupled with his "solemn interest" (twice), he is "calm and steady," and he looks at the rising sun "with reverently shaded eyes," as befits a man who has done with punch forever and drinks "nothing but a little coffee." When ordeals and difficulties have altered Dr. Manette's attitude, Dickens cannot have too many words to convey his restored determination: "strength and power . . . the kindled eyes, the resolute face, the calm strong look and bearing . . . his persevering purpose . . . a new sustaining pride . . . forces . . . he took the lead . . . a steady hand, confident in his power, cautiously persistent . . . never doubting . . . a steady hand" (III, *iv*). In the same character's notorious blood-and-soot letter, there is a marked (though perhaps unintentional) accumulation of the vocabulary of self-pity; the first paragraph contains, "I . . . unfortunate physician, . . . write this melancholy paper in my doleful cell . . . under every difficulty. . . . Some pitying hand may find it there, when I and my sorrows are dust" (III, *x*). These words are of slight value; they add nothing to the pathos of the narrative; they do not lend it increased pungency, but increased mawkishness. They can only serve to reinforce the picture of a state of mind.

In other cases, the cumulative process is clearly used for the creation of atmosphere. The quietness of the Soho corner (II, *vi*) is suggested by "quiet . . . quaint . . . retirement . . . cool spot, staid but cheerful . . . a very harbour . . . a tranquil bark . . . little was audible . . . shunned by all . . . a lonely lodger." The gradual trapping and imprisonment of Darnay in France (III, *i*) is emphasized by the constant hammering of many words: "barrier . . . closed and strongly guarded . . . prisoner

. . . escort . . . prisoner . . . escort and escorted . . . guard-room . . . gate . . . the gate was held by a mixed guard . . . ingress was easy enough, egress was very difficult . . . barrier . . . guard . . . barrier . . . escort . . . escorted . . . guard-room . . . guardhouse." And throughout the novel, in scene after scene, effects of light and darkness, often connected with the weather and also with noise and silence, are created by similar means, resulting in a kind of impressionistic or even *pointilliste* technique; the final paragraph of II, *xvi*, is a remarkable verbal jumble of conveyed sensations, visual and auditive, which cohere into an impressive picture or a prophetic vision: "darkness closed around . . . the ringing of church bells . . . military drums . . . knitting, knitting . . . darkness . . . another darkness . . . church bells . . . military drums . . . knitting, knitting . . . closing in."

The accumulation of cognate vocabulary is also to be found in a few prolonged or diluted metaphors. Lucie's apartment in the Dover Inn is lugubrious (I, *iv*), hence the sequence "dark . . . funereal . . . black . . . dark . . . gloomily . . . buried . . . graves . . . obscurity." The destruction of Dr. Manette's shoemaker's bench is treated with a similar luxuriance of words stressing the criminal nature of the undertaking: "mysterious and guilty . . . murder . . . grimness . . . burning of the body . . . wicked . . . destruction . . . commission of their deed . . . accomplices in a horrible crime."

Images and comparisons of all kinds, from the ordinary simile up to the most elaborate metaphors and symbols, form the third major stylistic device in the *Tale*. Its novelty in Dickens' work is not striking, yet a protest must be entered against one or two critical pronouncements, like Cockshut's complaint that Dickens "enjoyed over-obvious comparisons"[15] or John Gross's view that the novel is written in "a grey and unadorned style."[16] Other commentators have emphasized the treatment of the prison

theme in *A Tale of Two Cities,* both concretely and symbolically,[17] to which it will not be necessary to revert here.
Others again have stressed the personification of Saint-
Antoine, which might be placed in the same category as the
gradual metamorphosis of "Monseigneur" into a collective
entity (II, *xxiv*). On the other hand, it is true that there are
numbers of uncharacteristic and even worthless images, of
a trite or vague kind. We do not need Dickens to tell us that
a brooding mood sat upon Manette "like a heavy cloud" (II,
iii), that news travels "like a train of powder" (II, *xxii*), or
that Mr. Lorry is attached to the Bank "like strong root-ivy"
(III, *ii*).[18] Yet three points still require comment.

In the first place, the persistence of some traditionally
Dickensian methods is clearly to be observed. Images pro-
liferate in the *Tale* as elsewhere; even the stupidest characters, like the road-mender, are credited with some imaginative and metaphorical powers: "Some whisper this,
some whisper that; they speak of nothing else; even the
fountain appears to fall to that tune" (II, *xv*). The usual
anthropomorphic treatment of inanimate objects (mainly
houses, doors, and pieces of furniture) reappears again
and again:[19] "a loud watch, ticking a sonorous sermon" (I,
iv); "a door of idiotic obstinacy with a weak rattle in its
throat" (II, *i*); another door "grudgingly turned on its
hinges" (II, *ii*). Of this procedure there exist variants: instead of anthropomorphic an image can be zoomorphic
("the little . . . town of Dover hid itself away from the
beach, and ran its head into the chalk cliffs, like a marine
ostrich" in I, *iv*) or theomorphic (as in the legend of the
guillotine in III, *iv*). The anthropomorphic device is occasionally used in reverse, when a human being is treated as
an inanimate object: Jerry throws off "sarcastic sparks
from the whirling grindstone of his indignation" (II, *i*) and
behaves like "an animated bit of the spiked wall of New-
gate" (II, *ii*). Parts of the body can also be detached for
similar purpose: "Mr. Lorry shook his head; using that

important part of himself as a sort of fairy cloak that would fit anything" (II, *vi*). In addition to the successful images of this specific type, there are others which are pleasantly characteristic of Dickens' usual manner through their picturesqueness or their poetry: Jerry wears "an old cocked-hat like a three-cornered spittoon" (I, *iii*); Miss Pross's bonnet is "like a Grenadier measure, and good measure too, or a great Stilton cheese" (I, *iv*); the hail falls "like a pigmy charge of bayonets" (II, *xxiii*). Particularly original and telling is the description of Stryver "bursting out of the bed of wigs, like a great sunflower pushing its way at the sun from among a rank gardenful of flaring companions" (II, *v*).

Secondly, some images are used in specific ways to serve the special purposes of the *Tale*. There is a kind of symbolical color-scheme: red is the color of blood, of wine, and the setting sun. The point is, if not labored, certainly emphasized: "The sunset struck so brilliantly into the travelling carriage . . . that its occupant was steeped in crimson" (II, *viii*); "in the glow, the water of the château seemed to turn to blood, and the stone faces crimsoned" (II, *ix*); the French road-mender himself says that he saw some soldiers, and adds, "They were almost black to my sight—except on the side of the sun going to bed, where they have a red edge, messieurs" (II, *xv*). Several symbols and metaphors are worked into the chapter headings and into the dialogues, like Carton's "hand at cards" (III, *viii*).

Thirdly, the quality and the functional value of a number of images in the *Tale* are striking and original and exceptional. Most of them are sufficiently obvious not to need illustration here: the golden thread, the sea-ocean-waves, and the fire-fever images are permanent features of the novel; in the Revolution fire and water are, so to speak, reconciled, since the effects of both, in a conflagration or in a storm, are identically destructive. As Stoehr says: "Much of the total effect depends . . . on the texture of dreamlike images, the interweaving of symbols with the action."[20] Many allegorical and mythological references are also worked into the historical narrative: the Woodman, Fate, and the Farmer, Death (i, *i*), the Furies (ii, *viii*), the Gorgon's Head (ii, *ix*), the great grindstone, Earth (iii, *ii*), the dragon's teeth (iii, *iv*), and a few similar phrases, lend dignity and impressiveness to many passages. The life-journey image[21] is ever present; the fancy ball in Monseigneur's house is described on a grand scale (ii, *vii*); Dickens must have done full justice to such a scene in his public readings. All those procedures work together. The "choice of graphic symbols . . . used to emphasize the major theme of inevitability by recalling the past and suggesting the future" is, according to K. J. Fielding, the main source of the success of the *Tale*.[22]

Dickens' comments in the text of the novel on the workings of imagination and imagery are less interesting than his references to repetition. Yet one statement must be mentioned; when he shows us an image in the making, an image taking shape in Darnay's mind, he calls it "a wandering fancy" (iii, *i*). But no clearer distinction between imagination and fancy is to be expected from him.

The term "Revolutionary style" which I use to label the fourth category of specific stylistic devices in the *Tale* may not be the most adequate phrase, but it is a tempting one. Dickens is increasingly recognized as a revolutionary writer (in his treatment of language), although this went almost unperceived by most of his contemporaries and was resented by the rest. When he deals with the French Revolution, his theme, it seems to me, reinforces a tendency that was already in existence. At the core of this phenomenon is to be observed the interplay between rhetoric (which implies order and control) and exaltation (which involves irrepressible outbursts).

Dickens' mastery over his medium had never been so complete. His longest sentences remain clear; his handling of intricate syntax is skillful; his control is perfect whenever he wishes to exert it. He has recourse once or twice to what William F. Axton calls "grotesquerie,"[23] yet neither when he presents a grotesque scene of rioting in the streets of London (II, *xiv*) nor when Carton grotesquely acts the stage Englishman at Defarge's is the novelist merely indulging himself. Carton's fooling is a vital part of his vital plot; the London riot is but a comic rehearsal of the Revolution. Everything is deliberate and calculated.

The plentiful use of rhetoric—a code of rules ensuring orderliness so as to achieve effectiveness and persuasiveness—strengthens Dickens' superb control over his writing. In a book with a historical, philosophical, and political message, the author wants and needs to persuade the reader. Some of the devices already studied are rhetorical: repetition, symmetry, and imagery are parts of rhetoric. But there are other arts of persuasion whose use in the *Tale* must be described. They are probably what G. K. Chesterton had in mind when he wrote of the *Tale* that "in dignity and eloquence it almost stands alone among his books."[24] The composition of many paragraphs, the marshaling of the words in them, is eloquent; they are made for effect and they achieve it. The end, that is, the last three paragraphs of II, *v*, is a clear illustration, though too long for quotation. A briefer and proportionately neater example is to be found in II, *xiii:* "When Mr. Stryver . . . had carried his delicacy into Devonshire, and when the sight and scent of flowers in the City streets had some waifs of goodness in them for the worst, of health for the sickliest, and of youth for the oldest, Sydney's feet still trod those stones." Like most moderately good things, rhetoric can be overdone; there can be too much of it: Jerry's address to Barsad ("What, in the name of the Father of Lies, own father to yourself, was you called at the time?" III, *viii*) is highly improbable. But the rhetoric of the dying boy, as reported in Dr. Manette's sanguinary letter, though it wastes both

the dying youth's breath and the prisoner's blood (III, x),
has something to be said for it, as do also Madame Defarge's rhetorical questions: "How long does it take to make
and store the lightning . . . to prepare the earthquake?"
(II, *xvi*). Dickens' idea in such cases seems to be that
intense purposefulness and single-mindedness tend, especially in a Frenchman, to produce or reinforce rhetorical
inclinations. And that is true enough. The final sentence of
the book, spoken, not by a Frenchman, but by a character
with a French-sounding name, one who had studied in
Paris, is a perfect specimen of rhetorical symmetry: "It is a
far, far better thing that I do, than I have ever done; it is a
far, far better rest that I go to, than I have ever known."

Yet, under the influence of the vivid and contradictory
emotions created in him by the violence of the revolutionary episodes, Dickens seems to lose his fine control. He
becomes overexcited; his style is disrupted; his sentences
explode. It may be deliberate policy on his part thus to let
himself go or even to work himself up into a state of frenzy.
The result, at any rate, is striking. Edgar Johnson sees this
as a "strange flame of ex*u*ltation."[25] I, for one, had rather
speak of ex*a*ltation. But perhaps we mean pretty much the
same thing. The genesis of the revolutionary style in the
Tale is easy enough to follow in the curious chapter (II,
xxi) that takes the reader out of the peace of Soho to plunge
him at once into the turmoil of the other city, around and
in the Bastille. One of the earliest sentences referring to the
revolutionary happenings is remarkable by its lush "verb-
fulness"; it concerns Defarge who, within three lines, "issued orders, issued arms, thrust this man back, dragged
this man forward, disarmed one man to arm another,
laboured and strove." Such is the initial impulse; once it
had been given, the Revolution is set going and acquires its
own momentum. Hence the new and more properly revolutionary style, in which the most violent actions are described in conspicuously verbless sentences, through the

juxtaposition of brief separate vignettes, like the storming of the Bastille: "Deep ditches, double drawbridge, massive stone walls, eight great towers, cannon, muskets, fire and smoke." It is as though Dickens had invented a kind of cinematographic technique: each image is motionless, but their quick succession produces an impression of motion. In the Bastille scene, extraordinary vividness is imparted to the description by the narrator's attitude: he is not merely creating images—he is himself looking at them and they assume in his eyes the haunting power of a vision. In his overexcited, almost frantic, state, the visionary narrator issues a proliferation of diseased images: "A forest of naked arms struggled in the air like shrivelled branches of trees in a winter wind . . . a whirlpool of boiling waters . . . the sea of black and threatening waters"; his vocabulary becomes vehement, angry, and macabre: "Demented . . . raging . . . maniacal bewilderment . . . remorseless . . . headlong, mad and dangerous" (II, *xxi*). The scene is made present by the use of the present tense for the few remaining verbs, by the vivid exclamatoriness which, when worked into the texture of the narrative without inverted commas, associates the reader with the excitement: "Villain Foulon taken, my sister! Old Foulon taken, my mother! Miscreant Foulon taken, my daughter!" (II, *xxii*). In the grindstone scene, Dickens' excitement has again risen by several degrees, and he displays fantastic, almost insane, energy: "Faces . . . more horrible and cruel than the visages of the wildest savages in their most barbarous disguise . . . hideous countenances all bloody and sweaty, and all awry with howling, and all staring and glaring with beastly excitement" (III, *ii*). Yet the novelist's own excitement is not beastly enough not to yield to horror and detestation; he denounces soberly enough "mad joy" as well as "mad ferocity" in this "butchery so dreadful" (III, *iv*) and "the devouring and insatiate Monsters" (with their indignant capital M, III, *xv*). It is obvious that, toward the end of the novel, when he achieves emotional identification, it is with the fugitives from Paris (their flight is narrated in the first person plural in III, *xiii*) or with Carton's religiosity and sublimity in sacrifice, that is, with two forms of escape from a reality now fully recognized as hideous and hateful.

When the revolutionary disruption is combined with other devices (rhetoric, imagery, cumulative vocabulary, and repetition), a few genuine prose poems can be the result of their association. The end of II, *ix*, relating the death of the Marquis, and Carton's night walk through the streets of Paris (III, *ix*) are remarkable pieces of elaborate and, on the whole, felicitous writing. As for Carton's death itself (III, *xv*), if one concentrates on the wording without reacting to the complex of emotions involved, it may be regarded as a miniature masterpiece in that kind. After a final repetition of the Gospel phrase about the "Resurrection and the Life," it consists merely in this: "The murmuring of many voices, the upturning of many faces, the pressing on of many footsteps in the outskirts of the crowd, so that it swells forward in a mass, like one great heave of water, all flashes away. Twenty-three."

I suppose no competent critic of Dickens would care to commemorate the centenary of his death by putting forward in favor of *A Tale of Two Cities* claims like Mrs. Boas' that, thanks to "the simple beauty of the home life" in London, the "charm of Dr. Manette," "the pathos of Carton," that novel gives us "the full enjoyment we expect from one of Dickens's novels."[26] Few would refuse to admit that the *Tale* is very much a contrived product. It should, however, in all fairness, be stated that the contrivance is less obvious in passages of dialogue or ordinary description of things and gestures than in narrative and comment; that the contrivance is usually superb; that it is entirely intentional, part of the author's deliberate attempt at stylization and connected with the authoritative tone he usually adopted after *David Copperfield*. If one objection to the *Tale*, proffered by people who like Dickens better in his relaxed Pickwickian mood, is that it is a tense book, it may be confessed that it is so; but on comparing G. H. Ford's phrase ("one of the most strained of Dickens' works")[27] with George Gissing's ("the novelist here laid a restraint upon himself"),[28] we realize that they do not differ much, and by *restraining* exuberance one inevitably produces a *strained* impression. But I now believe that the "bloody horse," as Roy Campbell has it, is still there.

Finally, I am reminded of Dickens' own letter of 15 October 1859 to Philoclès Régnier, in which he said of the *Tale*, "I hope it is the best story I have written."[29] Admittedly, this was written on the spur of the moment, in the excitement of recent completion, of released creative energy, and it could be contradicted by similar statements about the author's other temporary favorites. Also, it was written to a Frenchman, an actor whose help Dickens hoped to enlist in securing the performance in Paris of a stage version of the *Tale*. As it stands, at any rate, the statement falls ludicrously wide of the mark. But what I hope I have at least begun to show in this essay is that we should be prepared to discuss a slightly modified statement such as "I hope it is the story I have best written." Even this would certainly not have carried unanimous conviction, but it would not have been, to me, ridiculous.

NOTES

Foreword

1. Sir Arthur Helps, "In Memoriam—Charles Dickens," *Macmillan's Magazine*, XXXI (July 1870), 176–77.
2. *Times* (London), 20 June 1870), p. 9.
3. Noel Peyrouton, *Dickens Criticism: a Symposium* (Cambridge, Mass., 1962), pp. ix–x.
4. George H. Ford, *Dickens and His Readers* (Princeton, 1955).
5. G. M. Young, ed., *Early Victorian England*, 2 vols. (Oxford, 1934); Humphrey House, *The Dickens World* (London, 1942); G. M. Trevelyan, *English Social History* (New York, 1943). These books were selected because they are relatively early; a complete list of books on the Victorian background to literature would be dozens long.
6. "The Late Charles Dickens," *Illustrated London News,* LVI (18 June 1870), 639.
7. "Charles Dickens," *Spectator*, quoted in *Littell's Living Age*, CVI (1870), 119.
8. A. O. J. Cockshut, *The Imagination of Charles Dickens* (New York, 1962), p. 11.
9. David Masson, untitled review in *North British Review*, reprinted in *Littell's Living Age*, No. 374 (19 July 1851), pp. 97–111.
10. Walter Bagehot, "Charles Dickens," *National Review*, VII (July–October 1858), 458–85.
11. "The Death of Mr. Dickens," *Saturday Review*, reprinted in *Littell's Living Age*, CVI (1870), 120–22.
12. "Charles Dickens," *Fraser's Magazine*, LXXXII (1870), 130–34.
13. Helps, p. 176.
14. With the possible exception of the anti-Victorian debunkers of the 1920's and 1930's.
15. Peyrouton, pp. 10–11.
16. *Ibid.*, pp. 21–23.

Dickens' Self-Estimate—*Collins*

1. J. Hillis Miller, *Charles Dickens: The World of His Novels* (Cambridge, Mass., 1958), p. 250; K. J. Fielding, *Charles Dickens: A Critical Introduction,* 2nd ed. (London, 1965), p. 216.

2. John Forster, *Life of Charles Dickens,* ed. J. W. T. Ley (London, 1928), p. 646.

3. *Ibid.,* p. 88.

4. See Monroe Engel, *The Maturity of Dickens* (Cambridge, Mass., 1959), chap. 1, "The Strategy of the Novel"; and Richard Stang, *The Theory of the Novel in England, 1850–1870* (London, 1959), pp. 19–28.

5. See my "Significance of Dickens's Periodicals," *Review of English Literature,* II (1961), 55–64.

6. *Life,* pp. 625–26.

7. I tried not very successfully, to discuss this in "Queen Mab's Chariot among the Steam-engines: Dickens and Fancy," *English Studies,* XLII (1961), 1–13.

8. *Letters of Charles Dickens,* ed. Walter Dexter (London, 1938), III, 461–62.

9. *Ibid.,* II, 679–80. The story (by Miss Emily Jolly) appeared in *Household Words,* XII, 97–186 *passim,* incorporating these suggestions.

10. *Life,* pp. 473, 737.

11. I have argued this more fully in "Dickens's Public Readings: The Performer and the Novelist," *Studies in the Novel,* I (1969).

12. Letter of November 1839, in *Memorials of Thomas Hood,* ed. by his daughter [Frances F. Broderip] (London, 1860), II, 41.

13. *Letters,* II, 150.

14. *The Way of All Flesh* (1903), chap. 34.

15. *Life,* pp. 617–18.

16. *Ibid.,* p. 39.

17. *Ibid.,* pp. 481, 635, 761.

18. *Ibid.,* p. 89; but cf., on this letter, *The Pilgrim Edition of the Letters of Charles Dickens,* ed. Madeline House and Graham Storey (Oxford, 1965), I, 280–82 and notes.

19. See Michael Slater, "Dickens (and Forster) at Work on *The Chimes,*" *Dickens Studies,* II (September 1966), 106–

40; and John Butt and Kathleen Tillotson, *Dickens at Work* (London, 1957), chap. 5.

20. *Examiner* (London), 9 October 1836, p. 667; 4 September 1836, p. 563.

21. *Life*, pp. 89, 214; but see n. 20 above.

22. *Dictionary of National Biography*, xx, 17.

23. *Life*, pp. 122, 308.

24. *Examiner*, 20 July 1861, p. 452.

25. Forster had offered to review *The Chimes* in the *Edinburgh Review;* his review appeared there in January 1845, LXXXI, 181–89. See the *Wellesley Index to Victorian Periodicals 1824–1900*, ed. Walter E. Houghton (Toronto and London, 1966), I, 494. He therefore invited Leigh Hunt to help him with suggestions for a review for the *Examiner* (Maggs Brothers' *Catalogue No. 443*, 1923, item 1042, cited by Michael Slater in "*The Chimes:* Its Materials, Making, and Public Reception" [Ph.D. diss., Oxford, 1965]). The review in the *Examiner* (21 December 1844) is manifestly in Hunt's style, not Forster's.

26. The strength of Forster's loyal concern for Dickens was noted by someone who saw them together in 1853: "It was almost pathetic, the look of affectionate concern with which he [Forster] watched the other's every movement. I have never seen anything like it, before or since." See Richard Renton, *John Forster and his Friendships* (London, 1912), p. 130.

27. *Man in the Moon*, I (1847), 158.

28. Forster, p. 88, quoted in n. 26 above. E.g., see the review of *Oliver Twist* in the *Examiner*, 10 September 1837, p. 581.

29. *Examiner*, 27 October 1839, pp. 677, 678.

30. *Examiner*, 26 October 1844, p. 675. In his 1844 Preface to *Chuzzlewit*, Dickens remarked that he had tried "to keep a steadier eye upon the general purpose and design. With this object in view, I have put a strong restraint upon myself." One minor puzzle: Forster was remarkably dilatory in writing his reviews of this novel and its successor *Dombey* (*Examiner*, 28 October 1848), four and seven months respectively after the serialization ended. He refers to these delays, with jocular embarrassment, in both reviews. I cannot surmise why, on these two occasions, he kept his readers (and his friend Dickens) waiting so long.

31. *Examiner,* 28 October 1865, p. 682. Cf. the conclusion of the review of *Hard Times:* "Its many beauties blind us, as they will blind other generations, to its few defects" (9 September 1854, p. 569). The defects are not specified.

32. *Examiner,* 8 October 1853, p. 644. Forster shared the general partiality for Dickens' heroines, and presumably encouraged Dickens to commit more of them: "Imogen, Desdemona, or Sophia Western are not truer or more lovable women than many of Mr. Dickens' heroines. His Agnes is the finishing grace of *Copperfield*" (14 December 1850, p. 798).

33. *Life,* pp. 559–60, 743.

34. *Examiner,* 20 July 1861, p. 452, reviewing *Great Expectations.*

35. *Examiner,* 14 December 1850, p. 798. Cf. *Life,* p. 554.

36. See *Examiner* on *Bleak House* (8 October 1853, p. 644), *Hard Times* (9 September 1854, p. 568), *Little Dorrit* (13 June 1857, p. 372), *A Tale of Two Cities* (10 December 1859, p. 788), *Great Expectations* (20 July 1861, p. 452).

37. *Examiner,* 28 October 1865, p. 681. "Latinized races" are brought into the argument, no doubt, because Forster already had Hippolyte Taine on his mind. Taine's *Histoire de la littérature anglaise,* containing the celebrated chapter on Dickens, had just been published and was being much discussed in England. Later, of course, Taine was to co-star with G. H. Lewes as the critical villain of Forster's *Life of Dickens.*

38. *Life,* p. 291; cf. 1844 Preface to *Chuzzlewit.*

39. *Examiner,* 8 October 1853, p. 644, reviewing *Bleak House.*

40. *Examiner,* 28 October 1848, p. 692.

41. *Examiner,* 8 October 1853, p. 645.

42. *Examiner,* 28 October 1848, p. 692.

43. *Examiner,* 13 June 1857, p. 372, reviewing *Little Dorrit.*

44. *Examiner,* 10 December 1859, pp. 788–89.

45. *Life,* p. 761; *Examiner,* 8 October 1853, p. 644.

46. *Life,* p. 560. Dickens makes this point in his 1857 Preface to *Little Dorrit* and his 1865 Postscript to *Our Mutual Friend.*

47. *Examiner,* 8 October 1843, p. 644. Cf. 9 September 1854, p. 568; 13 June 1857, p. 372; 10 December 1859, p. 788; and references in following notes.

48. *Examiner*, 28 October 1865, p. 681.

49. *Examiner*, 20 July 1861, p. 452, 453.

50. *Life*, p. 737.

51. *Examiner*, 20 July 1861, p. 452. E. S. Dallas made some of the same points in his review of *Our Mutual Friend* in the *Times* (London) (29 November 1865) which so pleased Dickens that he made the remarkable gesture of giving Dallas the manuscript of the novel: "He is in greater force than ever. . . . We hear people say, 'He has never surpassed *Pickwick*' . . . [but *Our Mutual Friend* is] infinitely better than *Pickwick* in all the higher qualities of a novel. . . . In all the 600 pages there is not a careless line."

52. G. K. Chesterton, *Charles Dickens* (1906; reprint ed., London, 1956), p. 138.

53. *Life*, pp. 552, 561, 566n., 625, 627, 731, 743–44, 825–61. For fuller discussion, see Sylvère Monod, "John Forster's *Life of Dickens* and Literary Criticism," *English Studies Today*, 4th ser. (Rome, 1966), pp. 357–73.

54. *Times* (London), 2 January 1847, p. 6.

55. *Examiner*, 19 December 1846, p. 819; *Life*, p. 436.

56. Charles Gavan Duffy, *Conversations with Carlyle* (London, 1892), p. 75.

57. *Examiner*, 9 September 1854, p. 568; *Life*, p. 566.

"The Story-Weaver at His Loom"—*Patten*

1. Edgar Johnson, *Charles Dickens: His Tragedy and Triumph* (New York, 1952), I, 298.

2. Texts of letters through 31 December 1841 are taken from the Pilgrim Edition, *Letters*, ed. Madeline House and Graham Storey (Oxford: The Clarendon Press), I, 1965; II, 1969. Thereafter, the source is The Nonesuch Dickens, *Letters*, ed. Walter Dexter, 3 vols. (Bloomsbury: The Nonesuch Press, 1938). If the date is supplied in the text, no further reference is given. See Addendum, p. 205.

3. John Forster, *The Life of Charles Dickens*, ed. J. W. T. Ley (New York [1928]), II, *vi*, 139.

4. Pilgrim *Letters*, I, 681.

5. Pilgrim *Letters*, I, 565, 570; Forster, II, *vi*, 142.

6. Pilgrim *Letters*, II, 4, to Forster [?10 January 1840].

7. Pilgrim *Letters*, II, 24–25 [?12 February 1840]. The

story promised is "Mr. Pickwick's Tale" of John Podgers, originally planned for number III, which ran "into no. 4" (Pilgrim *Letters*, II, 35, to Chapman and Hall 28 February [1840]), and was thrown "over to 4, 5, or 6" on 9 March (Pilgrim *Letters*, II, 41, to Chapman and Hall). It eventually appeared in *Clock* V and VI. Dickens sent to Cattermole on 12 February most of number II; in the remainder of the week he worked on the "witch story" promised Cattermole, and which was originally designed for *Clock* III. See Addendum, p. 205.

8. Cf. Pilgrim *Letters*, II, 7–9, to Cattermole [13 January 1840]; II, 13, to Macready [29 January 1840]; II, 26, to Thompson [13 February 1840].

9. Pilgrim *Letters*, II, 31.

10. Pilgrim *Letters*, II, 40 [?8 March 1840], dated 4 March by Forster, but Dickens and Forster were both in Bath on this day.

11. Pilgrim *Letters*, II, 42 [?9 March 1840].

12. Victoria and Albert Museum, MS., Forster. Quoted by permission.

13. Johnson, I, 297.

14. Reproduced in *The Dickensian*, VI (1910), 226, and Arthur Waugh, *A Hundred Years of Publishing* (London, 1930), facing p. 48.

15. Pilgrim *Letters*, I, 570.

16. William Charles Macready, *Diaries*, ed. William Toynbee (London, 1912), II, 56.

17. Pilgrim *Letters*, II, 50 to [Hall, ?7 April '40].

18. Johnson, I, 306–7.

19. Charles Dickens, *Master Humphrey's Clock* (London, 1840–41), vol. I, number IV, *The Old Curiosity Shop* [chap. 1], p. 47.

20. Forster, II, *vii*, 146.

21. Dickens, *Clock*, vol. 2, XXXIV, *liii*, 94.

22. Cf. J. C. Reid, *The Hidden World of Charles Dickens*, The Macmillan Brown Lectures, 1961, University of Aukland Bulletin No. 61, English Series 10 ([Auckland, N.Z.], 1962), p. 40: Dickens "first conceived the short story as little more than a touching sentimental episode, exploiting contrast."

23. I quote from the edition of 1841 (British Museum G. 18069). For the editions of 1848 and 1868 minor changes were made, especially in punctuation.

24. Forster, II, *vii*, 146.
25. *The Athenaeum*, 7 November 1840, p. 887.
26. London, 1848.
27. Dickens, *Clock*, vol. 1, XV, *xv*, 172.
28. Dickens, *Clock*, vol. 1, VII, 75.
29. Dickens, *Clock*, vol. 1, VIII, *iii*, 90.
30. Preface to the 1841 edition.
31. See the preface to the Cheap Edition.
32. Dickens, *Clock*, vol. 2, XLV, 224–25.
33. The idea that Grandfather Trent is wealthy received confirmation in the manuscript of chapter 1, where Nell tells Master Humphrey that she has been out selling diamonds. But Dickens excised this revelation in proof.
34. Preface to the 1841 edition.

Laughter and Pathos—*Kincaid*

1. Both J. Hillis Miller, *Charles Dickens: The World of His Novels* (Cambridge, Mass., 1958), pp. 95–96; and Larry Kirkpatrick, "The Gothic Flame of Charles Dickens," *Victorian Newsletter*, No. 31 (1967), p. 20, argue that the ironic identification of rural "escape" with death functions as a criticism of the ending of *Oliver Twist*.
2. *The Letters of Charles Dickens*, ed. Walter Dexter (London, 1938), I, 305, to Thomas Latimer, 13 March 1841.
3. The phrase is Aldous Huxley's in *Vulgarity in Literature* (London, 1930), p. 57.
4. This phrase is Swinburne's in "Charles Dickens," *The Quarterly Review*, CXCVI (1902), 22.
5. The best historical argument is by Edgar Johnson, *Charles Dickens: His Tragedy and Triumph* (New York, 1952), I, 323–24. He argues that "we live in a different emotional climate from theirs" and that "our response is the deviation." Our fear of sentiment, in other words, is far more unnatural than the Victorians' attraction to it. Justifications of Nell on artistic grounds ordinarily emphasize the ironies which attend her and deny sentimentality altogether; see A. E. Dyson, "*The Old Curiosity Shop*: Innocence and the Grotesque," *Critical Quarterly*, VIII (1966), 112. For a documented account of the outpouring of grief occasioned by Nell's death see Johnson, I, 303–4.

6. *Anatomy of Criticism* (Princeton, 1957), p. 217.

7. For a fuller exploration of the implications of suicide in the novel see Warrington Winters, "*The Old Curiosity Shop:* A Consummation Devoutly to Be Wished," *Dickensian,* LXIII (1967), 176–80.

8. This point is made and explored briefly by Miller, *Charles Dickens,* p. 95.

9. I am very much indebted to Pearson's article in *Dickens and the Twentieth Century,* ed. John Gross and Gabriel Pearson (London, 1962), pp. 77–90, particularly to his conception of the novel as being defined by the three forces of Nell, Quilp, and Dick. Though I do not agree that Dick's humor is a "subversive commentary" (p. 87) on the other two forces, I think his general view of Dick's relation to Nell and Quilp is accurate, and I have used it here.

10. *Ibid.,* p. 90.

11. The conception of laughter used here is generally that given by Freud in *Wit and Its Relation to the Unconscious,* trans. A. A. Brill (New York, 1916). In addition to the aggressive component of laughter, Freud later suggested a more positive assertion of pleasure, which he called humor and which is, in this novel, particularly applicable to Dick Swiveller; see Freud, "Humor," *International Journal of Psychoanalysis,* IX (1928), 1–6.

12. See my article, "Laughter and *Oliver Twist,*" PMLA, LXXXIII (1968), 63–70.

13. Notice how misleading the term "trotters" is. Trotting is the characteristic activity of Dickens' mercantile philanthropists from the Cheerybles to Mr. Boffin. In this novel it becomes particularly ugly.

14. This same "delusive impulse toward safety" is discussed briefly by Monroe Engel, *The Maturity of Dickens* (Cambridge, Mass., 1959), p. 100.

15. G. K. Chesterton has the best and most evocative description of this irony: "All the good fairies and all the kind magicians, all the just kings and all the gallant princes, with chariots and flying dragons and armies and navies go after one little child who has strayed into a wood, and find her dead," in his *Appreciations and Criticisms of the Works of Charles Dickens* (London, 1911), pp. 53–54.

16. Johnson (*Charles Dickens* I, 326–37) is one of the few critics to take seriously the commercial and economic im-

plications of the novel's theme. He argues, interestingly, that it is, in part, based on a current boom in stock-market speculation, but he sees that behind all this is the attack on "acquisitive greed callous to the suffering it caused." Reid, *The Hidden World of Charles Dickens*, pp. 34–47, does offer a similar reading, but it seems to me somewhat weakened by being so self-consciously "archetypal" in approach.

17. This descriptive term is used by Steven Marcus and discussed at some length in *Dickens: From Pickwick to Dombey* (New York, 1965), pp. 135–42.

18. Marcus also sees Quilp as the polar opposite of Nell and notes that he is her "other half" (p. 151), though he does not pursue this suggestion.

19. Dyson (*Critical Quarterly*, pp. 115–17) discusses this point and other interesting aspects of Quilp.

20. John Forster, *The Life of Charles Dickens*, notes by A. J. Hoppe (London, 1966), I, 119.

21. J. B. Priestley interestingly and wittily discusses Dick's reliance on phrases and roles; see *The English Comic Characters* (London, 1925), pp. 227–39.

22. Marcus (pp. 165–68) argues for Dick's role as a hero but sees him finally as "too light and supple" for the "dead weight of the novel's great theme."

David Copperfield's Carlylean Retailoring—*Dunn*

1. Although we have no proof that Dickens ever read *Sartor Resartus*, Mildred D. Christian has shown that Dickens was "acquainted in greater or lesser degree with every important social pronouncement of Carlyle between 1829 and 1843" and that he read all of Carlyle's important later works. "Carlyle's Influence upon the Social Theory of Dickens," *Trollopian*, I (March 1947), 27–36; II (June 1947), 11–26.

2. Thomas Carlyle, *Sartor Resartus* (New York, 1921), I, 7, 45. Further reference from this edition is included in the text, citing only book and chapter numbers.

3. George Levine, in *The Boundaries of Fiction: Carlyle, Macaulay, Newman* (Princeton, 1968), p. 23, summarizes the differing readings of *Sartor*'s form and himself adapts Northrop Frye's terms to consider *Sartor* "a fiction belonging to the complex class of 'confession-anatomy-romance.' "

4. See G. B. Tennyson, *Sartor Called Resartus: The Genesis, Structure, and Style of Thomas Carlyle's First Major Work* (Princeton, 1965).

5. Samuel Davey, *Darwin, Carlyle, and Dickens; With Other Essays* (London, 1875), p. 61.

6. Charles Dickens, *David Copperfield*, ed. George H. Ford (Boston, 1958), p. 9. Further reference from this edition is included in the text, citing only chapter numbers.

7. James Anthony Froude, *Thomas Carlyle; A History of His Life in London, 1834–1881* (New York, 1884), II, 19.

8. John Forster, *The Life of Charles Dickens* (Philadelphia, 1886), I, 53.

9. *The Hero in Eclipse in Victorian Fiction*, trans. Angus Davidson (London, 1956), p. 127.

10. "The Undisciplined Heart of *David Copperfield*," *Nineteenth-Century Fiction*, IX (September 1954), 81–108.

11. "Carlyle is a man of feeling striving yet failing to translate his feelings into thought. This striving explains his irascibility and the fantastic rhetoric in which it finds expression." Holbrook Jackson, *Dreamers of Dreams* (London, 1948), p. 63.

12. The essay first appeared in *Frasers*, number 27 (April, 1832).

13. "Varnhagen Von Ense's Memoirs," in *Critical and Miscellaneous Essays* (New York, 1901), IV, 25.

14. "*David Copperfield*," *Yale Review*, XXXVII (June 1948), 659–60.

Bleak House and the Graveyard—Fielding and Brice

1. Mowbray Morris, "Charles Dickens," *Fortnightly Review*, N.S. XXXII or O.S. XXXVIII (December 1882), 762–69. Compare also with the review by George Brimley, *Spectator* (24 September 1853), p. 923, which says that the suit of Jarndyce & Jarndyce "is lugged in by the head and shoulders, and kept prominently before the reader, solely to give Mr. Dickens the opportunity of indulging in stale and commonplace satire upon the length and expense of Chancery proceedings."

2. John Butt and Kathleen Tillotson, *Dickens at Work* (London, 1957), pp. 177–200; use of the same material was

made by John Butt in *"Bleak House* in the Context of 1851," *Nineteenth-Century Fiction*, x (1955), 1–21.

3. Review of *Narrative of the Expedition sent by her Majesty's Government to the River Niger, under the command of Captain H. D. Trotter, R.N., by Captain William Allen, R.N., Commander of H.M.S. Wilberforce, and T. R. H. Thomson, M.D., one of the medical officers of the Expedition* in the *Examiner* (19 August 1848), pp. 531–33.

4. *The Speeches of Charles Dickens*, ed. K. J. Fielding (Oxford, 1960), in his speech to the Metropolitan Sanitary Association (10 May 1851) when he dated a "strengthening" of his interest to "twelve or fifteen years ago," probably meaning about 1839 or 1840.

5. Edwin Chadwick (1800–1890), reformer; the first sanitary commission had been appointed at his instigation, 1839; secretary to the Poor Law commissioners, 1834–46; one of the commissioners to the General Board of Heath, 1848–54.

6. University College, London, MSS., Chadwick.

7. Charles Dickens, *Collected Papers* (London, n.d. [1915]), p. 298.

8. *Speeches*, pp. 104–10, 127–32.

9. *Ibid.*, p. 129.

10. Henry Austin (1812–61), civil engineer; see *Letters of Charles Dickens* (Oxford, 1965), i, 21.

11. They are quoted here, from MSS in the Pierpont Morgan Library, by kind permission; reference is by date. With a few exceptions, they have not been published before.

12. The fullest account is by the present authors in "Dickens and the Tooting Disaster," *Victorian Studies*, xii (December 1968), 227–44. See also A. W. Brice, "Ignorance and its Victims," *Dickensian*, lxiii (1967), 143–47; Fielding and Brice, "Charles Dickens on 'The Exclusion of Evidence,'" *The Dickensian*, lxiv (1968), 131–40, and lxv (1969), 35–41.

13. John Phillips was one of two chief surveyors to the Commission, whereas Austin was Acting Consulting Engineer. Both submitted plans, but, though Austin's was backed by Chadwick, bitter divisions within the Commission brought its activities to a standstill. Eventually the place of the first Metropolitan Commission of Sewers was taken by a smaller body excluding Chadwick and members of the warring factions. See S. E. Finer, *Edwin Chadwick and the Public Health Movement 1832–54* (London, 1952).

14. Henry Fielding's *Life and Death of Tom Thumb the Great* was a favorite with Dickens, who put on a production at home for his children; the names of Coodle and Doodle (*Bleak House*, chap. 12) derive from it. The Upas tree is frequently referred to, including "The Sunday Screw," *Household Words,* I (22 June 1850), 289–92. The part the army played in the survey stems from its conduct by the Board of Ordnance.

15. *Speeches*, p. 106.

16. "Intramural Interment," *Examiner* (8 September 1849), pp. 561–62; see also "Public Health and Nuisances," *Examiner* (1 September 1849), p. 546. The burial ground belonged to St. Clement Danes.

17. *Letters of Charles Dickens*, ed. W. Dexter (London, 1968), III, 642, to Miss Palfrey, 4 April 1868. See also W. Dexter, "Poor Jo's Churchyard Identified," *The Dickensian,* XXV (1929), 143; Trevor Blount, "The Graveyard Satire of *Bleak House* in the Context of 1850," *Review of English Studies*, N.S. XIV (1963), 370–78. The latter article covers some of the same ground as the present study, but documents the "satire" entirely by reference to George Walker's earlier works (going back chiefly to 1839) without showing any direct link with Dickens other than the letter to Miss Palfrey.

18. J. H. Stonehouse, *Catalogue of the Library of Charles Dickens from Gadshill, Reprinted from Sotheran's "Prices Current of Literature,"* (London, 1935), p. 88, under "PAMPHLETS Various." There were six volumes of pamphlets in Dickens' library, 8vo, bound in half calf, substantial in size, each of which would have had his bookplate. Their contents were mostly, but not entirely, listed; and the present authors would be grateful for information about their whereabouts today.

19. There are too many contributions dealing directly or indirectly with the sanitary question for it to be profitable to list them. One is of some interest in view of the phrase in *Bleak House* (chap. 11) that Nemo is interred in "a beastly scrap of ground which a Turk would reject as a savage abomination, and a Caffre would shudder at." This is "Heathen and Christian Burial," by W. H. Wills and George Hogarth (Dickens' father-in-law), in the second number, 6 April 1850, which includes references to Mahommedans and to the barbarities of the "Caffres."

20. *Household Words*, 18 May 1850, collected in *Reprinted Pieces*, 1858. The letter is mutilated by a gap cut out of

it of about seven lines. But in the part that is left Dickens implies that, even for him, there was some difficulty in combining fiction and taking part in this controversy: "gaps and trapdoors of advocacy, that open unexpectedly when I have my hands (and head) full of other work."

21. "Mr. Booley's View of the Lord Mayor's Show," 30 November 1850.

22. Chadwick, Lord Shaftesbury, and the Earl of Carlisle (formerly Viscount Mospeth) had been appointed as the three Commissioners of the General Board of Health in September 1848. Southwood Smith was appointed as the medical member very soon afterwards. He and Dickens were often actively associated.

23. See *Letters from Charles Dickens to Angela Burdett-Coutts 1841–1865*, ed. E. Johnson (London, 1953); further unpublished letters in the Pierpont Morgan Library; and K. J. Fielding, "Dickens's Work with Miss Coutts: Nova Scotia Gardens and What Grew There," *The Dickensian*, LXI (1965), 112–19.

24. See Fielding and Brice, "Dickens and the Tooting Disaster," pp. 227–40.

25. *Uncle Tom's Cabin, Bleak House, Slavery and Slave Trade*, 1853.

26. John Forster, *The Life of Charles Dickens*, ed. J. W. T. Ley (London, 1928), pp. 727–28.

27. Edmund Wilson, *The Wound and the Bow* (London, 1942), p. 37.

28. Forster, p. 564.

29. Ten manuscript title pages in the Victorian and Albert Museum, Forster Collection, read as follows:

Tom-All-Alone's / The Ruined House

Tom-All-Alone's / The Solitary House /
    [That never knew happiness] / That was always shut up. /
                Bleak House Academy / The East Wind

Tom-All-Alone's / Building / That got into chancery /
          Factory   and never got out
          Mill
      The Ruined House

Tom-All-Alone's / The Solitary House / where the grass grew

Tom-All-Alone's / The Solitary House / That was always shut up /
                        never lighted

Tom-All-Alone's / The Ruined Mill / That got into chancery /
                    and never got out

Tom-All-Alone's / The Solitary House / where the wind howled

Tom-All-Alone's / The Ruined [Mill] House /
                That got into chancery and never got out

Tom-All-Alone's / The Ruined House / [In Chancery] /
                That got into chancery / and never got out. /

Bleak House / and The East Wind /
                How they both got into chancery / and never got out. /

Bleak House.

Dickens' manuscript shows that the title provisionally decided on while he was writing the first and second number was, in fact, *Bleak House and the East Wind*. By chapter 8, the first of the third number, the title was fixed on and Dickens had Jarndyce bring the two together with his explanation to Esther that, when he inherited the house, it was in a state of decay much like Tom-All-Alone's itself, because, though "not in Chancery, its master was."

    30. *Examiner* (12 January 1850), p. 19. For the full story see Fielding and Brice, "Charles Dickens on 'The Exclusion of Evidence,'" *Dickensian* LXIV (1968), 131–40, and LXV (1969), 35–41. Part of its point is to show that Dickens may have written this article in the *Examiner* and another comment on the same case in the *Household Narrative*. Both have links with *Bleak House*. It is also suggested how representative a figure Jo was of the dilemmas of the time which were felt by men who were no more sure about the other world than Jo.

    31. *Nineteenth-Century Fiction*, XXII (1967), 145–54.

    32. See chap. 11 for the inquest; the end of chap. 19 and the end of chap. 22 for his ignorance of the New Testament, which he had "never heard of. Its compilers and the Reverend Chadband were all one to him"; and chap. 16 for the drover's dog.

    33. *Saturday Review* (17 December 1859), pp. 741–43, reprinted in *The Dickens Critics*, ed. George H. Ford and Lauriat Lane, Jr. (Ithaca, 1961), pp. 41–42.

Little Dorrit: A World in Reverse—*Stang*

    1. *Dickens, A Collection of Critical Essays*, ed. Martin Price (Englewood Cliffs, N.J., 1967), p. 147, reprinted from *The Opposing Self* (New York, 1955).

2. *Little Dorrit* (London, n.d. [1925]). All references to *Little Dorritt* will be from this edition and will refer successively to book, chapter, and page: 1, *xx*, 252.

3. See the excellent discussion of Mrs. Clennam's role in the plot in Ross H. Dabney, *Love and Property in the Novels of Dickens* (Berkeley and Los Angeles, 1967).

4. It is interesting that the image of the lamp and the candle had been earlier introduced when Arthur Clennam described himself to Mr. Meagles as a victim of his parent's religion, " 'a gloomy sacrifice of tastes and sympathies that were never their own. . . . I have no will. . . . Will, purpose, hope? All those lights were extinguished before I could sound the words.' " " 'Light 'em up again!' said Mr. Meagles" (1, *ii*, 22–23). This key statement will be taken up again further on in this essay.

5. See II, *xiii*, 616: "That it is at least as difficult to stay a moral infection as a physical one; that such a disease will spread with the malignity and rapidity of the Plague; that the contagion, when it has once made head, will spare no pursuit or condition, but will lay hold on people in the soundest health, and become developed in the most unlikely constitutions—is a fact as firmly established by experience as that we human creatures breathe an atmosphere. A blessing beyond appreciation would be conferred upon mankind, if the tainted, in whose weakness or wickedness these virulent disorders are bred, could be instantly seized and placed in close confinement (not to say summarily smothered) before the poison is communicable."

6. On the way Dickens connects his various social groups by theme and image, as well as plot, see Martin Meisel, *Shaw and the Nineteenth-Century Theater* (Princeton, 1963), p. 69, where Shaw speaks of his purpose as a dramatist, "to shew the connexion between things that seem apart and unrelated in the haphazard order of events in real life." See also in the same book Shaw's definition of melodrama, which so well describes Dickens. Of course Shaw owes a good deal to Dickens: "It should be a simple and sincere drama of action and feeling, kept well within that vast tract of passion and motive which is common to the philosopher and the laborer, relieved by plenty of fun and depending for variety of human character, not on the high comedy idiosyncrasies which individualize people in spite of the closest similarity of age, sex, and circumstances,

but on broad contrasts between types of youth and age, sympathy and selfishness, the masculine and the feminine, the serious and the frivolous, the sublime and the ridiculous, and so on. The whole character of the piece must be allegorical, idealistic, full of generalizations and moral lessons, and it must represent conduct as producing swiftly and certainly on the individual the results which in actual life it only produces on the race in the course of many centuries."

7. G. K. Chesterton, in *Appreciations and Criticisms of the Works of Charles Dickens* (New York and London, 1911) and A. O. J. Cockshut in *The Imagination of Charles Dickens* (London, 1961) see Dickens in *Little Dorrit* as a believer in an almost complete determinism.

8. On this point see Edgar Johnson, *Charles Dickens, His Tragedy and Triumph* (New York, 1952); John Butt and Kathleen Tillotson, *Dickens at Work* (London, 1957); and Richard Stang, *Theory of the Novel in England, 1850–1870* (New York and London, 1958).

9. The grotesque comedy of this part of the book makes one think of Kafka, as it does of Gogol too. For example, consider passages like the following: "So he went back to the Circumlocution Office, and once more sent his card up to Barnacle Junior, by a messenger who took it very ill that he should come back again, and who was eating mashed potatoes and gravy behind a partition by the hall fire" (I, *x*, 121). Or the long passage on the next page:

> He entered the apartment, and found two gentlemen sitting face to face at a large and easy desk, one of whom was polishing a gun-barrel on his pocket-handkerchief, while the other was spreading marmalade on bread with a paper-knife.
>
> "Mr. Wobbler?" inquired the suitor. . . .
>
> Both gentlemen glanced at him, and seemed surprised at his assurance.
>
> "So he went," said the gentleman with the gun-barrel . . . "down to his cousin's place, and took the Dog with him by rail. Inestimable Dog. Flew at the porter fellow when he was put into the dog-box, and flew at the guard when he was taken out. He got half a dozen fellows into a Barn, and a good supply of Rats, and timed the Dog. Finding the Dog able to do it immensely, made the match, and heavily backed the Dog. When the match came off, some devil

of a fellow was brought over, Sir—Dog was made drunk—
Dog's master was cleaned out."

"Mr. Wobbler?" inquired the suitor.

The gentleman who was spreading the marmalade returned, without looking up from that occupation, "What did
he call the Dog?"

"Called him Lovely," said the other gentleman.

10. This aspect of the novel is thoroughly treated in
Lionel Trilling's essay on *Little Dorrit* in Price, ed., *Dickens*.

Some Stylistic Devices in *A Tale of Two Cities*—Monod

1. R. C. Churchill, in *Pelican Guide to English Literature*,
ed. Boris Ford (New York, 1958), VI, 133, accounts for it by
saying that "it is one of those books we first read in childhood,
and the spell so early cast upon us we can never, even if we
wished it, be fully shaken off."

2. George H. Ford, in *Dickens and His Readers* (Princeton, 1955), p. 172, points out that "by 1944, no less than sixty
different editions of *A Tale of Two Cities* were published by
presses in Great Britain." Incidentally, as there is no authoritative edition of the novel, my references are to book and
chapter, not pages.

3. *Saturday Review*, 19 December 1859, quoted by F. G.
Kitton in *Dickensiana* (London, 1886), p. 283.

4. In *Dickens and the Twentieth Century*, ed. J. Gross
and G. Pearson (London, 1962), p. 194.

5. *The Flint and the Flame: The Artistry of Charles
Dickens* (Columbia, Mo., 1963), p. 250. Chapter 12 of Earle
Davis' book, "Recalled to Life," contains one of the best studies
of the *Tale* so far.

6. Admittedly the printers and proofreaders of the Everyman's Library edition I use (London, 1906) contributed more
than their fair share of errors. I am not charging Carlyle with
the repeated use of *viola* (raped) for *voilà*, or for "De Launay
has been profuse of beverages" as translation of *"prodigua des
buissons"* (bushes instead of drinks). But the printers cannot
have invented all the mistakes.

7. See K. J. Fielding, *Charles Dickens: A Critical Introduction*, 2nd ed. (London, 1965), p. 201.

8. *Dickens* (London, 1935), p. 117.

9. *Life of Dickens*, Everyman's Library, II, 283: "There was probably never a book by a great humorist . . . with so little humor."

10. Gross, p. 195: "The book is notoriously deficient in humor. . . . As comic characters the Crunchers are forced and mechanical."

11. Both in *Charles Dickens: His Tragedy and Triumph* (New York, 1953) and in a brilliant introduction to the Pocket Library edition of the *Tale* (New York, 1954) from which my quotation is taken, p. vii.

12. Edward Wagenknecht, *Dickens and the Scandal-mongers* (Norman, Okla., 1965), p. 129, makes the interesting comment that, while he finds this description "exceedingly unpleasant," he must "recognize the existence of historical evidence which shows that children have died just in this way."

13. Gross, p. 196.

14. Yet Mrs. F. S. Boas, in her introduction to the *Tale* (p. xxv) in the World's Classics edition (London, 1903 and 1960), says that Stryver "elbowed his way successfully through life."

15. A. O. J. Cockshut, *The Imagination of Charles Dickens* (London, 1961), p. 185.

16. Gross, p. 194.

17. See Johnson, *Charles Dickens*, and Cockshut, *The Imagination of Charles Dickens*.

18. Unfortunately this is only a small sample from a very large collection of examples.

19. Taylor Stoehr, *Dickens: The Dreamer's Stance* (Ithaca, 1965), p. 200, sees this in the personification of Saint-Antoine. I think it is in fact quite a different case: the church, or the houses, or even the district of that name do not become human individuals; the thousands of inhabitants act as one person.

20. *Ibid*. The word "dreamlike" is to be taken with a grain of salt, as Stoehr's theme is "The Dreamer's Stance." But his comment, without the dreamlike, or nightmarish, connotation, seems valid.

21. Excellently analyzed by C. A. Bodelson, "Some Notes on Dickens's Symbolism," *Essays and Papers* (Copenhagen, 1964), p. 31.

22. Fielding, pp. 198–99.

23. *Circle of Fire: Dickens' Vision and Style and the Popular Victorian Theater* (Lexington, Ky., 1966).

24. *Charles Dickens* (London, 1906), p. 230. What Chesterton actually wrote, or what was actually printed, is "among his books by Dickens."

25. Introduction to Pocket Library ed., p. xii.

26. Introduction to World's Classics ed., p. viii.

27. Ford, p. 204.

28. *Charles Dickens: A Critical Study* (London, 1898), p. 67.

29. "Une amitié française de Charles Dickens: Lettres inédites à Philoclès Régnier," *Études Anglaises*, XI, No. 2 (April–June 1958), 221.

ADDENDUM to "The Story-Weaver at His Loom"—*Patten*

I believe that the letter to John Forster which the Pilgrim editors conjecturally date 20 April and surmise refers to correcting proofs of number VII (in which the *Shop* is resumed) may equally plausibly be dated 13 April and refer to proofs of number VI, the manuscript of which only reached Chapman and Hall around 9 April (see letter to [William Hall, ?7 April 1840]). If the *Shop* was expanded partly in response to falling sales, then it is a little more likely that the partners waited until sales of number III (18 April) were in before changing direction. During the week between publication of II and III, Dickens wrote two letters saying the *Clock* was going well (Pilgrim *Letters*, II, 57); according to Thackeray, by the first week in May sales had slumped by 20,000 (*Letters and Private Papers,* ed. Gordon N. Ray, 4 vols. [Cambridge, Mass.: Harvard University Press, 1945–46], I, 444). Whether Dickens resumed the *Shop* after *Clock* II or *Clock* III appeared, the point that he decided to expand it before his readers had seen the first installment remains valid.

INDEX

Key to abbreviations in the Index:

CD	Charles Dickens	LD	*Little Dorrit*
AN	*American Notes*	MC	*Martin Chuzzlewit*
BL	*The Battle of Life*	MHC	*Master Humphrey's Clock*
BH	*Bleak House*	ED	*The Mystery of Edwin Drood*
DC	*David Copperfield*	NN	*Nicholas Nickleby*
DS	*Dombey and Son*	OCS	*The Old Curiosity Shop*
GE	*Great Expectations*	OT	*Oliver Twist*
HT	*Hard Times*	OMF	*Our Mutual Friend*
HM	*The Haunted Man*	PP	*Pickwick Papers*
HW	*Household Words*	TTC	*A Tale of Two Cities*